DEFIANCE: GREECE AND EUROPE

If Europe gets torn apart, it will start at the bottom corner. Greece, the first country in modern times to elect a radical left-wing government, faces economic war from Brussels and a tide of refugees from collapsing states to its east. At this critical moment Roger Silverman's book views the origins of the Greek crisis using the lens missing from most media coverage: class, class conflict and the problems of a democratic system balanced on deep corruption and oligarchic power.

Paul Mason, Economics Editor of Channel 4 News, formerly Economics Editor of Newsnight, author of *Postcapitalism: A Guide To Our Future* and *Why It's Kicking Off Everywhere*

In the last 4-5 years, I have been asked many times by friends from Europe and even Latin America to recommend them a book on postwar Greece. Unfortunately, I always had to answer that there is no such book, not at least in the major European languages, and that there is an enormous gap in the international bibliography of modern Greece. Now Roger Silverman's book not only fills this gap but goes even further, by covering Greece's recent political and economic turmoil with up-to-date first-hand information. But this is not its only virtue. Silverman prefers to give the floor to the protagonists and actors in these cataclysmic Greek events, leaving the reader free to judge and draw the lessons of this emblematic modern Greek tragedy. It goes without saying that such a book, written not only for specialists but accessible to almost anyone with an interest in the recent Greek crisis, needs to be translated into other languages as soon as possible.

Yorgos Mitralias, Athens. Journalist and member of the Greek Debt Truth Commission.

Roger Silverman's excellent and most accessible book engages with the exciting advances and the devastating setbacks of Greek popular movements facing down the powerful and vindictive forces of international finance over the last five years. His analysis of the real possibilities in the first year of the SYRIZA Government is developed from a much needed popular history of the resistance of the Greek people from the War of Independence in 1821 to the present, and from an appreciation of similar developments across the world today.

Paul Mackney, Co-chair, Greece Solidarity Campaign, Former General Secretary, National Association of Teachers in Further and Higher Education (now part of UCU).

Roger Silverman's book is the only one I have found which answers the fundamental questions I wanted answered about the tragedy of the Greek people. Nothing happens without reasons, but there are few writers who know how far back to go to provide a clear, honest and readable analysis of the corruption and mismanagement which led to a whole country being pauperised. Clearly written and with hair-raising details of the crisis which has brought Europe close to disintegration, this is a book to learn from.

Bill Boyle, Editor, *DatacenterDynamics*

Defiance:
Greece and Europe

Defiance: Greece and Europe

Roger Silverman

Winchester, UK
Washington, USA

First published by Zero Books, 2016
Zero Books is an imprint of John Hunt Publishing Ltd., Laurel House, Station Approach,
Alresford, Hants, SO24 9JH, UK
office1@jhpbooks.net
www.johnhuntpublishing.com
www.zero-books.net

For distributor details and how to order please visit the 'Ordering' section on our website.

Text copyright: Roger Silverman 2015

ISBN: 978 1 78535 398 7
Library of Congress Control Number: 2015960865

A CIP catalogue record for this book is available from the British Library.

The cover photo shows a section of the crowd at the final OHI rally on the eve of Greece's
historic referendum in July 2015. Photo by Aggelos Kalodoukas, Athens.

Design: Stuart Davies

Printed and bound by CPI Group (UK) Ltd, Croydon, CR0 4YY, UK

We operate a distinctive and ethical publishing philosophy in all
areas of our business, from our global network of authors to
production and worldwide distribution.

CONTENTS

In memory of comrades Nicos and Deirdre Remoundos, whose hospitality, humour and courage remain an inspiration.

How many hearts wept in those black years
That we lived in slavery, treated like dirt?
How many young bodies and lives wiped out
And houses shut up without cause?
Let them take a good look at what made our hearts burn
While they got rich and had fun on our helplessness.

From "The Black Years", a rembetika song by Stratos Payioumdzis, 1946, translated by Gail Holst and included in her book *Road to Rembetika: music of a Greek sub-culture, songs of love, sorrow and hashish*, published by Denise Harvey.

Introduction

The Greek people today find themselves doubly trapped by the human consequences of twin aspects of a single catastrophe: a capitalist crisis which is simultaneously both stripping them of the elementary requirements of civilised life, and driving millions of global refugees onto its shores in flight from the wars, civil wars and environmental degradation it has left in its wake.

Greece has always uneasily straddled the border between Europe and the "global south". Even since the Second World War, while the rest of Europe enjoyed a healing respite from the horrors of the past in half a century or more of relative peace, Greece was facing yet more war and repression. As in Korea, Vietnam and the Philippines, fighting continued for many more years against overwhelming odds as a war for independence. Greece's postwar history belongs more to Asia than Europe; it bears especially uncanny parallels with that of the Philippines. In both countries, a ragtag wartime guerrilla resistance movement had overthrown a fascist occupation army virtually single-handed; in both, it was forced to continue its struggle, this time against the world's strongest economic and military superpower and its allies within the local elite, among them outright wartime quisling collaborators. And where the conflict in Korea ended in a draw, and in Vietnam a humiliating defeat for US imperialism, in both Greece and the Philippines the guerrilla struggle was ground down by a relentless war of attrition. In both cases, later generations were to rise up in massive popular mobilisations that brought new dictatorships crashing to their downfall: the Greek colonels fleeing for their lives and the Marcoses clambering on to their palace roof to the helicopter that lifted them to exile.

Today the old neat tripartite partition of the postwar world between two rival superpowers and a so-called "third world"

1

has long since vanished. Stalinism has crumbled into history; capitalism is reeling from a downturn comparable to the 1930s. It is Europe now that is staggering from one crisis to the next, and tracts of Asia where capitalism still fitfully flourishes – above all, paradoxically, in Mao's China, whose Stalinist state bureaucracy had cleared the path to development by sweeping away the blight of landlordism. On a world scale, the rich have got stupendously and senselessly richer than ever before in history, largely nowadays by parasitic speculation; the poor stripped bare of the most basic means of subsistence and nowadays even of a viable homeland, as they roam the seas in leaky boats and trudge barefoot across continents.

This is the consequence of a breathtaking concentration of wealth. 1% of the world's population now own more wealth than all the other 99% combined. According to the latest report from Oxfam, the world's richest 62 people own as much wealth as half of the world's entire population. (Only five years previously, in 2010, the equivalent number was 388 people.) These 62 masters of the universe had seen their wealth grow within five years by half a trillion dollars to $1.76 trillion. Meanwhile, between 2010 and 2015, despite a population increase of 400 million, the total wealth of the poorest 50% fell by an astounding 41%.[1] Nowhere in the world have the poor got poorer so catastrophically fast as in Greece; and nowhere have they stood up so boldly for their rights.

This book is frankly partisan. It expresses a consistent interpretation of past as well as current events that is controversial, and that will no doubt be contested by others. I don't claim to be an expert on Greece, though I have tried to justify my assertions with references to sources. My interest in Greece is as a fellow campaigner against austerity, and as a champion of the Greek people's inspiring stand against it.

I remember in the 1960s, during my early political awakening, reading with fascination reports of building workers marching through Athens in their thousands demanding the right and means to defend themselves against the impending military coup [2], then observing with horror the sheer brutality of the junta once it had seized power; and in the early 1970s, watching in awe the courage of the youth at the Polytechnic as they defied the guns and tanks of the regime, and greeting with jubilation the subsequent flight and disgrace of the overthrown colonels.

These were stirring times, defining the period as one of revolutionary change. Almost simultaneously, along with the Greek colonels, the Portuguese dictatorship had collapsed after almost half a century; in Spain, Franco's bloodthirsty regime was on the point of crumbling at last; and the memory was fresh in the mind of the 1968 uprising in France, when ten million workers had occupied their workplaces and festooned them with red flags and insurrectionary slogans, while the ageing de Gaulle fled Paris to hunt desperately for loyal troops. Further afield, as a generation of conscripts at home were tearing up their army draft cards and downtrodden youth in the ghettoes were rioting, the USA was suffering its first ever military defeat at the hands of a ragged army of peasant guerrillas in an obscure backwater of South-East Asia; the heroic youth of Soweto were rising up against South Africa's slave-labour apartheid system; and cracks were bursting open throughout the East European Stalinist monolith...

Not for the first time, it was the Greeks who were in the vanguard of this wave of revolt. In the exciting times following the downfall of the junta, I had the rare privilege as a full-time political activist to visit Greece often, for a period almost commuting regularly between London and Athens and engaging in heated but always enlightening political debates.

Gradually I came to learn more about Greece's history of endless wars, coups and civil wars; its liberation from Ottoman rule; the meddling intrigues of the European great powers; the rout of Mussolini's invasion; popular resistance to the Nazi

3

occupation and its historic overthrow; British and then American military occupation; the civil war and its aftermath; strangulation by the EU and the German banks.

These days were vividly recalled when I witnessed the Greeks' recent mobilisations in Syntagma Square; their avowedly internationalist slogans calling on the other countries of Europe, in their own languages, to wake up and join them; the rise to power of a previously obscure dissident group pledged to fight the austerity plague; and the subsequent months of real panic that gripped the institutions that ruled Europe and the world.

Defiance seemed the best word to describe the consistent response by ordinary Greeks to invasion, occupation, domination, dictatorship, exploitation and bullying. True, it hardly describes the current posture of the SYRIZA government towards the troika; but it defines the unmistakable mandate of the Greek people in July's referendum. And, with the clock ticking towards a new world financial crisis, the Greek story is by no means over. Strikes and protest demonstrations are back, and the government today is barely clinging on to its majority.

The Greeks' misfortune is that they launched their struggle a little ahead of the rest of us and found themselves facing the enemy alone. There is nevertheless a certain symmetry at play. The rise of SYRIZA had helped spark up a frisson of hope throughout Europe, as shown in the growth of PODEMOS, the Corbyn upsurge, and the election of a coalition government in Portugal claiming opposition to austerity; a mood reflected even across the Atlantic in the Sanders phenomenon. Prior to taking office, Tsipras had toured Latin America to consult the "left-leaning" governments of Argentina and Brazil. Conversely, SYRIZA's subsequent capitulation to the troika has left its mark by contributing to a lowering of morale internationally, as indicated in sharp reverses for the left in Argentina, Brazil, Venezuela and Bolivia; the rise to power of xenophobic governments in Hungary and Poland; and the ominous growth of the

4

Front National in France and the Lega Nord in Italy. It is a trajectory parallel to the horrific tide of communal barbarism that drowned the flicker of hope aroused by the "Arab spring". Without a bold counter-offensive, the world could find itself stumbling towards catastrophe.

And yet the experiences of the Greeks directly affect us all; we can learn alike from their achievements and their failures. Nothing has been resolved by SYRIZA's defeat. As markets once again slide into recession, all the expectations are that there will be a fourth debt crisis, a fourth bailout deal, a fourth memorandum, and a new Euro crisis. And if the lessons are not learned from last time, then the sinister shadow looms ahead of Golden Dawn and its ugly counterparts throughout Europe. It is a threat we ignore at our peril.

There are some excellent books about each of the momentous chapters in Greece's history, but throughout these years I wanted so much to be able to read and recommend to others a single straightforward account of Greece's story; to draw people's attention to the rich historical background to today's news. And since, as I discovered, there wasn't one, I thought maybe I should have a go.

In tackling this task, I found especially useful the gripping blogs and commentaries of Paul Mason, Michael Roberts, Yanis Varoufakis, Stathis Kouvelakis, Costas Lapavitsas, Nasos Iliopoulos, Panayiotis Lafazanis, Maria Pendaraki and others, and Kevin Ovenden's history of SYRIZA.

Above all, my sincere gratitude to all those who read my manuscript at various stages and offered me their invaluable expertise, ideas and advice. Special thanks are due to Eric Toussaint of the Committee for the Abolition of Third World Debt for his patience in clearing up my confusion over the origins of the Greek debt; to Yorgos Mitralias and Zoi Konstantopoulou in Athens for their painstaking verification of historical details; to Paul Mackney and Cherry Sewell of the

Greece Solidarity Campaign; to Themos Demetriou, Andros Payiatsos, Sonia Mitralias, Yiannis Tollios, Yorgos Baskozos, Mick Brooks, Finn Geaney, Felicity Dowling, Julian Silverman, John Pickard, John Reimann, Ed Bober and my co-thinkers in the Workers' International Network, all of whom helped me gain a clearer insight; also to Aggelos Kalodoukas in Athens for the cover photo and to Dominic James, Stuart Davies, Douglas Lain, Emma Jacobs and everyone at Zero Books for their support. All the ideas expressed here, including all the mistakes and omissions, are of course entirely my own.

I would welcome comments, contributions and constructive criticisms from readers at https://rsilver100.wordpress.com/.

—Roger Silverman, February 2016

Chapter 1

Rebirth

The future of Europe, with a population of 500 million and a gross domestic product of €13 trillion, depends on the self-sacrifice of 11 million Greeks in its south-eastern corner – or so we are told. If this seems to place an inordinate burden on a population 46 times fewer and a GDP 60 times smaller, then for the Greeks that is nothing new.

Like so many other nations within the Ottoman empire, and also the Russian and later the Austro-Hungarian empires (or the Kurds, Basques and Palestinians today), the Greeks were until the early nineteenth century a stateless and scattered people with a rich culture of their own and a growing yearning for statehood. Modern Greece is a product of revolution. Over three centuries, lawless *kleftes* or bandits had been defying the Ottoman rulers, together with defectors from the security forces (*armatoloi*) and their commanders (*kapetanioi*). Greece's rebirth was impelled by the radical wave that swept Europe in the wake of the French revolution. Inspired by the continental-wide aspiration for liberty, equality and fraternity, early Greek insurgents stood for a multi-national state where Greeks, Turks, Albanians, Slavs and all the other Balkan ethnic groups would participate as equals. Their pioneer Rigas Feraios translated the Marseillaise into Greek and appealed to Napoleon for military support. After his execution, the secret society *Filiki Etaireia* (Society of Friends) was founded to prepare an armed uprising alongside "the people of Europe, fighting for their own rights and liberties". Tens of thousands of Greeks were massacred during 11 years of guerrilla struggle. Since then, Greece has always been Europe's simmering volcano.

The Greek revolution was closely monitored by the "Great

Powers", seeking to play off their rivals. Britain, France and Russia intervened decisively at the battle of Navarino to destroy the Ottoman fleet, while failing to raise the siege of Athens. The British were content to patronise a new Greek mini-state limited initially to the Peloponnese region.

Liberation from Ottoman rule did not free the Greeks from foreign domination, nor from constant coups, wars and civil wars over the following century and a half. In the 193 years since its foundation, Greece has had no fewer than 186 governments – some of them concurrently.

The ruling powers of Europe were wary from the beginning of these unpredictable Greek brigands. In London in 1830 it was decided that Greece's "independence" would take the form of rule by a king chosen by officials of the British Empire from one of the royal families of Europe. It was standard practice for British imperialism either to impose its rule through home-grown local chiefs and maharajahs or to foist surrogate hand-picked royals on those peoples not directly incorporated into its empire – the Hashemites, the Sauds, the Pahlavis[3] and the rest. That is what it did in Greece repeatedly over the following 150 years.

First a spare prince from Saxe-Coburg was approached, and when he passed up the offer, Otto, a Bavarian teenager, was persuaded to accept. The British simultaneously appointed two imperial overlords to command Greece's naval and military forces.

Greece fell under the patronage of the British establishment, which soon found itself incapable of containing the implicit instability of the new state. The new puppet monarchy was propped up by Bavarian troops until new revolts in the 1840s forced Otto to concede cosmetic reforms, which gave him no more than a breathing space. In 1862, Otto was overthrown and fled the country. The "protecting powers" promptly began the search for a new king of Greece, first proposing Victoria's second son

Alfred, but following objections from France and Russia, settling instead on another teenager: this time a Danish prince named Glucksburg (the grandfather of "our own" Prince Philip), who assumed the title George I.

The new Greece had a population of 700,000, which still left two million Greeks living under Ottoman rule, or that of other foreign powers (including Britain itself). To assuage anti-royalist sentiment, Britain later ceded the Ionian islands and granted Greece a formally democratic constitution, although it was not until 1951 that women would achieve the right to vote. By the time of the Crimean War, the British were now in alliance with the Turks, and actively suppressed any support for uprisings of Greeks still under Turkish rule.

It was largely left to the British government to determine the new boundaries of Greece. In doing so, it excluded the majority of its current territory. Even today, Greece's northern border is completely artificial: Greeks, Serbs, Bulgarians, Jews, Albanians, Gypsies and Turks were scattered all over the Balkans and moved freely throughout the area. Years later, there was still semi-clandestine movement across the border. (It was not until 1947 that Greece was to extend to its current boundaries, which were drawn in line with NATO's Cold-War considerations: its need to cut off the newly-established states of Bulgaria, Yugoslavia and Albania – all falling at least potentially within the Soviet sphere of influence – from access to the Mediterranean.)

From the very start, class conflicts were already raging, with the shipping magnates demanding huge compensation for their losses, and landowners blocking the attempts of the new government to distribute land previously owned by the Turks to the Greek poor. Between 1865 and 1875 Greece had seven general elections and 18 governments. It was only from 1875 onwards that Greek political life settled down for a while to a British-style alternation of rival establishment politicians: the "westerniser"

Trikoupis and the "panhellenist" Deliyannis.

However, even this temporary stability was not to last long. Not only the government but the very borders of Greece were in constant flux. The drive for Pan-Hellenic unity – the Megali (big) Idea – remained powerful. In the 1860s, the people of Crete rose up under the demand for *enosis* (union with Greece) – a demand rejected by the "protecting powers". After Russia beat Turkey in a new war in 1878, the Ottoman Empire continued to crumble. Bulgaria gained independence and there were renewed claims on areas populated by Greeks. Britain gained overall responsibility for Cyprus, though it was to remain formally under Turkish sovereignty. In 1881, there were more uprisings which forced Turkey to cede more Greek-populated territories to Greece. In 1885, as Greece mobilised its armies for a new war to liberate other compatriots still under the Ottoman heel, the British government sent warships to impose a blockade.

Well before the end of the century, Greece found itself in a predicament that is easily recognisable today. The combination of Trikoupis' domestic liberal reform programme and Deliyannis' foreign expansionist military adventures had drained the treasury dry. No further taxes could be squeezed out of an already impoverished population. Not for the last time, Greece fell under the clutches of foreign bankers. By 1893, half of revenues were going to service external debts; then came a succession of agricultural failures. Greece was bankrupt.

Another familiar consequence of the crisis was the wave of emigration by young Greeks fleeing unemployment and decay at home. Between 1890 and 1914, 350,000 Greeks – one sixth of the then population of Greece – emigrated, mostly to the USA. Greece staggered on, surviving on the remittances of its emigrant workers.

Into the whirlwind

There followed half a century of wars, coups and civil wars. First came simmering conflict with Bulgaria over Macedonia – a melting pot of nationalities including Greeks, Bulgarians, Turks, Albanians, Gypsies, Jews and Vlachs. Then in 1897 Greece finally went to war with Turkey over the status of Crete. A Greek invasion of Turkey was repulsed, and once again it was the grossly misnamed "protective powers" who established a Commission of Control to enforce the payment of Greek indemnities to Turkey.

By the early 1900s, a combination of economic collapse, military disaster and national humiliation had led to a growing rebellion against the foreign-imposed monarchy. In Crete, the politician Venizelos led a daring revolt which captured the public imagination, and in 1909 a group of mutinous officers known as the Military League led a coup. In 1910 and again in 1911, Venizelos won two successive general elections with massive landslide majorities. He introduced substantial social and military reforms, formed the Balkan League alliance, and, following the defeat of Turkey by Italy, launched a military campaign. The first Balkan War forced Turkey to surrender nearly all of its European territories, and the second pitted Greece and Serbia against Bulgaria. Greece emerged with its population expanded from 2.8 to 4.8 million, and its land area extended by 70%. But three million Greeks were still left languishing under foreign (mostly Turkish) rule. Meanwhile, in Turkey, the Ottoman Empire was crumbling and the "Young Turks" were gaining influence.

In 1913, King George I – by that time the longest-reigning monarch in Europe, having somehow managed to survive on the throne for 50 years – was assassinated. He was succeeded by his son Constantine I.

The outbreak of the First World War plunged the monarchy even deeper into crisis. Constantine's sympathies (and those of his chief-of-staff, General Metaxas) lay with his brother-in-law Kaiser Wilhelm of Germany, rather than with his cousins King

George of Britain and Tsar Nicholas of Russia, while those of his prime minister, Venizelos, were with the Triple Entente. When Venizelos won another election in June 1915, and started preparations for war, he was dismissed by the king. New elections were called for December 1915, but they were nullified by a mass boycott. By 1916, Greece was close to civil war. August 1916 saw an anti-royalist military coup in Thessaloniki; royalist reprisals in Athens; and Venizelist counter-reprisals in the north. French and British forces landed at Piraeus to enforce a military ultimatum and blockaded the southern ports, bringing starvation to Athens. King Constantine fled the scene and, having failed to persuade his son George to take his place, finally managed to dump the crown on to his second son Alexander. With Greece now firmly back under British control, Venizelos was restored to the premiership in June 1917, and in July Greece entered the war on the Entente side. There was a purge of royalists and pro-German officers from the army and civil society, including Metaxas. May 1918 saw Greece's first military engagement in the war.

The end of the World War brought no respite to the chaos and flux of Greek politics. At the Paris peace talks, Venizelos staked a claim for the territories around Smyrna (Izmir) in Asia Minor, which was the home of a Greek population greater than Athens. As a cynical bargaining counter, he volunteered Greek troops to aid the French intervention in the Black Sea, part of the multi-national armed intervention against the Russian revolution. Faced with fierce resistance by the newly mobilised Red Army, the Greek forces suffered heavy losses, along with the British, French and other interventionist armies.

In May 1919, Greek forces landed in Smyrna, sent to police the area on behalf of the British and the French – supposedly until a referendum could eventually be held to determine its fate. The atrocities they are said to have committed there against the local Turkish population aroused national resistance. The presence of the Greek army in Smyrna was disastrous for other reasons too.

Anxious to secure the region's stability, it was determined to enforce the rule of both the Greek and Turkish ruling classes, and – being more efficient than the Ottoman authorities – was seen also by the Greek population less as liberator and more as the new oppressor.

While in 1920 the Treaty of Sevres handed over to Greece all the Greek-populated islands except for the Dodecanese, which were still occupied by Italy, Turkey refused to cede any territory on the Turkish mainland, above all Smyrna.

Meanwhile, although the new young king, Alexander, had suddenly died of blood poisoning, having met with an unfortunate accident (he had been bitten by a gardener's pet monkey in the palace grounds), the monarchy was still trying in vain to reassert its dominance. In 1920, there was a royalist assassination attempt on Venizelos, and in November he lost an election. The country was exhausted by years of wars and mass poverty. There was a succession of weak and short-lived governments. For the fifth time, Rallis became prime minister; in February 1921 he was replaced by Kalogeropoulos, to be succeeded in April 1921 by Gounaris, who himself lasted only until May 1922. Koumoundouros was appointed prime minister no fewer than ten times in 17 years.

A grossly rigged plebiscite was held in which, by a highly improbable margin of one million to ten thousand, the throne was restored – if only briefly – to Constantine, and a wave of reprisals rocked military and civil society.

Soon came disaster. In March 1921 a new offensive was mounted against the Turks. This time, Greek armies succeeded in penetrating beyond Smyrna almost into Ankara. With an overstretched supply line in areas devoid of Greek populations, the Greek army crumbled and the adventure ended in disaster.

In August a fierce counter-attack by Ataturk drove them back, and in September 1922 the Turks retook Smyrna. Thirty thousand Christians were massacred, and 250,000 Greeks and other

Christians fled to Greece. The defeat had become a full-scale rout. A counter-coup was staged by the Venizelists, forcing Constantine to abdicate in favour of his son George and move back into exile. There followed a new purge of royalists, and a round of executions of former generals, politicians and prime ministers.

By 1923, Greece had lost half of its "historic" land and suffered huge human losses. The Treaty of Sevres had honoured Lloyd George's promise of territory for Greece in return for support in the fight against the Ottoman Empire... but now it was shamefully abandoned under the Treaty of Lausanne, which formally rescinded it. Venizelos represented Greece at the negotiations and was forced to accept the treaty which established the current boundaries of Greece and Turkey (apart from the Dodecanese, which were only transferred to Greek sovereignty in 1947, following the defeat of Italy in the Second World War).

There followed a massive population exchange – one of the biggest mass migrations in modern history, comparable to the later expulsions of the Crimean Tartars or the Sudeten Germans. Four-hundred-thousand Muslims living in Greece were relocated to Turkey, while a massive 1.3 million Greeks were forced out of Asia Minor to settle in Greece. Refugees came streaming in, swelling the population by 20%. Between 1914 and 1923, an estimated 750,000 to 900,000 Greeks had died at the hands of the Ottoman Turks: yet another of the forgotten genocides of the twentieth century.

In 1923 a new royalist coup led by General Metaxas was suppressed, and the king and queen were driven out of the country. In January 1924, Venizelos won new elections, but resigned after just one month in a dispute with his allies over the future of the monarchy. In March 1924, the National Assembly voted to discard the monarchy and establish a republic. Soon afterwards, a national plebiscite approved this decision by a two-thirds majority. The monarchy – that symbol of national humiliation – was overthrown.

And still the political instability continued. Between Venizelos' resignation in February 1924 and his return to office in July 1928, there had been ten different prime ministers and several military coups. In 1925, General Pangalos took power; in 1926, General Kondylis overthrew him. It was only with the return of Venizelos, who again held office from 1928 to 1932, that even a brief breathing space of temporary stability was restored. Venizelos normalised relations with Greece's Balkan neighbours and reached an agreement with Ataturk.

Then came the Great Depression. Greece was hit hard by the slump in exports of its agricultural produce and by the drop in remittances from Greek workers in exile. Venizelos resigned in May 1932, and Greece once again witnessed a revolving-door succession of five prime ministers in the following ten months. In March 1933, the royalist Tsaldaris came to power; there was an abortive pro-Venizelist coup, followed in 1935 by another, which also failed. There were new purges by the royalists, and Venizelos slunk into exile, where he died soon afterwards. In new elections, the royalists (masquerading under the name Populists) won a landslide victory – though for the first time the Communist Party also won 10% of the vote. In October 1935, Tsaldaris was replaced by the more extreme royalist Kondylis, who then staged another rigged plebiscite (this time conjuring up a vote of 1.5 million to 32,000!) to restore to the throne George II, who returned in triumph in November 1935. The royal card had been dealt yet again. Worse still was to come.

New elections in January 1936 brought an indecisive result, with the Communist Party holding the balance of power with 15 seats. When King George appointed the fascist General Metaxas prime minister in May, there were widespread protest strikes. Metaxas declared a state of emergency, dissolved parliament, suspended human rights, and refused to set a date for new elections. In an echo of the nomenclature of the Third Reich, Metaxas labelled his dictatorship The Third Hellenic Civilisation (after ancient Greece and the Byzantine Empire). Political parties were forcibly liquidated, press censorship was imposed, trade unions were outlawed, the secret police were granted unlimited powers, and a fascist-style youth movement was launched. Thirty thousand people were jailed or fled into exile.

Chapter 2

Resistance

The rout of Greece in Asia Minor in 1922 had brought years of renewed turmoil: the overthrow of the monarchy and a new series of coups, counter-coups, successive short-lived dictatorships and foreign adventures (including a border skirmish with Bulgaria known as the War of the Stray Dog). Then, on top of these years of instability came the terrible scourge of the Great Depression, which sent the value of Greek exports plunging by a catastrophic 70%.

Against this grim background, the restoration of the monarchy on a fraudulent referendum in 1935 encountered little opposition from a demoralised and starving population. Within a year, the new king was presiding over a military dictatorship far harsher than anything that had come before, under General Metaxas. The impotence of the liberals was finally exposed when they tamely acquiesced in this coup rather than form a bloc with the fledgling Communist Party of Greece (KKE), which had begun to gather support.

But where the peddlers of fine phrases had capitulated, the workers were now ready to join battle. Like the Asturian miners in 1934, the Greek workers rose up in May and June 1936 in a heroic bid to escape the fate of the Italian, German and Austrian workers before them. In Thessaloniki, police opened fire on striking tobacco workers. The next day, a general strike brought the city to a standstill; brutal police attacks on marching strikers left twelve workers dead and 32 injured; and when army units were drafted in, many soldiers deserted to the workers' side. Within days the workers had won all tbeir demands: an eight-hour working day, pensions and health insurance. There were similar outbreaks in other cities.[4]

The dictatorship avenged itself by building up a formidable apparatus of terror, using spies, infiltration, police dossiers, forced declarations of loyalty, forgery, and the torture and imprisonment of up to 100,000 people. The people were temporarily stunned. But soon an opportunity arose to seize their chance to fight, no matter how hopeless the international background.

Thirsting for instant glory, Mussolini had invaded Albania in April 1939. In August 1940, Italian warships started harassing Greek shipping, and on 28th October, Mussolini issued an ultimatum demanding that Greece allow Italy a free hand to occupy certain unspecified locations in Greece. It was then that Metaxas – conscious, despite his pro-fascist sympathies, that his royal patrons owed their allegiance and their throne to the British – issued his famous proclamation: *Ohi* (no)! Italy launched an immediate invasion of 200,000 troops by land, sea and air.

There was an immediate national response. Metaxas even received a message from Zachariades of the KKE in his prison cell pledging unconditional support (see below). Within days the Greeks were counter-attacking. By 2nd November, the Greek army under the command of Papagos had driven the Italians back into Albania and were chasing in hot pursuit. By early December, Greece had captured towns in Northern Epirus (Albania) with an ethnic Greek population. The Italian forces had been routed. This was the Axis forces' first defeat of the Second World War – and it was a mass popular uprising which had swept them back, celebrated not just as a national but also as a class victory. So widespread was the cry "Down with Fascism!" that the Metaxas press nervously insisted: "Greece is fighting not Fascism but Italy."

In January 1941, Metaxas died, and the banker Koryzis replaced him. Nazi forces were by now already in the Balkans (in Romania, Hungary and Bulgaria, and soon afterwards Yugoslavia) and were edging closer. Koryzis accepted the offer of British troops which had earlier been turned down by Metaxas for fear of provoking Hitler, and 63,000 British squaddies arrived. In April 1941, the Nazi invasion began from the north. The British escaped to the south, but Greek forces were caught in a pincer movement between German and Italian troops, and in April they surrendered. Koryzis committed suicide. Athens came under heavy attack from air and land, and by the end of April Athens fell. The king, the government and the remnants of the Greek and British forces escaped to Crete in the Mediterranean, which was still under British naval control; and when the Nazis invaded Crete by air attack, albeit with heavy losses, the king and government fled onward to Egypt.

Despite Greece's time-honoured commitment to the interests of British imperialism, the Greek ruling caste was so shaken by fear of popular mass resistance that, as in France, it chose to capitulate to Hitler rather than find itself perched uneasily at their head. The King was whisked out to safety in Cairo. The rulers of Greece absconded, leaving the people at the mercy of Hitler and a handful of quisling collaborators.

The KKE

Purged of all dissidents, like the Communist Parties worldwide the KKE was by now in effect an auxiliary agency of Moscow diplomacy. However, when Mussolini launched his invasion in October 1941, with half of the KKE's 2000 members in prison or in exile, the remaining leaders were thrown into confusion. The so-called "Old Committee" of former KKE leaders still at large considered the conflict "an imperialistic war" in which communists should not participate. Another faction called for collaboration with the German and Italian dictatorships in accordance with the currently prevailing non-aggression pact between Hitler and Stalin. A third, including after some dithering Zachariades (the KKE's general secretary, who was still in jail) and Siantos (the acting general secretary, who had escaped) argued that the KKE should support the Metaxas regime in spite of its persecution of the KKE.[5]

The Nazi invasion of Greece in April 1941 threw the KKE still deeper into confusion. When Germany occupied Greece, there were still two months to go before Hitler was to tear up the Hitler-Stalin pact and launch the invasion of Russia. Fully purged of all dissidents, the KKE was by now a thoroughly reliable agency of the Kremlin; so much so, that initially it failed to resist the Nazi invasion, Germany and Russia still being allies.

On entering Greek territory, the German occupation forces promptly released many of Metaxas' KKE prisoners, though Zachariades was whisked away to the notorious Dachau concentration camp for the entire duration of the war.

As soon as the pact with Hitler was broken, Stalin duly switched sides to form an alliance with the British. The KKE now found itself paradoxically in an uneasy and fragile partnership with its own former jailers and heirs of Metaxas, with EAM/ELAS, under the political control of the KKE, constantly seeking an elusive working relationship with the British.

The removal of the top Party leader had left room for a certain leeway, and there were some differences within the remaining leadership, with Ioannidis (another prominent KKE leader) generally supporting the Moscow line and Siantos often dissenting from it.

The German invasion in April 1941 resolved all doubts. On the very day that Hitler attacked the Soviet Union on 22nd June 1941, the KKE launched "the struggle to defend the Soviet Union and the overthrow of the foreign fascist yoke".

Right up to the mid-1930s, the Greek Trotskyists – independent communists who were not subservient to the cynical twists and turns of the Kremlin bureaucracy – had actually been stronger than the Stalinist KKE. The 2000-strong so-called Archeio-Marxist group had been the largest section of Trotsky's International Left Opposition, and the founder of the united Trotskyist party Pandelis Pouliopoulos was a truly heroic revolutionary, who campaigned courageously for internationalist principles as a soldier in the Balkan wars; went on to become the KKE's first general secretary; broke away from the crystallising Stalinist stranglehold to form an independent revolutionary group; defied successive kangaroo courts; organised militant resistance against successive dictatorships; built the strongest section of Trotsky's incipient Fourth International; translated the works of Marx and Engels into Greek; and died at the age of 43 in a concentration camp in the Italian occupation zone, having made such an eloquent impassioned speech in Italian to the firing squad assembled to execute him that they refused to open fire, and it was left to their commanding officer (or, according to alternative accounts, the Italian special police squads the *carabinieri*) to carry out that assignment.

For all their shining record, the Trotskyists never recovered from the repressions of the Metaxas regime, followed by the relentless persecution they suffered at the hands of the KKE's resistance police force OPLA.[6] It is estimated that some 800 Trotskyists opposed to collaboration and appeasement of the British were executed during the occupation at the hands of the KKE.

In practice, resistance to the Nazis was left almost entirely to the underground Communist Party (KKE), which in September 1941 created EAM (the National Liberation Front) and ELAS (the National Popular Liberation Army) – a broad anti-Fascist resistance movement and its armed wing respectively – adorned with various token liberal figureheads at the top. The KKE now found itself paradoxically on the same side as its own former executioners and torturers of the Metaxas dictatorship, and EAM/ELAS, under the political control of the KKE, made strenuous though largely futile efforts to work in harmony with the British, in line with Stalin's new diplomatic alignment.

By June 1941, Greece was under occupation by Germany, Italy and Bulgaria, with Germany taking Athens, Piraeus,

Thessaloniki, Crete and other strategic areas. The brutality wrought in western Thrace and Macedonia by Bulgaria – a residue of the Balkan wars – forced 100,000 Greeks to flee to other areas. A collaborationist puppet government was set up under General Tsolakoglu, who had earlier commanded troops against the Italian and German invasions; he was later replaced first by Logothetopoulos and then by the notorious Greek Quisling Ioannis Rallis – the son of a previous monarchist prime minister.

Under the Nazi jackboot, there was outright plunder of Greece's agricultural and other resources to feed the German armies, while a British naval blockade was concurrently stopping all imports. The outcome was mass starvation and soaring inflation. By the end of the winter of 1942, 100,000 Greeks had died of starvation. Even after the arrival of at least a dribble of aid relief, people were still dying of the effects of food shortages and hyperinflation right up to the end of the occupation in late 1944.

Under Occupation

The first guerrilla band was formed early in 1942 under the legendary hero Aris Veloukhiotis. The guerrilla war which it launched in the mountains performed feats little short of miraculous. With the sole exception of neighbouring Yugoslavia, not one of the countries under Nazi occupation put up such outstanding resistance as Greece.

The KKE had a broadly liberal anti-monarchist programme. In areas under its control, it organised elections, ran education programmes and promoted women's rights. By 1944, EAM supporters numbered up to two million, and there were about 60,000 active fighters in the ranks of ELAS.

The Nazi occupation forces exacted ferocious reprisals for every guerrilla ambush. For every German who was killed, 50 Greeks would pay the price. Many Greek villages suffered total destruction. Rallis mobilised brutal Greek security battalions composed of the dregs of society, criminals and royalists, numbering 18,000, to terrorise the population.

The peasants afforded protection to the partisans in the teeth of savage reprisals from the Nazis, including the burning down of whole villages with their inhabitants trapped inside, and the tossing alive of men, women and children into the local bakers' ovens.[7]

The workers in the towns were no less heroic. As early as May 1941, two Greek teenagers – Manolis Glezos and Lakis Santas – defiantly tore down the swastika from the iconic Acropolis flagpole flying over Athens and instantly became legendary folk heroes. Both became fighters for ELAS and suffered years of exile and persecution under the triumphant post-civil-war adminis- tration. Glezos, still a living revolutionary today, survived successive death sentences under the German, Italian and pro- US regimes and continuing persecution after the civil war. He left the KKE in despair at its policies, joined PASOK and then left that party too to join SYRIZA well before it became a sizable force. Glezos has only just retired from a seat in the European Parliament and, as a fierce critic of SYRIZA's concessions to the troika, joined Popular Unity in August 2015. Santas' daughter is a full-time activist for SYRIZA.

In Athens and Ioannina, many Greeks risked their lives to protect their Jewish neighbours from the quisling government's collusion in the Holocaust. Forty-seven thousand Jews (98% of the Jewish population of Thessaloniki, and one fifth of the city's total population) were exterminated; only Poland's Jews suffered a higher death toll.

The Nazi occupation forces were stopped in their tracks more than once by unarmed mass workers' risings. Threatened in 1943 with civil mobilisation – the rounding-up of the male population for the slave camps in Germany – a vast crowd of Athens workers surged forward bare-handed in their tens of thousands on the Ministry of Labour. Marching forward into the line of fire of the German guards' machine guns, their first ranks faced certain death. Wave after wave replaced them, to be chopped down in their turn, until by sheer force of numbers, the sea of humanity engulfed the guards, tore the guns out of their hands and stormed the Ministry. The files were burned and the Nazis had to cancel their plans.[8]

The resistance of the Athens workers was avenged by massacres in Kaiseriani and other red working-class districts. (The very first act of Tsipras on assuming office in 2015 was to pay homage to the martyrs of Kaiseriani.) Whole populations were driven out of their homes onto the public squares, where hooded informers marched up and down their ranks picking out known militants. Hundreds were shot on the spot and thousands deported to concentration camps.

The warlords themselves were stunned by the fighting capacity of the Greek people, which was ultimately to prove crucial to the outcome of the war. By forcing Hitler to send his armies to Mussolini's rescue, the Greeks had fatally delayed the invasion of Russia, leading inexorably to the ultimate defeat of Germany in the Russian winter.

It was then that Churchill delivered his famous accolade:

Henceforth we will not say that Greeks fight like heroes, but that heroes fight like Greeks... If there had not been the virtue and courage of the Greeks, we do not know what the outcome of World War Two would have been.

That, of course, did not stop him from turning his forces against those very same heroes in the civil war that followed.

Stalin too, before himself betraying and abandoning the Greek people at Yalta, promised:

The Russian people will always be grateful to the Greeks for delaying the German army long enough for winter to set in, thereby giving us the precious time we needed to prepare. We will never forget.[9]

Field Marshall Keitel, chief-of-staff of the German Army, told the court at Nuremberg:

The unbelievable strong resistance of the Greeks delayed by two or more vital months the German attack against Russia; if we did not have this long delay, the outcome of the war would have been different.

Even Hitler himself, in a speech to the Reichstag on 4th May 1941, grudgingly admitted:

"For the sake of historical truth I must verify that only the Greeks, of all the adversaries who confronted us, fought with bold courage and highest disregard of death."

EAM and EDES

The Allied forces were becoming increasingly alarmed at the meteoric growth of ELAS. A token alternative pro-establishment anti-German guerrilla movement was therefore founded under British patronage, led by the Venizelist Zervas: EDES. For a time EDES was in alliance with ELAS, but soon it came into fierce rivalry with it. By early 1942, with British support, it too had widespread feats of sabotage to its credit. In November 1942, for instance, joint ELAS, EDES and British special operations forces destroyed the Gorgopotamus Gorge railway bridge and cut the German supply line to Rommel in North Africa.

The self-styled government-in-exile, a creature of the British government based first in London and then in Cairo, was royalist and implacably opposed to the KKE. It gave no help to the real resistance movement on the ground – ostensibly out of a professed concern to avoid Nazi reprisals against the Greek population. However, it could not ignore the fact that the resistance controlled substantial areas of territory; it was fighting the Nazi occupation, and, remarkably, in places winning. It became out of the question to ignore its role, and, grudgingly, the Allies were forced to recognise it. In July 1943, the British enlisted the support of ELAS to simulate fake preparations for an allied invasion from the Mediterranean. It made a deal to give ELAS/EAM official recognition, provided it would cease attacks on EDES and co-operate in the invasion simulation. In August 1943, meetings were held in Cairo with King George and the government-in-exile.

EAM's sole condition for co-operation was a demand for a post-war plebiscite on the return or otherwise of the monarchy, and control in any post-war coalition government of the ministries of war, justice and the interior (i.e. the armed forces and the police). These demands were rejected out-of-hand. ELAS returned to the mountains empty-handed, and a virtual civil war broke out between ELAS and EDES, foreshadowing events following the war.

While showering military aid to EDES, the British summarily cut off all supplies to ELAS; but once Italy had surrendered in September 1943 and was out of the war, ELAS was able simply to help itself to the plentiful abandoned weapons stores of the fleeing 15,000 Italian troops. In February 1944, a fragile truce was established between ELAS and EDES, confining EDES operations to the region of Epirus, and giving the vastly stronger ELAS complete freedom of operation throughout the rest of Greece. By this time, Germany was withdrawing its forces for combat elsewhere to replenish its losses in Russia, with the result that whole new territories were liberated by ELAS. EAM also created a complete range of civil domestic organisations: a trade-union federation, a youth movement, a secret police and a civil guard. EAM had established foreign relations with neighbouring Communist Parties as well as with the British. In March 1944, it set up the Political Committee of National Liberation (PEEA) as a government in the liberated regions. This rival challenge to the government-in-exile enjoyed huge public support. As far away as Egypt, Greek military units under British army patronage mutinied in support of PEEA – and were ruthlessly suppressed by British military personnel.

The British were rapidly losing any vestige of a popular base within the Greek population. They had formed a puppet government-in-exile, but in an effort to bolster support, in April 1944 they hurriedly replaced their first choice of nominal "prime minister"-in-exile, the son of Venizelos – who had been in post a total of 13 days! – and appointed in his place a staunch anti-communist but also a known anti-royalist: the tamed republican George Papandreou. So anxious had the Greek Communists been to reach an agreement with the British that Papandreou had actually already previously been offered the leadership of EAM. But he had refused, instead offering his services to the British in a grovelling memorandum counterposing "Anglo-Saxon liber-alism" to "Pan-Slavic communism". In any case, Papandreou was to serve only as an adornment, for it was rabid royalists and Metaxists who were commanding the Greek armies serving in the Middle East war. Repeated mutinies against these reactionary officers were still being crushed with the utmost ferocity by the British.

A "conference of national unity" was hurriedly convened in Lebanon in the hope of forming a joint coalition government with the support of both EAM and EDES. However, despite its overwhelming base of proven visible popular support within Greek territory, EAM was presented with an insulting offer of no more than five very minor ministerial posts. It refused co-operation point-blank.

However, the EAM leaders too bore some responsibility for their subsequent defeat in the civil war which was to follow. Their response to this blatant act of blackmail was meek submission to domination by the artificial British-sponsored government, which without their endorsement would have lacked any semblance of popular support. Thus, as we shall see, the way was paved for years of civil war.

ELAS had proved the most successful resistance force in Europe, along with Tito's partisans in Yugoslavia. Fifty thousand fighters had succeeded in holding down seven German divisions, as well as (initially) the 11th Italian Army. By the time Germany withdrew from Greece in October 1944, retreating through Yugoslavia, ELAS controlled virtually the whole of Greece outside the main cities. It had liberated virtually the whole of mainland Greece.

Victory had come at a terrible cost. Between 1941 and 1945, at least 8% of the Greek population had died. Some 2000 villages and small towns had been razed to the ground. Starvation was rife due to wholesale plunder by the Nazis. Trade was at a standstill; most of Greece's merchant marine was lying wrecked at the bottom of the sea; and motorised transport had been confiscated by the occupation forces. A country that already had the lowest per capita income in Europe had suffered the famine of 1941–2 in which 260,000 people starved to death, and later hyper-inflation; by 1944 a kilo of bread was costing 122 million drachmas. Altogether, Greece had lost a larger proportion of its population than any of the other occupied countries.

By 1944 the KKE had grown to 450,000 members; the EAM to at least two million (over a quarter of the population); and the guerrilla army ELAS from a handful in 1942 to an army of 75,000, which liberated 27 out of 31 provinces of Greece. The daring exploits of ELAS had cut off Rommel's supply line, tied down 300,000 occupation troops, and thus delayed the Battle of Stalingrad those fateful months into the winter, arguably changing the whole course of the war.

The resistance had triumphed despite the treachery of the British Command, perched in Cairo alongside the exiled king, which had sniped at ELAS, and set up rival guerrilla bands to attack it from the flanks.

But not even this was the last word. The Athens proletariat rose up yet again in a general strike which effectively overthrew the Nazis single-handedly in the last days as their military grip weakened. The Soviet Army began its drive across Romania in August 1944, and the German Army in Greece began withdrawing north and north-westward to avoid finding itself cut off in Greece. Hence, the German occupation of Greece ended in October 1944, leaving ELAS to take control of Athens on 12th October 1944.

Initially, the guerrilla struggle had been considered an auxiliary force, secondary to the resistance of the Athens and Thessaloniki proletariat. The leader of the *kapetanios,* Aris Velouchiotis, held no office in the KKE and was treated as something of a freewheeling maverick figure. The KKE leadership actually wanted ELAS to be placed under the direct command of the British General Head Quarters, based in Cairo.

The KKE strategy was based on the expectation that following liberation – as in the countries of Eastern Europe that came under Soviet domination (Poland, Czechoslovakia, Hungary, Romania, Bulgaria and Soviet-occupied Germany), and also initially in France, Italy and Belgium – "popular front" governments would duly be established, in which the Communist Parties would be allowed to play their due role. And as in the neighbouring countries of Eastern Europe, they were demanding possession of the crucial portfolios of defence and internal affairs – i.e. direct control of the police and army. This would have given them power to deploy exactly the same tactic as was to be used throughout Eastern Europe, following the flight of the Nazi armies and their quisling puppet regimes in Poland, Hungary, Czechoslovakia and the rest, including in East Germany – what Rakosi in Hungary wittily called the "salami tactic", whereby the Russian-controlled Communist Parties ran the police and army ministries and their bourgeois allies in other parties were then to be methodically sliced off the government one by one, until they alone were left holding monopoly control of the state.

While Siantos used his authority as a minister in the PEEA (ELAS-based) government to urge the kapetanios "to capture Athens as soon as you are instructed to do so", Ioannidis was insisting that "the mountain ELAS should not enter Athens". Zevgos of the KKE explicitly refused permission to the Attica-Viotia ELAS kapetanios to take over Athens before the expected arrival of British troops.

Aris Velouchiotis swore that "ELAS will not surrender its arms until the people of Greece become rulers in their own country". Meanwhile, the KKE Politburo assured the British sycophantically that "the brave soldiers of our liberal ally Great Britain will meet the warmest welcome and help from the Greek people".[10]

It was at this point of irreconcilable conflict between a KKE leadership subservient to Stalin's diplomatic machinations and Aris Velouchiotis, founder and hero of the *andartes* – along with Tito's partisans perhaps the most successful guerrilla army in history – that Aris died under mysterious circumstances, branded by Zachariadis and the KKE a "renegade", "adventurist" and "criminal", blown up by a grenade. His death was hastily reported as suicide – an improbable explanation for such a fighter – but there is powerful circumstantial evidence that he was murdered by the former bandit Drakos in collusion with both the KKE and government agents. The severed heads of Aris and a co-fighter soon ended up strung up on a double gibbet in a public square.[11]

There was no hope, however, of arriving at a compromise between the EAM government of the "mountains" and the government-in-exile in Cairo – and still less so following a spontaneous, though ultimately doomed, mass mutiny of the Greek troops under British command in North Africa. Greece's fate had already been sealed under the secret deal to divide Europe concluded by Churchill and Stalin.

Chapter 3

Civil War

The workers of Athens and the heroes of the resistance were the unwitting victims of a strange and unexpected twist. Far away in a room in Moscow's Kremlin in 1944, in an informal and almost casual conversation, Churchill and Stalin had been settling the fate of Europe for the following half a century. In his memoirs, Churchill recounts the conversation word-for-word. After a sumptuous dinner and numerous toasts of the best vodka, Churchill asked Stalin:

> So far as Britain and Russia are concerned, how would it do for you to have ninety per cent predominance in Romania, for us to have ninety per cent of the say in Greece, and go fifty-fifty about Yugoslavia?

Churchill then handed to Stalin the back of an envelope on which he had scribbled a list of countries in Eastern Europe and the Balkans which were then under Nazi occupation, outlining how much "influence" the respective super-powers should exercise there after the war. To secure freedom of operations in Greece, Churchill had offered Stalin control of Rumania and partially Bulgaria, plus a 50% interest in Yugoslavia. Churchill described his ally's reactions:

> I pushed this across to Stalin, who had by then heard the translation. There was a slight pause. Then he took his blue pencil and made a large tick upon it, and passed it back to us. It was all settled in no more time than it takes to set down... After this there was a long silence. The pencilled paper lay in the centre of the table. At length I said: 'Might it not be

thought rather cynical if it seemed we had disposed of these issues, so fateful to millions of people, in such an off-hand manner? Let us burn the paper.' 'No, you keep it,' said Stalin.[12]

With a stroke of his pencil Stalin had signed away the fate of Greece, together with that of half of Europe. This casual deal was formally ratified the following year at Yalta.

The workers had little time to celebrate their liberation. Hard on the Nazis' heels came a 6000-strong British occupation force, who entered Athens on 14th October determined to crush them. In deference to the Churchill/Stalin pact, ELAS desisted from simply walking into the cities and taking over, but held back to allow the British to occupy Athens and install George Papandreou in office. Hoping for a painless accommodation, they stood aside, abandoning the workers to another dose of military repression, this time from the British. Not only the troops, but the hated collaborationist Nazi security battalions and the fascist general Grivas' "Organisation X", were turned loose on the workers by Papandreou and his British commander-in-chief Scobie.

In accordance with the Lebanon agreement, ELAS's 60,000 men and women guerrilla fighters were to lay down their arms on December 10th. Papandreou suddenly demanded total demobilisation of all resistance fighters, including even the one elite fighting unit they were entitled to retain under the terms of the agreement. ELAS refused. It also objected to the new government's blatant refusal to prosecute and punish Nazi collaborators.

Greece was in a state of utter devastation. Starvation once again stalked the country, as agricultural labourers were driven from their homes to flee to the cities. Black marketeering, inflation and unemployment were rife. Greece's perennial political instability continued: between January and November 1945 there were four prime ministers. New elections held in

March 1946 were boycotted by the KKE, and in September 1946 yet another rigged plebiscite resulted in a vote for the restoration of the discredited monarchy by a margin of 68% to 32%.

In December 1944, the EAM ministers resigned from the government en bloc and staged a general strike and mass demonstration in Syntagma Square.

Churchill cabled to Scobie:

> Do not... hesitate to act as if you were in a conquered city where a local rebellion is in progress... We have to hold and dominate Athens... with bloodshed if necessary.[13]

Dekemvriana

On the morning of 3rd December 1944, hardly six weeks since Greece's liberation from Nazi occupation, a crowd of jubilant demonstrators gathered in Syntagma Square to celebrate victory. As they chanted support for the victorious resistance partisans along with the slogans "Viva Churchill! Viva Roosevelt! Viva Stalin!", under Churchill's direct orders British troops opened fire on them, and distributed arms to former Nazi collaborators. Twenty-eight demonstrators were killed – mostly boys and girls – and hundreds injured.

Titos Patrikios, a survivor of the massacre, recalled:

> I can still see it very clearly, I have not forgotten. The Athens police firing on the crowd from the roof of the parliament in Syntagma Square. The young men and women lying in pools of blood, everyone rushing down the stairs in total shock, total panic... I jumped up on the fountain in the middle of the square, the one that is still there, and I began to shout: 'Comrades, don't disperse! Victory will be ours! Don't leave. The time has come. We will win!'. Nobody expected a bloodbath.[14]

This was the start of the *Dekemvriana* (the December events) – a fateful new turning point in Greek history. The British brought 50,000 Italian reinforcements to Greece to "maintain order in Athens" and to "neutralise or destroy all EAM-ELAS bands approaching the city". At least 3000 supporters of the left were to be executed during and after the subsequent Civil War, and another 50,000 dispatched to concentration camps and "political re-education centres".[15]

Six weeks of fierce Athens street-fighting followed between ELAS and British troops. In the countryside, ELAS hunted down and killed collaborators, and in its own appointed sanctuary, Epirus, EDES was completely destroyed. Half a million people followed the funeral procession of workers shot by fascist murderers under British protection. The police opened fire on the unarmed demonstrators, and 16 were killed, with many more wounded.

On Christmas Day, Churchill and Eden flew to Athens. Churchill warned the King to stay away until a plebiscite could be held, and an Archbishop was appointed regent. Papandreou was hastily removed from office and replaced by the Venizelist former would-be dictator Plastiras. By January 1945, heavily reinforced British troops had quelled the uprising in Athens, and in mid-February the notorious Varkiza agreement was signed, whereby ELAS was to totally disarm its forces in return for an amnesty, and a plebiscite and new elections were promised. Of course, the moment ELAS had surrendered most of its arms, a bloodthirsty "White Terror" was launched. Over the following two years, thousands of leftists were murdered, executed or jailed; meanwhile, no effort was made to hunt down wartime Nazi collaborators. Huge numbers of people went underground or fled to the mountains.

Yet even after the British had clamped their military stranglehold on Athens, EAM yearned for a compromise with its sworn enemies. Siantos, acting-secretary of the CP, said: "The conflict between the British and ELAS is the result of a regrettable misunderstanding." But both Churchill and Stalin were determined to keep Greece under the Western "sphere of influence", and in January 1945 Tito transmitted to ELAS Stalin's wishes that they surrender. As a result, the following month, ELAS signed the humiliating Varkiza agreement, voluntarily disarming the partisans. This surrender betrayed them to a remorseless terror campaign. The arms used by the fascist squads to kill partisans were the very ones surrendered by ELAS at Varkiza.

In March 1946, in a menacing atmosphere, rigged elections were staged on the basis of obsolete pre-war registers and boycotted by the opposition, with an abstention rate of about 40%. The monarchists and their allies won 80% of the vote, giving a semblance of legitimacy to the intensified murder campaign. The Allied Mission promptly deemed the elections "free", "fair" and representative of the "true and candid verdict of the Greek people".

In retaliation for yet another protest general strike, the government kicked out the elected trade-union leaders and replaced them with its own stooges. Tens of thousands of workers were arrested. The Minister of Justice even had the nerve to suggest that "the immense number of accused is the result of a deliberate manoeuvre on the part of the detained persons to overburden the judicial system"!

This victory was hastily followed up by a rigged referendum on the restoration yet again of the monarchy. For the third time, a royal family was foisted on Greece by force of British arms. It became again the figurehead of the corrupt hierarchy, its courtly sycophants dressing up the rule of the generals, blooded and brutalised in the Metaxas, collaborationist and civil-war regimes, hell-bent on a crusade against communism. It is ironic that George Papandreou himself was later to fall victim to its power.

Civil war

For sheer self-preservation, the partisans were forced back to the mountains. The civil war began again in conditions far less favourable to the EAM as a result of its blunders.

It started with the guerrillas facing hopeless odds. On the government side were 100,000 regular soldiers, 20,000 gendarmes, 6000 police, 200 paramilitary bands of "head-hunters", and 16,000 British troops – all ranged against no more than 4000 guerrillas. There were over 30,000 political prisoners, to say nothing of the 7000 refugees who had fled across the border into Yugoslavia. Industrial and agricultural production had slumped to somewhere between 20% and 50% below pre-war levels. Half the workforce of 600,000 were unemployed. Malnutrition was rampant. However, by February 1947 the guerrillas had swelled to an army of 13,000 and had lost only 100 dead compared to 500 on the government side.

Despite the humiliating defeat at Varkiza, the KKE still retained mass support among the workers and peasants, winning 71% in trade-union elections and major influence in the peasant co-operatives... but then began the White Terror of "monarcho-fascism". Fascists, Metaxas thugs, royalists, head hunters and outright collaborators exacted their revenge. Those who had collected taxes for the PEEA were accused and convicted of theft; judges at the popular justice tribunals, of murder; ELAS heroes were shot for having executed traitors. Woodhouse himself felt constrained to write:

> In 1944 I saw the freedom of the Greek people endangered by the extreme left. In 1945 I saw the freedom of the Greek people endangered by the extreme right. That is why I am against them.[16]

By 1947, its former empire melting away into oblivion, and gripped by post-war exhaustion and indebtedness, the British government announced its ignominious withdrawal from Greece. The growing cost in terms of money, arms, resources and army morale had become an intolerable burden on the by now drastically weakened power of an empire on which, according to its former boast, the sun never set. The British government – a majority Labour government which was simultaneously engaged in an ignominious retreat from India – decided it could no longer bear the burden of fighting the civil war in Greece, and relinquished its patronage of the Greek government to the USA. The strain of propping up this contemptible regime had proved too heavy.

When Attlee announced that Greece was to be abandoned, the US president Truman appealed to Congress for $300 million, stating that "without financial aid from America, Greece will fall under Communist domination within 24 hours". Truman promptly secured for the Greek operation $400 million in "aid", mostly in the form of military supplies, planes, tanks, artillery, advisers and personnel. Dollars poured in. Inflation reached 50% between March and August 1947.

The Americans were soon to turn Greece into a testing-ground for all the fiendish scorched-earth tactics that were later to become notorious in the Vietnam War and elsewhere: napalm, defoliation, strategic hamlets, concentration camps... The *New York Times* wrote: "Greece is our laboratory for policy towards other nations."

By 1948 the Democratic Army had 28,000 partisans, of whom 25% were women and 80% aged between 15 and 25. As Christophe Chiclet commented:

This was Greece's drama. The flower of her youth died on the peaks of Macedonia or withered in the island concentration camps. This blood-letting would fossilize Greek society for twenty years or more.[17]

The KKE was busily recruiting new members in the mountains, and supplies were coming in from new regimes initially favourable to the KKE's cause in neighbouring Bulgaria, Albania and especially Yugoslavia. In October 1946, Markos Vafiadis proclaimed the formation of the Democratic Army of Greece. Throughout 1946–7, Markos was winning significant victories in the mountains. The new Democratic Army's numbers never exceeded 28,000, and it was compelled to institute forcible conscription. Eventually 40% of its soldiers were Slav Macedonians. Nevertheless, throughout 1947 it controlled large areas of the countryside.

In the cities it was a different story. By June 1947 the trade unions had been purged by mass arrests of left activists. In July 1947 thousands of insurgents were arrested in Athens and exiled to the notorious island concentration camp in Ikaria. All the left parties were proscribed. It was not until the overthrow of the colonels' regime in 1974 that the ban was to be lifted.

From 1946 to early 1948, the DAG held a substantial proportion of Greek territory.[18] Martial law was declared. Nevertheless, the underlying weaknesses of the former partisan movement were beginning to show. Markos had declared the establishment of a Provisional Democratic Government in Konitsa, but proved unable even to capture his own nominated seat of government, and it was recognised by no one. There were increasingly fractious internal disputes within the KKE, and General Secretary Siantos found himself replaced by the veteran Party leader Zachariadis, newly released from the Nazis' infamous Dachau concentration camp. He abandoned the DAG's traditional military policy of daring guerrilla hit-and-run raids and initiated a strategy of conventional army warfare. The switch proved disastrous.

The KKE sought to protect the children from the horrors of the war by evacuating 23,700 of them across the borders to safety in Yugoslavia, Romania, Hungary, Bulgaria, Czechoslovakia and

Albania. This became the subject of a shameful slander. The US charge d'affaires wrote: "This issue can be turned into useful anti-communist propaganda", and the monstrous lie gained currency that the communists were kidnapping children. The Yugoslav government replied to this lie:

> In Yugoslavia there are no children brought by force; there are only children who have left with their mothers in the face of terror, or orphans – that is, children threatened with death by terror, cold and starvation.[19]

When Yugoslavia was expelled from the Stalinist bloc, and Zachariadis dutifully denounced Tito, the umbilical cord was cut and the supply lifelines destroyed. ELAS found itself abandoned. A terrible royalist revenge was coming. Thousands of guerrillas were killed in government offensives; hundreds of prisoners on Makronisos Island were beaten up, and several died; the former leader of the General Confederation of Labour was found hanged in his prison cell. On top of the 20,000 KKE guerrillas killed in battle, another 6000 were now shot by firing squad, and 20,000 more imprisoned.

And still the leaders of the KKE, obediently basing their policy on the strategy used in very different conditions in Eastern Europe, were pleading for a coalition with the butchers of Athens. The blood of the partisans was spilt recklessly, merely to score cheap bargaining points.

By now, Greece had expanded to its current borders, Italy having ceded the Dodecanese islands, including Rhodes, following its defeat in the World War. King George II had died and his brother Paul had succeeded him.

Another serious blow was the expulsion of neighbouring Yugoslavia from the Moscow-led Cominform. This political complication destroyed relations between Tito and the KKE, which still maintained its slavish allegiance to Moscow.

Yugoslavia soon sealed its borders to the KKE guerrillas, as did Bulgaria, on Stalin's orders. Vital supply lines and escape routes were blocked. Despite the bravery of the Democratic Army, after three years the odds against it were hopeless.

The USA was pouring troops, weaponry and millions of dollars in cash into Greece under the Marshall Plan, and by the start of 1949 the balance of forces was transformed. The Greek national army now had 200,000 well-equipped troops. Field Marshal Papagos assumed command and the DAG was in retreat.

A grisly manhunt was launched. A price was put, literally, on the heads of decapitated partisans which could be exchanged for cash prizes. Corpses were mutilated in order to furnish the press with faked "red atrocities". Hostages were shot in the prisons.

This was the gruesome outcome of a tragic drama of betrayal. A mass partisan army of workers and peasants had single-handedly overthrown one of the most bloodthirsty regimes in history. Only the machinations of political and diplomatic treachery stood in its way in establishing an independent socialist society.

Having been cynically granted a free hand by Stalin, Churchill had proceeded to declare war on the heroes of the Greek resistance and to reimpose royal rule by brute force. For its part, in deference to orders from the Kremlin, EAM had reluctantly signed the infamous Varkiza agreement and meekly surrendered its arms, thus opening the way to an era of brutal repression at the hands first of British and then American military forces.

Finding itself subsequently compelled to resume resistance – though by now in a severely weakened and isolated condition – its guerrilla forces found themselves once again beginning to regain momentum and score spectacular successes. This came to a sudden halt with the return from captivity in a German concentration camp of the KKE's former leader Zachariades, who promptly overruled ELAS to order an abrupt abandonment of guerrilla tactics and a switch to conventional warfare against the

British – a fatal decision which doomed it to defeat.

At least 600,000 Greeks had died in the convulsions of war and civil war: more than half a million killed during the occupation, and 80,000 more in the civil war. Thousands of heroic partisans and militant trade-unionists had been executed or jailed for life. Seven-hundred-thousand homeless refugees were stranded in camps; and 100,000 Greeks had fled to exile. Nearly one-tenth of the population of seven million had died fighting in turn the Italian, German, British and American occupations.

Although the civil war had been won in the name of "democracy", the survivors were left in no doubt as to the outcome. Thousands of political prisoners herded on the notorious Makronisos Island prison camp were harangued by the commandant:

> Communism fell at Vitsi and Grammos. Now it's going to eat dirt at Makronisos… We stop at nothing. We are the winners, you are the losers… The time has come to crush you… You submit or die. The army runs things here… We have all the rights and power and we want you to know it.[20]

Forty-eight hours' torture for the first batch of 3000 prisoners produced the following gruesome statistics: 17 dead, hundreds of attempted suicides, 600 bone fractures and 250 mental cases. That was the real face of the victors of the civil war and their "Anglo-Saxon liberalism".

Chapter 4

Riding the Tiger

In 1950, fresh from victory in the only contemporary civil war in Europe, Greece's armed forces were the biggest in Europe. A Greek government propped up by massive US intervention duly sent an infantry brigade and an airforce unit to fight alongside US forces in the Korean War, and in 1951 Greece joined NATO.

Now the civil war was over. Death sentences were passed upon about 3000 partisans – many of them heroes of the resistance. KKE leaders Beloyannis, Ploumpidis and many others were executed. The scale of reprisals on the vanquished was exceeded only by the bloody massacres perpetrated by Franco at the end of the Spanish civil war. Tens of thousands of political exiles were forced into emigration. Between 1955 and 1971, 1.5 million of the rural population left the land: 900,000 into exile abroad and 600,000 to the city slums.

For the following quarter-century, Greece was to be ruled by a regime of fear. The workers and peasants had been defeated at the hands of the royalists and former collaborators, but their will was not crushed. For all the grim reprisals, their political memory had not been obliterated by the kind of systematic annihilation accomplished, say, in Nazi Germany or Franco's Spain. In the 1950 elections, the left was already scoring 10% of the votes, and the far right less than 20%.

The post-civil-war regime was anything but stable. The regime that had emerged victorious was still insecure. In the three years of civil war (October 1946 to October 1949), the royalist administration had five prime ministers, and between October 1949 and November 1952, seven more.

No fewer than 44 parties contested the March 1950 general elections. The right-wing Populists – the biggest single party –

did not have enough seats to form a government on their own. A coalition was formed containing many of the old familiar names: the Liberals led by yet another Venizelos, the National Progressive Centre Union by Plastiras again, while another constituent party was actually called the "George Papandreou Party"! Venizelos became prime minister for a few weeks, then Plastiras for four months, then Venizelos again for a year, then new elections were held in September 1951. Again, Venizelos became prime minister for a couple of months, then Plastiras for 11 months, and then a certain Kiusopoulos for six weeks. Papagos' Greek Rally party supplanted the Populists on the right, and the EDA (United Democratic Left) appeared as a surrogate for the KKE.

Despairing of Greece's endless political instability even after victory in a civil war, the USA insisted on a change in the electoral law to provide for simple majority rule. It certainly achieved that. In November 1952, elections held under the new law brought Field-Marshal Papagos to power with a massive 247 seats out of 300. On a vote of 49%, he had won 82% of the seats. Papagos and his successor Karamanlis continued to hold uninterrupted power for the next 11 years, until 1963 – though the electoral law was routinely manipulated to fix subsequent elections.

It was against the background of an intensification of the Cold War that the US embassy had intervened to install as prime minister a man drenched in blood from the civil war. Field-Marshal Papagos had been the pre-war dictator Metaxas' chief-of-staff, commander-in-chief of the army throughout the civil war, and head of the generals' sinister secret society IDEA, which had been founded with the express purpose of suppressing the 1943 and 1944 mutinies of Greek troops under British command in the Middle East.

On Papagos' death in 1955, he was succeeded by an obscure backwoodsman hand-picked by CIA chief Allen Dulles as a pliant tool – Karamanlis, who remained prime minister from 1955 to 1963.

Papagos and Karamanlis presided over the devastated battle-field of Greece as IDEA perfected a shadowy police state under the camouflage of "emergency legislation". The officers exacted revenge on workers, who were duly blacklisted; on militant activists, who were assassinated; and on the political prisoners, of whom there were still a thousand languishing in captivity a decade and a half after the end of the civil war.

For now, at last a government had been elected with a rock-solid stable parliamentary majority; but beneath the surface, all the stresses and tensions of Greek society were still at play. The Papagos government continued to hound the left long after their defeat in the civil war, blacklisting them from employment and periodically setting thugs on them as a timely reminder. Greece remained a police state in all but name. It was not until August 1989 that a staggering 16 million personal files accumulated by the Greek security police were finally publicly burned in a steel plant outside Athens.

In the early 1960s, unemployment in the cities was 11%, and in the countryside anything up to 25%. There was a massive exodus from the countryside: a migration to the cities – more than half the population are now living in Greater Athens – and a flood of emigration abroad. From the mid-1950s to the end of the 1960s, 300,000 Greeks emigrated to Australia, the USA and Canada, and over 500,000 to Europe as "guest workers". Net emigration overtook the birth rate and the population actually declined. Wages were clamped down and Greece became a profit haven for foreign investment, which poured into construction, shipping and the tourist industries.

However, the wounds of the civil war were quickly healing. Following devaluation of the drachma by 50%, while the high cost of imports was hitting living standards hard, there was some development of the Greek economy: a growth of exports, an increase in foreign investment, low-interest loans to farmers, modernisation of the infrastructure, a boom in construction, industry and tourism, and the growth of huge merchant shipping fleets, owned by notorious magnates like Onassis and Niarchos. Development was promoted by a substantial public sector: by the early 1960s, one third of urban workers were state employees. On the basis of cheap labour, the national income was growing by 5.5% a year.

This feverish boom was giving the workers a new sense of their identity as a class. As early as 1958, EDA (the legal front for the banned CP) was winning 25% of the votes. At the same time, a safer channel of dissent emerged in the form of a new party, the Centre Union, under the leadership of the "old fox" George Papandreou and a descendant of Venizelos.

Meanwhile, a new terror campaign was unleashed, paving the way for the rigged elections of 1961 in which Karamanlis (who had replaced Papagos after his death in 1955 and renamed his party the ERE, or National Radical Union) increased his majority by 10% at the expense of EDA. This remarkable result was achieved by a military plan codenamed "Operation Pericles", involving the whole state machine, and masterminded by the intelligence agent and special liaison officer with the CIA, Colonel Papadopoulos – the same man who was a few years later to become Greece's military dictator. In the towns, 500,000 false names were added to the register. In the countryside, a wave of violence was unleashed to intimidate the voters, against the feeble protests of the Centre Union.

According to the official returns for the elections held in October 1961, George Papandreou's Centre Union came second to Karamanlis' party ERE, with EDA (surrogate for the banned KKE) winning 15%. There were claims from both the Centre Union and the EDA of widespread intimidation, manipulation and fraud. Papandreou mobilised mass support for new elections and an end to judicial and extra-judicial repression of the left. At the same time, the military were plotting an extra-parliamentary solution, and tensions arose between Karamanlis and the royal family over its closeness with the military. Popular anger reached boiling point in May 1963 when the popular EDA MP Lambrakis was murdered with police collusion in full public view at a street protest. Half a million people followed the coffin at his funeral parade.

By June 1963, Karamanlis' collusion with the Pericles ballot-rigging plot was exposed. He resigned in disgrace. Unproven rumours even circulated that Karamanlis had been a Nazi informer during the occupation who had been rewarded with the abandoned property of a Jew deported to Auschwitz. Such was the mass outrage that the King dismissed Karamanlis, who, having lost the subsequent election to Papandreou, literally had to slink out of Greece in disguise, under a false name and on a forged passport. It was only by remaining in exile in Paris in splendid isolation for the next 11 years that he managed to avoid becoming personally tainted with the intrigues of 1963–7 and the colonels' dictatorship of 1967–74, and was enabled to return home after their downfall in 1974 masquerading as the saviour of Greece from the dictatorship imposed by his own former arch-accomplice Papadopoulos.

Constitutional crisis

Greece was in ferment. Elections in November 1963 gave a majority to a potential alliance of the Centre Union and EDA, but George Papandreou refused EDA's call for a "popular front" coalition government with EDA, and instead – in pursuit of his "two-front struggle" – within three months forced new elections which gave his Centre Union a decisive 53% of the votes and a landslide majority. Yearning for an end to their relentless perse-cution at the hands of the triumphant victors of the civil war, EDA supporters had opted to vote for Papandreou. EDA too was flourishing. By 1964–5, EDA had at least 90,000 members and a youth movement of 60,000, and was winning up to 33% in its own right in municipal elections.

The king and ruling circles had judged it wise to let off steam by cautiously allowing the Centre Union – the more wily liberal face of Greek capitalism – to come to power. But in the disguised dictatorship that still ruled Greece, even a mildly liberal government, by boosting the workers' morale and curbing the worst excesses of the police, posed a threat to the precariously balanced power structure which kept the revolution at bay.

The new government introduced significant liberal reforms. Political prisoners were released, diplomatic relations were opened with Eastern Europe, and long-overdue educational reforms were introduced, including the replacement of the formal purist *katharevousa* language with demotic Greek as the medium of instruction. Under the influence of George's son Andreas Papandreou, social-welfare programmes were introduced for the first time. These led to frictions and a backlash from the party's right wing, led by Mitsotakis.

In an attempt to clip the wings of the military, Papandreou cut its budget by 10% to help fund educational and social reforms; launched an official investigation into the Pericles plot to rig the elections in 1961; and tried to dismiss the most suspect senior officers. This led to an immediate constitutional crisis.

In March 1964, King Paul had died, and was succeeded by the young Constantine II. Papandreou's own defence minister refused point-blank to carry through Papandreou's new policy; and when Papandreou tried in May 1965 to dismiss him and assume the role of defence minister himself, the king blatantly refused to appoint him. Apparently it was quite permissible for a liberal to remain token prime minister for the time being; but not to take over direct responsibility for the real power of the state: the armed forces.

A head-on conflict developed between the government and the king. Using bribery, flattery, bullying and blackmail, defectors were enticed to rat on the Centre Union. In July, Papandreou resigned over the issue, hoping thereby to call the king's bluff. To his surprise, his resignation was immediately accepted – and it turned out that his right-wing successor, appointed minutes later, had already been sitting in the anteroom, waiting to take over.

The king had summarily dismissed Papandreou's democratically elected government and brazenly refused to allow the prime minister to dismiss the army commander-in-chief who had masterminded the criminal Pericles coup, or even to take personal charge, as he had proposed, of the defence ministry.

It is worth bearing in mind here that the Greek monarchy was a direct British import modelled on British constitutional practice, and that King Constantine's actions were soon afterwards to be repeated by the Queen's official representative in Australia, who likewise summarily dismissed the reforming Labour prime minister Gough Whitlam.

It was an unprecedented situation. The whole population of Greece was drawn into open scrutiny of a conspiracy by the king and the military to subvert and if necessary remove from office a government elected with a clear popular mandate. It was a covert coup. There were massive demonstrations. One million people flooded the streets to greet Papandreou after his return from the palace, and a general strike was called. Building workers marched through the streets shouting "give us arms!"

Hurried attempts were made to cobble together a standby government. In July, a certain Athanasiadis-Novas was appointed prime minister; in August, Tsirimokos, a former EAM leader and now a defector from the Centre Union; and in September another defector, Stephanopoulos, formed a government including the right-wing ERE along with some renegade Centre Union members and even the EDA. This government staggered along for more than a year, but in December 1966, having lost the support of both wings of his government, it was replaced by the caretaker government of Paraskevopoulos. In April, this government too fell, and the new ERE leader Kanellopoulos was invited to form a temporary government to prepare elections scheduled for 28th May 1967.

There began a tussle between the two wings of the establishment. Karamanlis' successor Kanellopoulos appealed for renegades within the Centre Union to split it from within. Papandreou retaliated by publicly exposing the regime's dirty secrets relating to the 1961 Pericles vote-rigging plot. He was playing with fire. By exposing the role of the generals, he was shining a spotlight on the rottenness of the state machine, and setting in motion a scandal of the dimensions of the Dreyfus affair. Like a cornered rat, the king demanded the punishment not of the Pericles criminals, but of those officers who had dared to investigate them, on the grounds that they had "violated the hierarchical principle of army organisation"!

In a pre-emptive strike, the officer caste countered with an even more cunning ploy: the "Aspida" frame-up. A handful of democratically-minded junior army officers had quite understandably tried to set up a protective organisation – Aspida (the shield) – in the hope that it might help offer security against the danger of a future military coup. The right raged about a "red plot" and made the absurd accusation that Andreas Papandreou – a Harvard economist – was personally implicated. Eighteen officers were soon to be convicted in connection with the Aspida "conspiracy".

In foreign policy, too, Papandreou's hands were tied by NATO and the US government. Successive governments had played the Cyprus card to rally patriotic aspirations for the union of all Greek populations. Most of the Greeks in Cyprus, who made up 80% of the population, wanted *enosis* – union with Greece. This was also the ultimate goal of its president, Makarios. The British were determined to keep Cyprus as a strategic base for naval control of the Eastern Mediterranean and the Suez Canal. In

April 1955, the right-wing terrorist group EOKA – led by the notorious civil-war butcher Colonel Grivas – began a violent campaign against the British occupation. Its programme of *enosis*, its fiercely anti-communist posture and its collaborationist history in Greece played right into the hands of the British; and when in response they formed an anti-terrorist force (the Auxiliary Police Force) composed solely of Turkish Cypriots, in classic British "divide-and-rule" imperial tradition they succeeded in misrepresenting the crisis as an inter-communal conflict, their own professed mission being to protect the Turkish minority (who at that time numbered only 100,000). Actually, most of EOKA's victims were not Turks but those they considered Greek Cypriot "traitors" (by one estimate, 203) and British soldiers (104). Nevertheless, Turkish mobs attacked Greek enclaves in Istanbul and Izmir (Smyrna) and, on the island, leaders of the Turkish community were vetoing all government measures, with Makarios demanding curbs on their veto. There were fierce ethnic clashes and threats of military intervention by Turkey. British troops and later a UN emergency force policed the island. Grivas – now promoted to General – took command of Greek troops on the island and Turkish planes bombed Greek positions. Soon the US government imposed a settlement over Papandreou's head.

"Fuck your parliament!"

In the light of what was to happen to Greece soon afterwards, it is interesting to note the terms in which US President Lyndon Johnson dictated his solution to the Cyprus question. These were his words at the time to the Greek ambassador in Washington:

Then listen to me, Mr Ambassador: fuck your parliament and your constitution. America is an elephant. Cyprus is a flea. If these two fleas continue itching the elephant, they may just get whacked by the elephant's trunk, whacked good... We pay a lot of good American dollars to the Greeks, Mr Ambassador. If your prime minister gives me talk about democracy, parliament and constitutions, he, his parliament and his constitution may not last very long.[21]

The Centre Union was poised to win a crushing victory in new elections scheduled for 28th May 1967, with a popular mandate at least to curb the rule of the palace, the army and the US embassy. However, the real powers in Greece had other plans. Andreas Papandreou had even been given an explicit warning by a top US diplomat:

Unless the Centre Union were willing to lose the next election… it was inevitable that we would face a dictatorial solution; for the establishment would not tolerate an out-and-out victory of the Papandreous.[22]

The palace and the IDEA generals were faced with a delicate dilemma. If they allowed elections to go ahead, giving the Centre Union a massive majority, that would be a rebuff to the king; a denial of his right to maintain a state machine unaccountable to parliament. It could open the floodgates to revolution. On the other hand, as they were advised by Tsirimokos, a former EAM leader and by now a hated renegade, "when the people are on the go, one cannot tame them with dictatorships". It would be necessary first to tarnish and compromise the liberals, who after all were no less frightened than the conservatives at the tiger that they found themselves unwillingly straddling.

George Papandreou could not openly capitulate without losing all credibility, but he did all he could to appease the elite. He submitted tamely to the Paraskevopoulos government which had been undemocratically foisted on Greece, limiting himself to feeble slogans like "the King reigns, the people rule", "the army belongs to the nation", and "allies of the USA yes; satellites, no".

Even according to his son Andreas, "his tone towards the King was respectful, reserved. Every so often he would attack the left so as to offer palpable proof that a popular front was not in the making." By avoiding a showdown he "gave time to the King, IDEA and the para-government of the right to prepare their counter-attack". And, faithful to its mantra of moderation, the EDA simply trailed along behind him.

Nevertheless, as elections approached, the eyes of the masses were still pinned on the hope of striking a decisive blow against the right.

The palace had been working in accordance with a tentative contingency plan – elaborately prepared for possible use in all NATO countries, and known in Greece as "Operation Prometheus" – for a military coup to be put into operation, either just before the elections or soon afterwards, at a moment when it was judged that the Papandreou government was beginning to discredit itself and disappoint the hopes and expectations of its supporters. But such a measure was fraught with dangers. At best, the intention was to organise a "mild" coup along the lines of Gursel's putsch in Turkey in 1960; to postpone elections for one year on the pretext of "security dangers"; organise a new party firmly under the king's control, rig the registers, harass the opposition, and gamble on an electoral victory for the right.

Meanwhile, however, the cowboy operatives at the local CIA station, never renowned for their strategic subtlety, were urging the colonels involved in their own so-called EENA conspiracy (to whom they were closer, the palace still maintaining closer ties to British influence) to set the Prometheus mechanism in motion a little prematurely, and then present the king with a *fait accompli*. Let him face the choice of either relinquishing power to the new junta or mobilising popular resistance to it. There was little doubt which course he would take.

Chapter 5

Under the Jackboot

On 21st April 1967, tanks rolled on to the streets of Athens. A clique of officers seized power under "Operation Prometheus", led by Colonel Papadopoulos – the army's liaison officer with the 300-strong local Athens CIA station. The main roads to Athens were blocked, the parliament building was under siege, and all communications and defence facilities were seized.

For the workers, a seven-year nightmare began. The colonels imposed a regime of ferocious terror: of overcrowded concentration camps and bestial tortures. Ten thousand people were arrested, from the Papandreous (father and son) and the caretaker prime minister Kanellopoulos downwards, and there was a full-scale purge of officers whose sympathies might be in doubt. The press was heavily censored, trade unions banned, gatherings of more than five people outlawed. Military courts administered summary penalties to be routinely executed in the prison cells and torture chambers of Brigadier Ioannidis' dreaded secret police.

The attitude of these demented reactionaries towards more complex social issues was no less insensitive. They imagined that it was enough to stamp their feet like sergeant majors at a parade ground and scream at the class struggle to "stand to attention!" Among the junta's first decrees were the banning of beards, long hair and mini-skirts, the censorship of "immoral" literature (including several classic Greek tragedies), and the imposition of an archaic form of Greek for use in schools. Boys and girls were even compelled by law to go to church.

They treated the economy, too, like a regiment, barking peremptory commands and issuing constant "decrees": for instance, to freeze prices at a time of rampant inflation caused by their own profligate state-spending.

The king, his courtiers and generals were taken unawares by the coup. Their palace junta IDEA had its own blueprint for a more strategically planned coup, but they had been beaten to the finishing post. The KYP intelligence officer Makarezos had been circulating an alarmist report warning of an "impending communist armed uprising", but the general staff had correctly dismissed it as over-zealous scare-mongering and over-ruled his proposals. They were, however, concerned by the more realistic risk that Andreas Papandreou might carry out his rhetorical threat to form a parallel "popular government" in Syntagma Square outside the parliament building, and had therefore themselves decided that elections must be postponed for three to six months.

The colonels had now pre-empted them by putting into operation NATO's Prometheus counter-insurgency plan: mobilising the army, police and reservists; securing the ports and airports; occupying all public buildings; and arresting thousands of listed potential dissidents – only adding to their list those figures from the political establishment who might object. According to some accounts, Constantine declined to sign the proclamation of martial law, so the colonels simply forged his signature.[23]

The generals' mechanism for a coup had been prematurely hijacked by the colonels. But this alone was not sufficient to explain their misgivings. They were appalled at the likely social consequences of handing over power to these uncouth upstarts. As strategists and not mere field commanders, they had had a lifetime of experience at taming the revolution. They understood that sometimes a cut of the whip will only enrage the beast all the more. As serious strategists of the establishment, they were alarmed at the colonels' indecent haste. They realised that, since the junta had no broad social base, but could rule solely through brute terror, it could never hope to suppress resistance for long –

and that it would be a superhuman task to ride the storm once the regime disintegrated, as it inevitably would.

That is why figures like Karamanlis, perched aloof in exile; deposed prime minister Kanellopoulos; the newspaper publisher Eleni Vlachou – all pillars of the right, none of whom had been notably squeamish up to now about the use of authoritarian rule by the palace and the victors of the civil war – all loudly opposed the regime. Even the king was later to go through the motions of a half-hearted counter-coup to try to restore his flagging credibility. The fears of these most farsighted representatives of the Greek ruling elite were to be dramatically vindicated by events.

On the other hand, the local CIA spooks – hardly renowned for their subtlety – were jubilant. Mostly former NCOs of rich peasant stock, with backgrounds in the bloody school of the civil war, they had grown impatient at the atmosphere of guile and hypocrisy surrounding the palace, its fawning courtiers cocooning it off from reality. They had formed the secret society EENA, which the CIA's 300 agents in Greece had cultivated and perfected into a sophisticated intelligence tool. One high-ranking local CIA officer had crude advice for the colonels on how to handle Andreas Papandreou: "Shoot the motherfucker because he's going to come back to haunt you."

Beyond the borders of Greece, however, the true "masters of the universe" – the White House and the worlds of diplomacy and business – were appalled at the colonels' cavalier haste and irresponsibility. A telling insight into the response of the top layers even of the CIA is contained in Tim Weiner's Legacy of Ashes (a history of the CIA), which quotes a subsequent CIA chief Dick Lehmann describing the reaction of the then CIA director Richard Helms:

The only time I saw Helms really angry was when the Greek colonels' coup took place in 1967. The Greek generals had been planning a coup against the elected government – a plan we all knew about – and that was not yet ripe. But a group of colonels had trumped their ace and acted without warning... He was furious.[24]

The whole fragile system of cautious preparation for a coup, the devious schemes to compromise the liberals and confuse the workers, their tortuous pretexts to postpone elections – pathetically inadequate though they were – were all trampled underfoot by the colonels' jackboots. The vow to "stamp out communism" was a dangerous appeal to the brutal instincts of the civil war, just at that moment when the workers' morale was beginning to be lifted. By taking over without first preparing a broad social base for their regime, these boneheaded Colonel Blimps were putting a question mark over the very survival of the system.

This was the fear underlying all the mealy-mouthed protests of the most experienced guardians of capitalism's interests. At times they blurted out their true misgivings. Kanellopoulos warned that "unless freedom is reinstated soon, destructive forces will be unleashed that could undermine the foundations of the social regime". Karamanlis was even more explicit: "The situation is dangerous. If it is prolonged excessively, without any wise and bold measures to restore legality, it is liable to lead to communism."[25]

Andreas Papandreou, George's son and a minister in his government, recounts how following the coup he wondered:

What had gone wrong? What had happened to the Democratic Leagues? To our youth organisation? To the labour unions? Somewhere, we had failed. We had been taken by surprise.

And yet ample warning had been given: by the king, by the US embassy, by the workers themselves, who had after all witnessed the whole chain of events take place more than once before. George Papandreou had replied privately to warnings of a coup with the retort: "This is not the Congo!" Andreas, leader of the Centre Union's left wing, too, had stated: "In Europe in the year 1967, a military dictatorship was inconceivable."

So the workers were left defenceless. Andreas Papandreou admitted later:

> Had we given serious attention to the establishment of a clandestine, resistance-oriented organisation; had we formed the nuclei through the country; had we given clear instructions for action in response to a coup; had we distributed radio transmitters and mimeograph machines; and had we rented apartments under cover to protect the leadership of the organisation; then possibly we could have frustrated the coup within the first few hours... No one had emotionally accepted the possibility of a coup, although all the signs of an impending coup were there.[26]

Too late, Papandreou now had ample opportunity in his prison cell to reflect on the fatal illusions and concessions made by the Centre Union. Two banking complexes controlled 97% of finance, and 30 industrial companies 70% of credit, and yet like every liberal government squeezed between the rising demands of an insurgent working class and the interests of a hidebound ruling oligarchy, it had found itself reduced to plaintive effete appeals for a compromise:

> We did not estimate correctly the magnitude of the task confronting us... We placed many hopes, far too many, on the possibility of mobilising the private sector of the economy.

After the event, he admitted the futility of the Centre Union's inadequate reform programme:

> Certainly, such reforms would have led to a hostile reaction

on the part of the foreign investors, the Greek industrialists and the big merchants... What happened in fact is that our much milder programme – which had been intended to prevent the alienation of the establishment – created no less hostility... Since any reform was poison to them, we might just as well have gone further.[27]

The liberals' touching faith in the decency of the officer caste was linked to their unwillingness to start a chain reaction that could end up reaching far beyond the limits of liberal capitalism. They were not prepared at that stage even to pose the abolition of the monarchy and a break with NATO and United States domination.

Pressure

The seven unstable years during which the junta clung precariously to power amply confirmed their fears. For all its brutality, it was tossed helplessly from crisis to crisis, lurching in drunken zig-zags from one contradictory decree to the next.

There was at first no organised resistance within Greece, due to the shock of the coup and the brutal regime of intimidation. Under international pressure, in early 1968 a few of the more prominent political prisoners had been released under an amnesty. Andreas Papandreou left the country and formed a Panhellenic Liberation Movement in exile.

For all the scandalous unpreparedness of the liberals and the left, from the very first days of the junta there were heroic isolated gestures of resistance. The huge volume of muted internal opposition was soon demonstrated when half a million people turned out for the funeral of George Papandreou in November 1968. Around the same time, one student, Kostas Georgakis, immolated himself in a public square. Then Alexandros Panagoulis, a deserter from the army, made a single-handed attempt on Papadopoulos' life. The would-be assassin was sentenced to death. Under international pressure, his sentence was commuted, but he was brutally tortured both physically and mentally in jail.

(There is an intriguing postscript to this story. After the fall of the regime, Panagoulis was elected an MP, but died in a mysterious car accident in 1976 – just two days before he was about to release secret police files proving collaboration with the junta by prominent mainstream establishment politicians, including the former Foreign Minister Averoff.)

As for the view from the palace, King Constantine had at first passively complied with the colonels' *fait accompli*; but soon he was discreetly canvassing support among exiled politicians and generals for what turned out to be a farcical gesture of disavowal. His token counter-coup in December – a charade acted out mainly for public display – could have been a scene from a pantomime. The king – together with his family, jewellery, clothing, butler, servants, doctor, nurses, dog and prime minister – took to the hills, made a broadcast to the nation on a low-power transmitter so weak that it was hardly audible in Athens, and slipped out within hours to a comfortable refuge in the fleshpots of Rome, where he lived happily ever after as a playboy on a pension of £126,000 a year (nearly £2 million in terms of current purchasing power). He himself admitted later that he had not been prepared to take decisive action, because he "didn't want to provoke a civil war".

The defection of the king called into question the constitutional designation of the regime. Papadopoulos had already abandoned his initial claim that his rule would be only a "parenthesis" and now proclaimed it pompously "A National Revolution For A New Democracy Of New Men And New Ideas". The colonels had appointed a handful of token civilian ministers; and in May 1968 a constitutional commission was appointed to draft a new constitution under a system of so-called "guided democracy". However, even their draft was summarily rejected by the junta, whose own version was then ratified in a rigged referendum in November 1968, but never in reality fully implemented. Now, following the royal counter-coup, Papadopoulos appointed himself prime minister and General Zoitakis as regent, standing in for the fugitive king. Later Papadopoulos was to assume in addition to his role as prime minister the roles of defence minister, foreign minister, education minister and eventually also royal regent, so that at one point he was simultaneously both prime minister and surrogate king, before eventually casually declaring a republic and plumping modestly for the office of unelected president. Thus, within the seven years of "stability" imposed under a military code of order and discipline, Greece was in turn a monarchy, a regency and a republic.

As for foreign relations, the regime showed due deference by discreetly withdrawing from the Council of Europe before it could be expelled; however, Greece's continued membership of NATO never came into question. Faced with a *fait accompli*, US diplomacy soon easily reconciled itself to the reality of the regime. It enjoyed barely concealed support from the already doomed presidential regime of Richard Nixon in Washington, and especially from his doubly doomed Greek-American vice-president, Spiro Agnew.

When the Six-Day War broke out in the Middle East in 1967, a Soviet fleet arrived in the Mediterranean and the USA further consolidated its relations with the regime. In 1970, official diplomatic recognition of the junta came from the USA, followed by Britain and Turkey. In 1971, the brief US vice-president, Spiro Agnew, on an official visit made a conspicuous homecoming to his ancestral village, and in 1972 an agreement was concluded giving the US 6th Fleet home port facilities in Piraeus. At the same time, the regime also encountered no barriers to the establishment of improved relations with the so-called communist states of Eastern Europe.

The junta was looking nervously over its shoulder, not at the king but at the workers, desperately seeking to placate them by a feverish resort to the printing press, churning out banknotes to buy off their acceptance of the dictatorship. At first the economy continued to grow until 1972, largely through extravagant state expenditure on the infrastructure of roads, airports, etc., but this was financed by heavy borrowing, and by 1973 inflation reached 33%, the highest in Europe. The regime was perched on top of a volcano liable to erupt at any moment.

In its last two years, 1972–4, the economy reached an impasse. Inflation had eaten huge bites into living standards. Where previously up to 90,000 Greeks a year had emigrated to Germany and elsewhere, a new ban on foreign guest workers, together with the slump in the tourist market, hit Greece hard. A colossal proportion of the budget was meanwhile drained off into defence expenditure. To pacify the population, the regime helplessly issued repeated "decrees" to fix prices, and also raised pensions, redistributed some land and "required" government agencies to respond to complaints from the public.

The fifth anniversary of the coup on 21st April 1972 saw the first open demonstrations against the junta. About a hundred students sat on the steps outside Athens University chanting slogans for freedom and democracy. The regime reacted in panic. The police stormed the occupied law faculty and beat senseless everyone within reach: student protesters and innocent bystanders alike. A decree was issued permitting the use of firearms to disperse illegal demonstrations, and expelling from university all students who had been arrested. Arrested students had their identity cards taken off them and were ordered to report to their local police stations to collect them, where they were duly "processed" with merciless beatings. When students responded with more strikes and sit-ins, a decree was proclaimed empowering the defence ministry to revoke the deferment of national service for any students who stayed away from classes or incited others to do so; in the next two months, 130 students found themselves called up for military service. In case they were in any doubt about it, the treatment they were to receive was made plain to them when Papadopoulos commented publicly: "If I'd had them in my army unit, I'd have smashed their heads in with a revolver."

The student revolt was a sure warning of deeper fissures in the social order. Papadopoulos issued a provocative decree revoking deferments of military conscription for all students deemed deficient in their studies, and police violently broke up a sit-in at the University of Athens law school – the first organised protest against the junta.

The strains on this floundering regime were already reaching breaking point. Four retired generals issued a call for restoration of democratic rule. Soon afterwards, on 4th November 1973, 10,000 people would demonstrate on the occasion of the fifth-anniversary memorial service for George Papandreou.

Then in May, a Commander Pappas led a token naval mutiny in the name of the king, in which 20 warships were involved. It was planned to blockade Piraeus and Thessaloniki. After briefly waving the flag, the captain, together with six officers and 25 petty officers, sailed away to exile in Italy, mumbling: "My action could have been more dynamic, but I had taken no decision to provoke civil war..." As revolts go, it was fairly pathetic, but so precarious was the grip of the regime by now that it prompted yet another abrupt policy lurch. There followed a swathe of arrests of naval officers and royalist politicians.

Then, suddenly, like a cornered rat, Papadopoulos peremptorily abolished the monarchy and proclaimed the foundation of a presidential republic, while appointing himself sole candidate for president – a decree soon ratified in yet another rigged referendum. At the same time, he hedged his bets by abruptly lifting martial law, proclaiming a general amnesty and announcing his intention to hold elections – on the basis of an as-yet-undefined system of "guided democracy". Papadopoulos exploited the general contempt for the king by denouncing him as "a leader of adventurers, bankrupts, fellow-travellers, saboteurs and even murderers", almost casually adding: "And I promise before God and men that by the end of 1974 the Greek people shall elect its representatives for parliament in general elections." As it turned out, his promise was to prove more accurate than he himself probably realised.

This desperate combination of repression and concessions could almost have been deliberately designed to undermine the foundations of the regime. A deep rift was developing within the ruling clique, with the menacing figure of Brigadier Ioannidis, founder of the dreaded Greek Military Police (ESA), casting an ever darker shadow. ESA was essentially a freewheeling torture unit, virtually autonomous, with its own chain of command and its own transport and communications equipment.

The Polytechnic revolt

The panic of the junta, and the precious glimpse that had been gained into the widening split between its rival factions, led directly to the uprising of November 1973. Student protests were spreading fast. By October, there were scattered university demonstrations.

Then, on 14th November, students marched on the Athens Polytechnic and staged an occupation, barricading the perimeter and laying in supplies for a long siege. The next day a trade-union Workers' Convention held a joint press conference with them. Soon young workers were joining in, swelling the sit-in to thousands. A huge crowd massed outside the building to support them. Farmers, professionals and trade-unionists paraded outside with banners. A clandestine radio station was set up to broadcast appeals for the overthrow of the junta. Bus drivers shouted slogans to their passengers. The police cordon was broken repeatedly by workers and housewives offering food and medical supplies to the students and workers. Other public buildings were occupied. The Ministry of Public Order was besieged at night and pelted with missiles.

One eye-witness reported:

We could see hundreds and thousands of young people clinging to the iron railings round the Polytechnic buildings, massed behind the railings, massed along the pavements out in front, perched on the pillars of the entrance gate already placarded with slogans; all shouting out the words that nobody has dared speak publicly in Greece.

Thousands of demonstrators (by no means only students) were chanting more slogans from the railings, all rhyming and all in the same relentless tetrameter rhythm: 'We haven't got enough to eat, today it's them we'll gobble up. Wake up, people, move yourselves, they're eating up the bread that's yours! Down with Papadopoulos, a lunatic is ruling us!' Two other cries – 'Greece for Greeks in torture-chambers, Greece for Greeks in prison cells' – parodied the senseless monotony of the dictatorship's favourite motto, 'Greece for Christian Greeks.'

Soon about five thousand people were taking up the cry in front of the National Museum... The demonstration had spread to the next block, the wide area of curving drives, lawns and open-air cafes, now loud with the chant of 'Education, Freedom, Bread! General Strike, General Strike! Let us not bow down to them! All of us together, at last it's now or never!'

The avenue was one great river of faces bright under street-lamps... The rhythmic roar of voices never stopped. The megaphones over the central gate gave out a loud hush, then announced that Salonica and Patras Universities had both closed down, with their students demonstrating in support of Athens.

All through the daylight hours groups of farmers, builders, actors, lawyers paraded before the School with the banners of their trade; lanes would open for them suddenly through the cheering crowd.

And then the news that the offices of the Nomarchy of Attica, in Stadium Street, had been taken over by construction-workers.

Meanwhile the students had set up their own radio station. Through most of the next 24 hours Athens listened to the voice of a young man or woman reading news and proclamations, with every few minutes the urgent feverish refrain: 'Radio Polytechnic. Radio Polytechnic. The station of the free and fighting students, the voice of the free Greeks in their struggle...'[28]

The police responded with characteristic brutality. After failing to clear the building with tear gas, soon they were deploying rooftop snipers to fire indiscriminately on the crowds below. Ambulances whisking away injured protesters turned out to be manned by undercover police thugs, and taxis delivered escaping protesters into the hands of police units, where they were severely beaten. By nightfall on 16th November, troops and tanks had moved into the city centre, and by the early hours three tanks were parked outside and beginning to smash their way into the Polytechnic. As students fled the compound, police and security personnel clubbed them to the ground. After three days, troops were called in. Barricades were set up to block their paths. Marines, commandos, military police and tanks were thrown against the unarmed masses. There were instances of soldiers refusing to open fire on defenceless civilians. The revolt was crushed only after at least 39 people had been killed (according to the official estimate) and maybe thousands wounded.

The uprising was over... but the shock had split the regime

wide open. As always with a dying elite, one wing fled helter-skelter on the path of hasty reforms, while the other opted for a brutal crackdown; but neither appeasement nor repression could save it now. It was clear that the days of the dictatorship were numbered. The nominal reforms suddenly announced in panic by Papadopoulos had enraged his sinister *eminence grise* Brigadier Ioannidis. The junta was in convulsions as it fell victim to a coup-within-a-coup. In sheer rat panic, Ioannides elbowed Papadopoulos aside and imposed an even more brutal regime of terror. He knew all too well that, however rigged the promised elections, once the masses felt the grip loosening, his gang of torturers could well end up decorating the lamp posts of Athens.

The tanks were soon rolling again, and the island prisons were soon back in business. On Sunday 25th November, within a week of the suppression of the Polytechnic uprising, troops under Ioannidis' command cut communication links and seized the radio stations. Papadopoulos found himself under arrest, jailed by his former accomplice. Ioannidis became Greece's new military dictator, and his sidekick General Gizikis president. Martial law was restored and brutal repression meted out to thousands in the torture chambers of the ESA. This time it was Papadopoulos' turn to find himself under house arrest – though in rather more luxurious surroundings than most of his victims, in his seaside villa.

Intent on somehow whipping up a patriotic wave of public support, the new regime was hell-bent on a foreign adventure, namely a war with Turkey. In a vain search for patriotic glory, first provocations were staged over some oil deposits found in the Aegean Sea; then, within months, Ioannidis moved to undermine the president of Cyprus, Archbishop Makarios, whom he contemptuously dismissed as "the red priest". The plan was to overthrow Makarios and impose by force of arms *enosis*: in reality, the forcible annexation of Cyprus. To pre-empt their plot, Makarios had demanded the immediate withdrawal of the 650

Greek officers assigned under a previous agreement to the Cypriot National Guard; whereupon on 15th July 1974 these Greek officers, together with the junta-backed terrorist organisation EOKA-B, staged a coup. They made an assassination attempt on Makarios, who escaped to Paphos on the west coast, where the British escorted him to one of their naval bases and thence to London. Greece immediately recognised as president the seriously unstable gangster Nikos Sampson. Sampson had been leader of an execution squad during the EOKA days against the British, and was still flirting with Grivas and EOKA-B, though he was not a member and had even been an erratic supporter of Makarios. The choice of this madman by the colonels was accidental; they had failed to recruit any of at least three other prominent right-wing figures to their enterprise and had only turned to Sampson in desperation.

Greek-Cypriot civilians were no less horrified by the ensuing bloodbath than Turkish Cypriots. "Bodies littered the streets and there were mass burials... People told by Makarios to lay down their guns were shot by the National Guard." Rina Katselli, a Greek Cypriot MP, wrote:

My God!... Everyone is frozen with fear... The old man who asked for the body of his son was shot on the spot... The tortures and executions at the central prison... Everyone is frozen with horror. Nothing is sacred to these people, and they call themselves Greeks! We must not keep that name any longer.[29]

Nicos Sampson himself boasted later: "Had Turkey not intervened, I would not only have proclaimed *enosis*; I would have annihilated the Turks in Cyprus."[30]

The Cypriot insurgents were probably tacitly encouraged in this lunatic escapade by the Athens outpost of the CIA, which could see clear advantages in the partition of this vital military base. Whether the more strategically minded Secretary of State Kissinger would have recommended it is doubtful; no doubt he was preoccupied with the Watergate crisis at the time. Whatever his own preferences, once the invasion was underway he had little option but to accept the overthrow of Makarios, the Turkish invasion and the partition of the island.

The new Greek junta had dreamed of scraping together at least some sliver of much-needed support at home by basking in the glory of having finally extended Greece's borders to incorporate the last major population of the Greek diaspora. The result was just the opposite. Turkey called on the British to intervene under its statutory joint guarantor status, and when Britain chose to stand aside and do nothing, on 30th July – five days after the coup – Turkey invaded the island. It massed an invasion force of 40,000 soldiers and 200 tanks and was soon in occupation of 37% of the island territory. Some 180,000 Greek Cypriots fled south and 40,000 Turkish Cypriots fled north. The island became indefinitely partitioned. The EOKA-B massacre and the Turkish occupation had uprooted one third of the population from their homes. Greeks and Turks who for centuries had lived mostly in harmony were subjected to a vivisection of the island which continues to this day.

These bungling dictators now suddenly found themselves embroiled in a hopeless war with the Turks. Worse still, the mobilisation of reservists had placed guns in the hands of Greek workers. Then, when Ioannidis ordered the Greek army to mobilise and fight, the military commanders refused point-blank.

Within days, the regime fell to pieces in utter panic. On 23rd July – just eight days after launching this adventure – the junta collapsed. The regime's puppet ministers literally fled the country, without even bothering first to submit their resignations. One of them was quoted admitting: "We are a ridiculous government, a laughing stock. Even my own friends have stopped greeting me." The nightmare was over.

The token president, Gizikis – a sinister figure in dark glasses, stranded, deserted, the sole remnant of a fugitive government – convened an urgent *ad hoc* meeting of the remaining military commanders and assorted senior politicians, announcing: "Greece is without a government". Unanimously and with relief, the meeting agreed to summon Karamanlis from his retreat in Paris. On 24th July at 4 am, he was sworn in as prime minister. Ironically, the same man disgraced by his proven guilt in the Pericles plot was now seen as the politician with the cleanest hands, least stained by complicity in the colonels' crimes.

A coalition government of national unity was formed, which discarded the 1968 constitution and restored the post-civil-war constitution of 1952, ended martial law, released political prisoners, and even – for the first time since the civil war – legalised the Communist Party.

Following the Portuguese revolution of 25th April 1974, only two months previously, one respectable newspaper had observed: "48 years of authoritarian rule – and Portugal ends up with communists in the government!" It was a prophetic warning that Greece too was about to lurch towards the left.

Chapter 6

Deadlock

The fall of the junta had opened the floodgates. As the more strategically minded of the old establishment had warned, by their adventurism the colonels had only pushed all Greece to the brink of revolution. And sure enough, Greece was plunged into turmoil.

It was in the vacuum created by the hasty departure of the colonels that Karamanlis, the vote-rigging fraud forced to slink out of the country in disgrace 11 years previously, found himself flying back home to cheering crowds in Athens in the private jet of his friend Giscard d'Estaing, president of France. On arrival he was whisked from the airport and sworn into office by the gangster president Gizikis, who was still wearing military regalia and his trademark dark glasses, Pinochet-style.

Now awkwardly draped in the mantle of democracy, and posing as the saviour of Greece from the rule of terror installed by his very own shadowy accomplice of 1961, Karamanlis was the best "symbol of unity" the emergency cabal of generals and establishment politicians could come up with. Karamanlis was no less uneasy in his new unaccustomed role than his contemporary counterparts further west in Portugal and Spain, General Spinola and Adolfo Suarez respectively. They were renegade former officials of recently overthrown fascist dictatorships who now suddenly found themselves helplessly straddling a democratic upsurge. (Both of the rotting Iberian dictatorships had finally collapsed almost simultaneously with the Greek junta: in Portugal just two months previously, and in Spain the following year.) Karamanlis' party was hastily scrambled together out of a coterie of monarchists, former junta supporters, "resistance democrats" and conservatives, and graced with a remarkably appropriate title: the founders of "New Democracy" certainly were rather new to democracy.

"Law and order" had collapsed. The population were dancing in the streets; the police were skulking in hiding; and the officers had locked themselves up in the barracks to protect themselves from their own troops. The revolution could have triumphed without a shot being fired.

However, the fall of the dictatorship had found the ruling elite better prepared than the resistance. While their Portuguese counterparts, enmeshed at every level for half a century with the overthrown fascist regime, staved off elections as long as possible (only to see the left parties between them win two thirds of the votes); while in Spain, mock "democratic" parties were hastily cobbled together at elite clubs and dinner parties, none of which could have survived without the credibility lent to them by the left leaders… in contrast, the Greek establishment rushed to hold quick elections before alternative parties could take root.

The defeat of 1967 had wrought great changes in the underground workers' movement. The betrayals of the civil-war era had not faded in the minds of living generations. The junta had lacked a strong enough foundation to dare to massacre a new generation of workers, as under a real fascist regime, or even the newly installed Chilean military dictatorship, which had at least prepared for itself a certain social base before assuming power and murdering thousands of victims. The memories of the turbulent '60s still remained fresh.

The underground Communist Party had split after the defeat in 1967. The KKE's orthodox leadership retained a solid base of loyalty among the civil-war veterans and organised workers, but among sections of the youth it was distrusted for its Stalinist record and its ties with the USSR. Many of the younger generation felt abandoned by the unreconstructed Stalinists of the party leadership, most of them safely ensconced in Bulgarian exile while they languished under the colonels' dictatorship.

Within a year of the coup, younger activists who had succeeded under the dictatorship in putting up some limited resistance, mainly in the student field, had broken away to form the "Communist Party (Interior)". Discarding the old orthodox subservience to Kremlin foreign policy, the breakaway party adopted instead a "Eurocommunist" or social-democratic posture, hoping to reach an accommodation with the Centre Union in the style of Berlinguer and Carrillo, leaders of the rightward-moving Communist Parties of Italy and Spain respectively, by underwriting the democratic credentials of Karamanlis and other "patriots and progressives".

To complicate matters still further, the EDA – formerly the legal front for the banned KKE in the '50s and '60s – also extricated itself from its ties with the old party and briefly operated independently, before later joining PASOK.

All three fragments of the old KKE were anxious to demonstrate their loyalty to the new government. On Karamanlis' return, Drakopoulos of the mainstream KKE called on "all Greeks to unite to face the national crisis over Cyprus". The CP (Interior) expressed the hope that elections would be held "in an atmosphere of responsible dialogue", and Eliou of EDA "voiced support for the efforts of Mr Karamanlis and urged on his followers patience and prudence". None were ready to challenge the restoration of the Pericles conspirators.

In the elections of November 1974 – the first for ten years – the hastily assembled Nea Demokratia took 220 out of 300 seats, leaving the Centre Union 60, the newly formed PASOK 12 and the United Left (a joint platform of both wings of the KKE) 8. The political default by the left; the wily gambits of Karamanlis; the use of rigged election registers dating from the junta days (which excluded the youth under 21, a blacklist of named militants and the hundreds of thousands of Greek workers in exile); and in particular the bullying tone of his slogan – "It's me or the tanks!" – all combined to give Karamanlis a 54% share of the vote. Their eyes still blinking in the sudden glare of democracy, the peasantry and middle class had weighed up the alternatives and settled on Karamanlis. And yet it was a hollow victory.

Karamanlis used all his cunning to carry through a tricky manoeuvre. He had argued previously that the colonels' coup could have been avoided "if the political parties had followed the example of certain political formations in 1958 in France". He had in mind a previous moment, when the shambolic French Fourth Republic had finally crumbled in 1958. Then too, another lost leader had been recalled to office from a splendid exile in a bloodless coup. General de Gaulle had at first succeeded in imposing at least a few years of order (that is, until the sudden revolutionary upsurge of 1968), on the basis of a new constitution bestowing considerable powers on the president. Now Karamanlis was proposing for Greece too a Gaullist solution. Cautiously avoiding any commitment to the hated monarchy, he staged a referendum on its future which revealed the true balance of forces: 69% voted no. Just as King Constantine had feared, for all his perfunctory protests against the junta, he sank into oblivion together with it. Yet again, another historic rebuff had been dealt to a monarchy repeatedly imposed by foreign overlords on Greece. Out of seven kings of Greece between 1832 and 1974, four had now been overthrown.

So, without consulting the electorate, Karamanlis rushed through his packed parliament a mildly authoritarian Gaullist constitution which, on paper, seemed tailor-made for his purposes. But where concentration camps and torture chambers are not enough to tame a revolution on the move, constitutions are mere scraps of paper. What Karamanlis had failed to reckon with was the actual objective pre-revolutionary crisis gripping Greece. Instead of cheating history, he became its plaything.

An explosion of industrial struggle swept Greece. Long and bitter strikes rocked society. In 1975, 380,000 workers went on strike; in 1976, 1.25 million; in 1977, two million. In the first three months of 1976, as many as one fifth of the labour force were striking to claw back the rights they had lost under the colonels' jackboots. The strike wave flooded light and heavy industry, telecommunications, transport, steelworks, banking, building, printing, the power stations, the civil service, the mines and shipyards and every other sector of employment. Many were bitter and prolonged strikes, fought against overwhelming odds.

The government was thrown into confusion by this explosion of pent-up rage. It was veering between reform and repression, undecided which way to turn. Karamanlis tried in vain to stand firm against this tornado. He sent the gendarmerie and police tanks against striking miners, put airport workers under military discipline, deployed fascist thugs against union militants, invoked laws to threaten strikers with the sack and their leaders with jail, and in the aftermath of a general strike sacked 1800 militants, including 240 elected trade-union officials. However, the most he could achieve was isolated sorties against individual groups of workers.

Meanwhile, he hurriedly placated public opinion. In a flurry of reforms, the new government nationalised Greece's oil refinery and airline, formally regulated the banks, lowered the voting age, brought women into the police and army, liberalised the divorce laws, nationalised some church land and belatedly bestowed official status to the modern vernacular demotic Greek language rather than the archaic classical form *katharevousa*. The employers' federation SEV protested against what it denounced as the government's "social mania" and responded with an investment strike.

New Democracy was bursting at the seams, its rival factions thrown apart. A long trial of strength was in prospect, on political as well as economic issues. The workers and youth were enraged – and with every justification. They saw the former dictators lounging in five-star luxury "prisons", biding their time while they dreamed of a future recall in more favourable circumstances. Trivial sentences had been passed on the murderers who had killed a hundred young people at the polytechnic, and caused countless deaths in the abortive Cyprus coup. Torturers on trial were given free rein to interrupt harrowing accounts from their former victims with displays of raucous jeering from the dock. Police were still brutally repressing public demonstrations, and a free hand was given to fascist provocateurs to disrupt them. Most shocking of all was the murder of the popular hero Panagoulis, the attempted assassin of Papadopoulos, still bearing the scars of his years of torture, and now a liberal MP, just two days before he was due to expose the complicity of named members of the current government in the crimes of the junta.

The lessons of these events were hammered home. Time and again, Athens rang with the tramp of a million workers marching the streets – literally one million, out of a total national population of at that time nine million.

What were the options for the stabilisation of Greece in these circumstances? The right-wing paper VIMA pointed out: "the maintenance of democracy has become dangerously difficult as the government becomes daily weaker, with no sign of any alternative." Karamanlis himself – rather too obviously manufacturing for himself a convenient alibi for his own continuing dictatorial ambitions – pointed out:

> Democracy in Greece was always unstable. Periods of democratic government were brief, few and far between. Greece may be confronted with the dilemma between communism and dictatorship.[31]

The right wing hankered after a new dictatorship. But after the lessons of 1967, such a measure would be resisted to the last drop of blood. The Greek workers and youth were in no mood to submit without a fight. In any case, the army now would be entirely unreliable. A conscript army composed of radicalised young workers, repressed by the fascist officer caste bequeathed from the civil war, it was in no condition to be used against the workers. A new coup could only blow up in their faces. That was what the maverick General Spinola had discovered in Portugal in March 1975, whose own botched coup had only precipitated a further lurch to the left and the overnight nationalisation of the banks (prompting *The Times* to publish, a little prematurely, an editorial under the famous headline: "Capitalism is dead in Portugal"). That was also the lesson to be learned soon afterwards by Tejeiro and his fellow comic-opera colonels when they stormed the Spanish Cortes and held Spain's MPs at gunpoint. And yet the alternative prospect was hardly any better: yet another succession of weak coalitions, intriguing and jockeying for position in the shifting quicksands of parliament.

Sooner or later, it would be necessary to cede power temporarily to a government incorporating some or all of the left opposition parties, in the hope of compromising them and undermining their appeal. But in Greece above all, this could have unpredictable repercussions. Greece was the only country in Europe never to have had a government in which any workers' party had been allowed anywhere near the levers of power. The danger was that the arrival of such a government could only be seen by the workers as a green light for a wave of strikes and occupations. It would hold back the workers' fury for barely a moment before throwing their constituent parties into even deeper convulsions. But under the smokescreen of such a government, who knows? Maybe a new coup could be plotted.

Karamanlis, the arch-reactionary of the 1950s, had dressed himself awkwardly in democratic clothing – only to find himself attacked in turn by the capitalists for allowing Greece to be infected by a plague of "socialmania". Having tricked the electorate into giving him the power to impose a Gaullist constitution with provision for autocratic rule, he dared not risk trying to implement its powers. Fearful of a governmental crisis following his planned departure as prime minister, it was not until 1980 that he finally assumed his designated office as president. Meanwhile, playing for time, he beat the drum of Greek nationalism to divert popular hostility against the external enemy.

In the aftermath of Ioannides' disastrous adventure in Cyprus, Karamanlis also had a crisis in international relations on his hands. Turkey had consolidated its occupation of nearly 40% of the island's territory and had now declared the autonomy of Northern Cyprus, which it proclaimed an independent state in 1983. Turkey was immediately gifted with $1 billion worth of US military equipment (later under pressure partially offset by $700 million of aid to Greece). There were riots by Greek Cypriots and the US ambassador was assassinated. Under pressure, Karamanlis was forced to withdraw Greece from the military wing of NATO and place a question mark over the future of the US bases.

Chapter 7

The Pasok Years

Finding themselves without a stable traditional political channel, the workers were fighting out their battles on the industrial front. At the same time, without a unified independent trade-union organisation either – since the civil war, the frail official trade-union movement had been controlled by the government – there had been a spilling-over of industrial militancy into *ad hoc* action committees and semi-official factory councils, and to some extent a localised recapture of the official trade-union bodies. That too was an explosive factor.

The working population had a high political consciousness that was conspicuously at variance with the programmes of its political parties. Its awareness derived from its rich and varied experience, the sharp alternation of political regimes. The modern history of Greece is after all a classic study on the role of the state. The workers had gained in the hard school of experience ample instruction in the role of the monarchy, and also in the limits of the bourgeois republic; they were all too aware of the menace of the military, and also of the fraudulent nature of referenda and rigged parliamentary elections. After all, at every election in Greece a different system of proportional representation had been used, on every occasion in an attempt to tilt the balance to the right, to suit current circumstances.

They knew the record of each of the political dynasties. They remembered what Karamanlis had stood for in the days before the junta – and they remembered too the abject failure of liberalism in the 1960s. They had learned the need to resist a future coup – but many were learning too that courage and sacrifice are not enough, without a programme and a leadership that could be trusted. More and more were coming instinctively to the conclusion that, unless the fundamental power structure was changed, while the relationship of forces was still relatively favourable, then the regime that they had just overthrown might come to look like no more than a mild foretaste of the horrors to come.

Thus, a gaping vacuum existed to the left of the KKE. Those growing numbers with revolutionary aspirations were disenfranchised. But history moves in the most circuitous routes to overcome the obstacles put up by encrusted bureaucracies. It was the unlikely figure of Andreas Papandreou – an economist who had originally even renounced Greek citizenship to devote himself to an academic life at Harvard – who became a pole of attraction and champion to the radicalised youth.

Along with other "third-world" features, Greece has an ingrained culture of dynasticism. Until the arrival of SYRIZA, modern Greek politics was dominated by the intrigues of rival family empires – in recent decades, mainly those of the Karamanlis, Papandreou and Mitsotakis houses (the latter itself an offshoot of the illustrious Venizelos clan).

No less than the naked nepotism of tyrants the world over, like the Duvaliers, the Somozas, the Kims, the Assads, the sons of Saddam, Mubarak and Gaddafi... most parliamentary systems too, from the land of the Kennedys and Bushes downwards, are riddled with dynasticism. The elegantly choreographed confrontations between the Papandreous and the Karamanlises yet again give Greece an uncanny resemblance to Asia. In the Philippines, a recent three-way presidential election was fought between the latest generations of the Malacanang/Arroyo and Aquino families and Imelda Marcos, widow of the overthrown dictator. In Bangladesh, politics has for decades been a tug-of-war between Sheikh Mujib's daughter and the widow of the dictator Zia who replaced him; Sri Lanka was ruled for half its history by one or another member of the Bandaranaike family. And that's before we come to the Nehru/Gandhi dynasty in

India, the Bhuttos of Pakistan, the Sukarnos of Indonesia and now the Aung San family in Myanmar, all tinged with the faint afterglow reflected by the yearnings for liberation of generations gone by.

So too, in their way, the Greek dynasties faintly echo the distorted aspirations of the masses for a better life: Venizelos the liberal anti-monarchist and "father of the nation"; Karamanlis who had falsely, and bizarrely, posed as bringer of democracy; and the first and second-generation Papandreous who had respectively stood momentarily in the way of the dictators and brought a measure of affluence and self-respect to Greeks.

At the decisive moment, Andreas Papandreou had entirely misjudged the situation, shrugging off the junta's collapse as "the NATO solution". Like many of his kind, he correctly read the minds of the academics and politicians with whom he rubbed shoulders, but assigned to the ordinary working people only a passive role. And yet, like nature, politics abhors a vacuum, and in stepped Andreas Papandreou to fill the gap left by the break-up of the KKE. Thus was founded a new party in the image of the other southern European socialist parties created at the time in Spain, Portugal and France – all parties swept forward by the energies of youth, new or newly revived parties not yet stabilised by the crystallisation of a hierarchy of functionaries who could contain the creative exuberance of the rank and file. In Greece too, the youth were ready to flock to the banner of a new party and impel it initially to the left.

The end of the dictatorship had brought a new political ferment. The traditional opposition had fragmented. The liberal Centre Union was discredited; EDA (the legal front of the previously banned KKE) hopelessly compromised by its vacillations before the coup; and the KKE itself split into two warring factions.

It was largely the EDA and the KKE in their quest for liberal allies which had underwritten the credentials of the

Papandreous, father and son, and in particular built up Andreas' popularity during the constitutional crisis of 1963–7. Papandreou had gone on to found in exile the Pan-Hellenic Resistance Front (PAK). On setting foot back in his homeland in the turmoil following the collapse of the dictatorship, Papandreou was aware of the space left void by the absence of a party aligned with the traditions of European social-democracy; though, sensing the mood of the times, he stridently rejected that label.

On 3rd September 1974, Papandreou proudly proclaimed the foundation of the Panhellenic Socialist Movement: PASOK. Papandreou, a Harvard economist, had not originally been even a social-democrat, but a liberal, albeit one with enhanced prestige as a result of his skirmish with the colonels. But the irresistible pressures of the social crisis had swept him far to the left, and he found himself presiding over what was for a time perhaps the most radical mass party in Europe. A complex personality, Papandreou had briefly flirted with Trotskyism in his youth and for a time employed the former Trotskyist Michel Raptis (Pablo) as his adviser. The new party was greeted warmly especially by the youth, the generation of the Polytechnic, looking for a party untainted by the fudges and betrayals of the past and capable of articulating its aspirations.

As a general rule, workers are reluctant to abandon the parties that generations of their forbears have fought and died to build. Yet for all the blood and sacrifice historically invested in the KKE, over the last four decades successive generations of youth have shown a remarkable volatility, in switching their allegiance not once but twice, first to PASOK and then to SYRIZA, proving a clear exception to that rule. In this respect as in others, Greece may be only pioneering a process that is beginning to develop across Europe, reflecting the consciousness of a society that has experienced turbulence without respite: civil war, agitation, dictatorship, insurrection and economic collapse, embodying a living memory of militant struggles, bitter defeats and hard-won victories.

PASOK was a pole of attraction to a new generation. However, as a volatile new party it lurched from left to right, adventurist to chauvinistic, in unstable transition between the poles of revolution and reform, moreover in this case revolving very firmly around a single patriarchal personality.

Support for PASOK initially shot up, doubling its vote at every successive election: from 13.6% in 1974, to 25.3% in 1977, to 48.1% – its highest percentage ever – in 1981, when it first came to power, only seven years after its foundation. The sharp angle of its ascent was to be matched only by that of its catastrophic downfall in later years: from 43% in 2009, to 13.2% and 12.3% in the successive elections of 2012, to a derisory 4.7% in 2015.

Social-democracy had never acquired the base in Greece that it had achieved historically in Western Europe. With its succession of wars, civil wars, mass migrations, coups and military dictatorships, Greece lacked the stable ecosystem in which such parties sink their roots and flourish. Its history is closer to that of Asia than Europe. To recapitulate: routed by the Turks in Asia Minor, briefly victorious in driving out the armies of Italian fascism, then under Nazi occupation waging a heroic guerrilla struggle of popular resistance which single-handedly overthrew it, the Greek population then suffered years of civil war against an elite propped up first by the British and then the US army, followed by years of repressive rule under a pro-American quisling regime. Then, just as a renewed revolutionary upsurge was once again gathering pace, came the military dicta-torship of the colonels, which was itself eventually overthrown following a youth uprising. It was not until the election of the first PASOK government in 1981 and accession to the EU that a brief era came of liberal reforms: a faint parody of the substantial welfare gains won over generations in Western Europe.

That explains why, seizing the chance to fill the gap between Stalinism and conservative authoritarianism, PASOK began by presenting its most radical face and insisted that it was "a socialist party, not a social-democratic party". Forty years later, however, the party was in shreds, having become a helpless tool of European capitalism, its collapse as spectacular as its earlier rise. It was to end in farce, as the third-generation Papandreou walked out of the party his father had created with such bombast, and – in a futile ruse to siphon off enough votes from SYRIZA to deprive it of a crucial margin – proclaimed the formation of yet another little one-man party. By now he had become an object of ridicule with little hope of regaining any credibility.

PASOK's accession to office had coincided with Greece's entry into the EU, a period of rising living standards, enabling it to justify its initial radical slogans by assuming credit for very real reforms in the lives of Greek citizens. However, with the onset of the crisis, its fate was doomed. It could never hope to achieve the viability of a Western reformist party without the material economic base to sustain it.

It was perhaps the most volatile of a cluster of newly revived parties throughout southern Europe. The French Socialist Party had been reconstituted in 1969 on the bones of the moribund SFIO, brought back to life by the uprising of 1968, in which ten million workers – most of them previously unorganised – had staged a spontaneous general strike, occupied their workplaces and festooned them with revolutionary slogans and red flags. The Spanish Socialist Workers' Party (PSOE) and the Portuguese Socialist Party had burst back to life after decades of repression under fascist dictatorships in 1972 and 1974 respectively. Like them, in its initial freewheeling phase before the crystallisation of an entrenched bureaucracy and the corrupting lure of office, it articulated the hopes of wide strata of the youth.

PASOK's original founding Declaration of 3rd September was a fairly modest statement appealing to traditional sentiments of national independence. But the young militants who flocked behind its banner exerted ever stronger pressures on Papandreou. He found himself voicing bolder slogans. Four months after PASOK's foundation, Papandreou was already talking a new language:

We are not Social-Democrats... The difference between Social-Democracy and socialism is a qualitative and not a quantitative one. It is like black and white... Social-Democracy must be judged not by its proclamations. It must be judged by its actions... It has supported... monopoly capitalism in Western Europe... Our socialist movement, in contrast, is based on the principle that we must pass beyond capitalism to a socialist transformation... Capitalism today has entered a phase of decline... Without doubt the working class... will come to realise in the period which approaches that their economic demands are not going to be satisfied if they do not become politicised and join the course... towards social liberation... The fact that we have chosen a democratic path does not mean that we are historically naïve... We put the burden on the shoulders of our opponents... When the hour of majority comes, as it will come, for the majority to rule, and they refuse it to us, they will have abolished the political order... PASOK aspires... to create such an organisation at the base to act as a counterweight to the schemes of the foreign and domestic establishment.[32]

Unfortunately, these stirring words, spoken in the cloisters of a Central Committee meeting, were not matched by a public call to action. Papandreou responded to the imminent threat of war with Turkey, not with an internationalist class appeal to workers of Turkey and Cyprus, but in words that could just as well have come from Karamanlis, or indeed Colonel Papadopoulos:

We are ready, regardless of the policy of our party, to shout 'present!' in every national struggle. The Greeks will defend their right to national independence, our territorial integrity, whatever the price might be... The time has come for the nation to find its soul and the people their course.

It was not long before the political contradictions within PASOK were matched by organisational convulsions. Apparatchiks were appointed from above, some of them not even party members but reliable cronies of the leadership, while waves of expulsions drove out potential rebels unwilling to accept PASOK as the personal property of its founder and seeking to turn it into an agency for revolution. In January 1975, Papandreou had made pious and solemn promises:

It is imperative that differences and tendencies exist. If they did not exist – if somehow we had managed either with brainwashing or with policing (these are the only methods I can imagine) to agree unanimously, then we would end up with a bureaucratic type arrangement – something which our movement condemns explicitly. For then we would have found a home in some Communist Party of Greece.[33]

Unfortunately, at its very first test, his implicit promise of democratic control by the rank and file failed. For all his initial gush of enthusiasm for the existence of "differences and tendencies", in practice Papandreou was wary of any spontaneous activity by the rank and file, and in particular by the Marxist wing grouped around the paper XEKINIMA, which could act as a catalyst in polarising the party. So once a coherent opposition tendency had developed, it was not long before this self-proclaimed democratic party embarked on a wave of arbitrary expulsions and mass closure of branches. So afraid was Papandreou of the rank and file that he even appointed personal friends who were not party members to police it as regional officials.

Nevertheless, after three years some kind of structure was beginning to take shape. Area and Pan-Hellenic conferences were held – but not before certain prior precautions had been taken, including a purge of the left, the dissolution of some of the most thriving branches, the appointment of bogus delegations, rigged debates, appointed chairpersons, the harassment of critical delegates. Despite its early protestations, the party apparatus turned out to be hardly less bureaucratic than the KKE. This process went largely unchallenged because of the party's predominantly middle-class active composition, the small-scale artisan nature of a large proportion of the working class, and above all the absence of any political traditions of internal democracy within the labour movement.

The dominance of a ruthless KKE bureaucracy over half a century had left deep scars. The despotic methods of Stalinist Russia and the atrocities of the Nazi occupation and the Greek civil war all combined to uproot any norms of democratic debate within the labour movement. One graphic and barely credible incident will be enough to illustrate the consequences. It is alleged by the foremost historian of the wartime resistance, Dominic Eudes, that on the death of the veteran KKE leader Zachariadis in a Siberian labour camp (ironically, himself a victim of the *gulag*), his house was found to contain a secret cell in which was incarcerated the corpse of Karageorgis, a missing KKE central committee member who had dared to raise criticisms of the party's civil war strategy.[34] Such was the merciless victimisation by the Stalinists of dissidents.

PASOK could have led the way towards the establishment of a new tradition. It was not the whim of a political celebrity that had really created PASOK, but the creative aspirations of the youth. But on the basis of erratic zig-zags by an arbitrary bureaucracy, it could only eventually disintegrate.

Reform

In May 1980, Karamanlis retired as prime minister and finally assumed his long-coveted customised office of president. The following election in October 1981 brought an unprecedented (and never to this day repeated) landslide to the left, with PASOK (then still considered a left socialist party) winning 48% of the vote, and the KKE 11%. Seven years after the collapse of the junta, the left had won a crushing 59% of the popular vote, under the slogan *Allayi!* (change). This was part of a wave of socialist party victories throughout southern Europe, alongside the elections of Francois Mitterand in France (1981), Felipe Gonzalez in Spain (1982) and Mario Soares in Portugal (1983).

PASOK's victory ushered in a period of reform and wealth redistribution, especially during its first year of office. A national health service was launched; wages and pensions were raised; trade-union laws were liberalised; price controls were established; a minimum wage and unemployment benefit were introduced. Other reforms included the granting of pensions to wartime resistance fighters, the legalisation of civil marriage, abolition of the dowry system, simplification of the divorce process, the decriminalisation of adultery, reform of universities, an end to triumphalist civil-war victory commemorations, a long-overdue amnesty for exiles from the civil war, and a modernisation of the written language (the adoption of *monotoniko*).

Soon, however, these initial reforms were partly clawed back, with controls on labour relations reasserted, a failure to implement indexation of state employees' pay, and new limits on their right to strike.

For all his earlier denunciations both of NATO and the EU, once in power Papandreou dropped his opposition to Greek membership of both. (Greece had joined the EU just before his election.) He softened his previously suspicious attitude towards Europe, and proved a skilful EU negotiator in securing generous terms for Greece, even using as a bargaining counter the threat to veto the accession of Spain and Portugal. After two successive devaluations of the drachma, the government went on to adopt tough anti-inflation measures and a "strong drachma" policy, in preparation for entry into the single currency, taking maximum advantage of all the EU's grants and agricultural subsidies on offer. He also relented on his previous threat to leave NATO, and even signed an agreement renewing the leases for US army bases in Greece.

Papandreou's radicalism was largely limited to tokens. He objected to NATO's deployment of Cruise and Pershing missiles in Europe; opposed its sanctions following the imposition of martial law in Poland; defied the EU by ostentatiously paying a visit to Poland's new military dictator General Jaruzelski (a curious choice, since this was, after all, the Polish Papadopoulos) and later supporting Serbia's Milosevic; muted the EC's criticism of the shooting down of a South Korean airliner by the USSR; offered verbal support to the Sandinistas in Nicaragua and the Palestine Liberation Organisation; vetoed the siting of NATO headquarters at the Larisa military base; restricted radio broadcasts from Voice of America to Greece; strengthened diplomatic relations with the Soviet bloc; and laid himself open to charges of leniency towards the November 17th terrorist gang. (This group, named after the date of the Polytechnic uprising, ended up mounting over a hundred attacks and assassinating 23 US, British and Turkish diplomats, forcing the USA state department to spend more on security for its diplomats in Athens than in any other world capital.) At the same time, Papandreou loudly thumped the nationalist drum, staging a provocative visit to Cyprus, mobilising the armed forces, and branding Greece's NATO ally Turkey its greatest threat. Papandreou balanced his caution in domestic policy with grandiloquent anti-Western foreign-policy gestures which burnished his reputation for radicalism while costing little; it was a classic populist act.

Meanwhile, after an initial year of tangible reforms, the PASOK government began retreating. Taking office as the rate of inflation reached 25%, and public debt at 25% was already causing disquiet (by 2014 it had reached 175%), it launched the first austerity programmes, borrowed heavily from the EC and devalued the drachma, not once but twice. Inflation continued to rise, along with unemployment and debt. The welfare programme stalled.

Nevertheless, at the next general election in June 1985, PASOK was re-elected. The left still had a clear majority, with PASOK on 46% and the KKE 10%. The leadership of New Democracy passed to Mitsotakis, who prior to the coup had been a right-wing rival to Andreas Papandreou within the Centre Union, branded a traitor for defecting and thus opening the way to the collapse of the government and the subsequent military coup. Meanwhile, Karamanlis' five-year term as president had just the previous month come to an end. Having promised at first to support his re-election, Papandreou suddenly executed a brilliant manoeuvre, nominating Christos Sartzetakis instead. This was a humiliating snub to Karamanlis. Sartzetakis had been the lead magistrate investigating the assassination of the popular left-wing politician Lambrakis in 1963, and was considered a hero, while Karamanlis was almost certainly personally impli-cated in the murder. Karamanlis was furious, and to avoid the almost certain humiliation of losing, resigned two months before the expiry of his term of office. Papandreou went on to amend Karamanlis' Gaullist constitution to remove presidential powers of veto and the right to dissolve parliament – not that either of the two successive presidents in office had ever chosen to exercise these potential authoritarian powers.

While the economy was kept afloat by surges of foreign investment and tourism, the Papandreou government became tainted by scandal. In 1988, Papandreou rushed to London for emergency heart surgery while continuing to "govern by fax" –

taking with him an air stewardess less than half his age and announcing from there his intention to divorce his wife Margaret, who was well respected in her own right for her campaigns for women's rights. Worse still, he became implicated in the Koskotas scandal involving the embezzlement of over $200 million from the Bank of Crete. It was alleged that briefcases containing in total up to $30 million had been handed over weekly to PASOK officials. Papandreou was later to be charged with colluding in Koskotas' embezzlement in return for kickbacks to PASOK, and with unauthorised wiretapping. It is a measure of his popular support and his confidence in it that when he was summoned to appear in court for the scandal, he flatly refused and challenged the Government to arrest him if they dared; they didn't. He was eventually acquitted of all charges relating to the Koskotas affair, though two of his ministers were jailed and another died before the verdict was reached. Koskotas himself served a 12-year prison term.

Papandreou responded to the scandals by manipulating the election rules in a shady practice also used by previous governments, to create 100,000 new public-sector jobs on the eve of new elections in June 1989. The renegade Mitsotakis won a plurality of votes, but failed to command a majority in parliament. To its lasting shame, it was the KKE that came to his rescue by volunteering to prop up a short-lived New Democracy government in order to keep out PASOK. New elections in November 1989 brought another indecisive result, and in April 1990, following the third election in ten months, New Democracy finally achieved a majority of one seat after gaining the support of a smaller right-wing party. In May, at the age of 83, Karamanlis succeeded Sartzetakis and resumed his presidency. For the moment, the right wing was back in the saddle.

With the collapse of the junta and the humiliation of the establishment, Papandreou had found himself an ideal freedom of manoeuvre for grandiose demagogy and populist gestures, all the more so given the scattered composition of the working class, in a society made up largely of small farmers, self-employed artisans, small family businesses, and participants in the "black economy". Even the *Financial Times* accepted that

> PASOK purports to be a socialist party but it owed little to classical socialism... What he [Papandreou] built was a machine that churned out votes, loaded the state with debt and oiled itself with the language of populism.[35]

Yes, Andreas Papandreou was a shameless populist and a demagogue; and his legacy could be written off as a performance of mere grandiloquent speeches masking gross nepotism and favouritism. But the era that he stands for in the popular memory is one of soaring living standards, international stature, and respite from the endless cycle of war, despotism and bloodshed. By acknowledging the heroic role of the resistance, Papandreou brought about the healing of the wounds of the civil war; and by exploiting the opportunities for lavish borrowing, he lifted Greeks out of their age-old abject poverty and gave them a glimpse of a decent life. He restored to the Greek people their self-respect.

His failing health and ultimately his death brought an era to an end. His successor Simitis eagerly submitted to the prevailing neoliberal agenda and, amid economic reverses and scandals, his government fell. New Democracy returned under the leadership of Constantine Karamanlis' nephew Costas.

PASOK was not at all a typical social-democratic party. Replacing both fragments of the discredited KKE, it had started life as an avowedly radical party. When Simitis later tried to turn it in effect into a kind of "third-way" "New PASOK" modelled on New Labour, but in conditions of growing catastrophe, it ceased to fulfil any purpose.

Chapter 8

Greece and Europe

The new Mitsotakis government had announced a "tough" programme for economic recovery – reducing state expenditure, cutting the state payroll, a programme of privatisations, a crackdown on tax collection, etc. However, it was so unpopular (including within New Democracy itself) that it hardly bothered. Corrupt practices flourished under New Democracy just as under PASOK. What remained of an austerity programme – a freeze on public-sector pay and the levying of new taxes – was bitterly resisted, with major strikes against privatisations in 1991 and 1992.

In 1992, the Maastricht treaty was signed. As the poorest country in the EU, with the highest inflation, the highest interest rates, and already at that time the highest-percentage budget deficit, Greece did not expect to join the single currency.

Meanwhile Greece was rocked by the shockwaves sweeping through its neighbouring countries following the collapse of the Stalinist regimes. There was an influx of Albanian refugees, punctuated by intermittent mass expulsions; Yugoslavia broke up in a series of wars and civil wars; Macedonia proclaimed independence, provoking a dispute with Greece over its use of the name. Antonis Samaras, then the Foreign Minister, adopted an extreme nationalist position and split from New Democracy to form his own party (Political Spring), thus depriving the government of its majority.

PASOK won the subsequent elections in October 1993, still with an impressive 47% of the popular vote. Papandreou kept nationalist tensions bubbling, initiating a trade embargo with Macedonia, border skirmishes with Albania, and enforcing a 12-nautical-mile territorial limit with Turkey. While denouncing

Mitsotakis' economic programme, however, Papandreou in practice continued it, provoking some defections from PASOK. In January 1996, Papandreou resigned and died soon afterwards. Immediately following the arrival of his successor Simitis, from the right wing of PASOK, Greece came close to war with Turkey, over a disputed Aegean island and a missile programme in Cyprus. Simitis initiated a ten-year armaments programme and proclaimed his determination to bring Greece into compliance with all the required criteria to join the single currency: a tough austerity programme, enforcement of tax collection and wholesale privatisation.

When early elections were called in September 1996, PASOK still won 41% of the vote, but Simitis' economic programme met with fierce resistance and strikes, from farmers, teachers, public-sector workers, even police and diplomats. The staff of Olympic Airways and the Ionian and Popular Bank resisted privatisation; school students staged sit-ins in protest at proposed educational reforms.

Once again, the response of the PASOK leadership to protests at its unpopular domestic policies was to divert attention with adventurist acts of foreign policy. Tension was raised over the deployment of F-16 fighters and Russian missiles at air bases in Cyprus. Then came an incident over Greece's granting of sanctuary in its ambassador's residence in Kenya for the Kurdish Workers' Party leader, Ocalan. He was ordered to leave, but was intercepted by Turkish secret police and flown back to Turkey to face trial. The Foreign Minister resigned, along with two other ministers, and was replaced by the young George Papandreou, who adopted a more emollient attitude towards Turkey. Temperatures rose again with the US bombing of Serbia for 78 days in 1999, which aroused anger among the Serbs' fellow Eastern Orthodox Greeks.

In April 2000, yet again PASOK narrowly won new elections, still committed to continuing the austerity programme in preparation for monetary union. By January 2001, Greece was deemed to have finally met the criteria for membership of the Euro: inflation had been cut from double digits to 4.2%, and interest rates were down to 4.75%. Later, between 2004 and 2006, it was announced that the budget deficit had fallen from 8% to 2.6% – a figure within the EU's permitted limits. On 1st January 2002, Greece joined the new currency along with 11 other countries, and from March, drachmas were no longer legal tender.

A euphoria was setting in. As one commentator put it,

> Greece has demonstrated a stability that eluded it throughout much of its modern history... All these factors bode well for Greece's future... As a fully-integrated member of the European Union... it has earned the respect of nations throughout the world... The outlook for the years ahead is better than it ever has been.[36]

Another was nearer the mark with his comment:

> Modern Greek history has been punctuated by periods of overwhelming cosmic optimism followed by defeat and disillusion.[37]

Greece's sudden swing from jubilation to despair can be compared to its victorious expansion into Ottoman Asia Minor followed by the catastrophe at Smyrna in 1922.

In reality, Greeks were to pay a heavy price for the convenience of easier trade and travel. They were paying European consumer prices out of Greek wages. Having experienced a boom following initial entry into the EU, once Greece had joined the single currency the tourism market was damaged by an end to cheap prices, with added competition from Turkey whose cheap lira was undercutting the rising euro. As inflation and unemployment rose (especially youth unemployment), support for PASOK was slipping away. In March 2004 elections were held – once again a contest between a Papandreou and a Karamanlis, this time between Andreas' son George and Konstantinos' nephew Kostas – and New Democracy won with a big majority; it went on to win the 2008 elections too.

The euro

The euro was conceived primarily for political reasons: to create a bipolar world pitting Euroland against the USA. Even at that late stage, its architects had not yet woken up to the rise of China, which within a decade was to become the world's second biggest economy. The haste to establish the euro received added impetus with yet another unexpected development: the collapse of Stalinism in Russia and Eastern Europe. Prodi (one of the principal champions of the Euro) admitted in so many words in 2002 that "the euro is not economic at all. It is a completely political step."[38]

It is not as if there had not already been ample warning of the risks. Since the Second World War, fixed exchange rates had been linked through the dollar to gold under the Bretton Woods agreement. With the ending of that arrangement in 1973, exchange rates were in flux. West Germany had become Europe's largest economy and main exporter. This was due to the wartime destruction and post-war reconstruction of its old industries, its receipt of aid under the Marshall Plan, dramatic leaps in productivity in industrial manufacturing, and – as with Japan – the "peace dividend" of enforced demilitarisation. To allay the haunting memory of hyper-inflation, the Bundesbank underwrote the deutschmark. With the strengthening of the deutschmark, various experiments were made to contain currency fluctuations and restore some stability. First the so-called "snake" model imposed a maximum deviation around an agreed norm. This broke down due to repeated devaluations of the French franc, disguised as revaluations of the deutschmark.

Then came the European Monetary System, and specifically the Exchange Rate Mechanism.

In 1992, Britain found itself forced out of the Exchange Rate Mechanism by international currency speculators. Within months, the Italian lira also left; the Spanish peseta and Portuguese escudo were devalued twice; and the Irish pound soon followed. The EU was compelled to concede a maximum margin of 15% fluctuation in exchange rates.

There had been other warnings too. Germany especially had already had a special foretaste of the dangers of imposing a currency union without the required precondition of a prior convergence of common economic, cultural and social factors: the currency union formed by the decision to concede parity of the deutschmark with the Ostmark when East and West Germany suddenly merged. This had put a severe strain on the former West German economy.

A currency union represents a positive attempt partially to overcome the reactionary effects of the survival of the nation state, an obsolete relic of a bygone era. Among its benefits, it cuts out the parasitic role of the money-changers – hence the ongoing hostility to the euro from the City of London and successive British governments, which thrive on this totally unproductive practice.

Nevertheless, such efforts to overcome the consequences of a prevailing system are constantly prone to crisis, as is seen today in the current strains on the euro.

These previous experiments were hardly encouraging omens. Within months of the signing of the Maastricht treaty, which had set out a strategic plan for currency union, the project's prototype had conspicuously failed. Widespread opposition to the treaty left Britain and other countries flatly opting out. Of the three countries allowed a referendum in 1992, Denmark and Ireland initially voted no, and France voted yes only by a margin of less than 1%. There was widespread opposition in Germany, including legal challenges, with many experts warning against undue haste or neglect of the agreed convergence criteria. However, the German government saw surrendering the deutschmark as a price worth paying for European approval of German reunification.

This was not even the first time that Greece had been involved in the experiment of a single multinational currency. A Latin Monetary Union with a common gold- and silver-based currency had been established in 1865, including France, Italy, Belgium, Switzerland and Greece (it was later extended even to some countries in South America and to France's North African colonies). The arrangement finally collapsed only in 1927, on the eve of the worldwide financial crash. Greece had had its own problems with this currency too, even incurring temporary expulsion after having debased its coinage by adulterating its precious metal content.

Yet another ominous historical precedent for Greece's participation in the euro was the case of Argentina. In 1983, hyperinflation had led Argentina to abandon the peso for the austral, and then to reinstate it in 1991 at a rate of 100 million to one, introducing convertibility at a fixed rate of 1 peso = 1 dollar. Like Greece, Argentina had previously languished under a dictatorship which had collapsed after indulging in a spree of military adventurism. Like Greece, Argentina had then relinquished control over its own monetary system by pegging its currency to a stronger foreign currency. In 1991, Argentina had frozen its currency to parity with the US dollar; in 2001, Greece to the euro. In both cases, stabilisation of the exchange rate had given an impetus to investment, construction and personal consumption. By 1994, Argentina was enjoying a 5.8% growth rate and a manageable inflation rate of only 4.2%; Greece was experiencing a boom in shipping, agriculture and real estate. In both cases, government spending and borrowing soared.

Yet both in Argentina and in Greece, following initial success, in the long run this strategy had only made it all the more vulnerable to external economic crises, once they came: the Asian crisis of 1998, and the US/European financial crisis of 2008 respectively. Both Argentina and Greece suffered overwhelming debt problems, and both were forced to submit to intervention from the IMF. The parallel process that had taken place in Argentina only one decade earlier had ended in the biggest default in history. People were blocked access to their own savings, and for a time there were around 20 alternative currencies circulating there. In Greece we see today the wreckage of the economy and the near-certainty of eventual default.

The architects of the euro had originally insisted on the need to guarantee measures of fiscal as well as monetary union – precisely the measures now belatedly demanded by the German government – but at that time political considerations dictated that the common currency should be launched straight away, regardless of all such scruples. Pressure to peg currencies to the rising deutschmark kept interest rates high, and helped precipitate the recession of 1990–2. The project was bitterly resisted all along by eurosceptics motivated by xenophobia, and – in the case of the City of London – by a very material pecuniary interest in maintaining separate currencies in which to speculate.

The five convergence criteria set out in the Maastricht treaty were largely independent of government control: strict limits to the budget deficit (3% of GDP), the public debt (60% of GDP), the inflation rate (within 1.5% of the lowest three), long-term interest rates (within 2% of the lowest three) and exchange rates (within ERM margins). In the early years of the euro it was Italy and Belgium (and later, France and Germany themselves) that were tacitly violating the Stability and Growth Pact rules.

There was irresistible pressure, not just in Greece but in all the eurozone countries, to massage the statistics. Specifically in relation to Greece, as late as in May 1998, the European Commission had ruled that Greece did not meet the criteria for entry, due to its public-sector deficit. However, in November 1999 it repealed its ruling and in May 2000 it approved Greece's application (while still rejecting that of Sweden). It later turned out that this was because the requirement that the public-sector deficit be kept within 60% had been surreptitiously diluted, so that entry would now be permissible so long as the debt was "in the process of falling" and it was "approaching the reference value at a satisfactory pace".

Complicity in the watering-down of criteria for entry into the new currency suited German capitalism down to the ground. The adoption of a single currency in which the strong deutschmark could be diluted by amalgamation with the weak drachma, peseta and lira brought incalculable benefits to German industry and commerce, by lowering the currency in which it traded its exports. So indifferent were the leaders of the EU to the eligibility of the weaker economies for entry into the euro that when the euro was first launched, there were actually no powers in place at all to subject the data reported by the governments of member countries to any objective independent audit.

Just as in the subprime crisis of 2008 good and bad mortgages had been bundled together and sold as investment-grade packages, so too the euro had mixed together sound and shaky currencies into a single marketable package. The European single currency was treated as a hard currency while including weak economies such as that of Greece. And as with securitised mortgages, so too in the case of the euro, the ratings agencies (who were of course in the pay of their client governments and banks) reacted only once it was too late.

There is a clear analogy between the financial crisis of 2008 and the Greek crisis that began in 2009. As Richard Koo of Nomura put it:

Goldman Sachs was criticised for selling financial instruments containing home mortgages for which the lender had not verified the borrower's income. If Greece's structural problems were as bad as they have been made out to be, the Western European financial institutions that ignored these problems in a search for higher yields should surely bear a similar responsibility. In that sense… a kind of collusive denial existed between the borrower and the lenders. Lenders thought that Greece would continue to muddle through despite its many problems, and Greece assumed that there would always be buyers for its debt even if it continued to run substantial fiscal deficits.[39]

Yes, the ratings agencies had certified these loans viable; they had awarded AAA credit ratings to the toxic assets of the banks, too. The ratings agencies are subject to conflict of interest: like company auditors, they are paid by the institutions they rate.

The banks justified their gamble by relying on Germany's apparent obligation to stand by ready to pay up. HSBC, for instance, said: "The big difference between Greece and Iceland or Dubai is its membership of the single currency."

The euphoria with which entry into the eurozone had been greeted was further hyped up by the staging of the Olympics and the unexpected bonanza of victory in the European football championship in 2004.

Dominated by corrupt oligarchic conglomerates such as those of the shipping tycoons Onassis and Niarchos, the Greek economy was booming. For the rich, the good times had arrived. Greece has the highest owner-occupancy rate in Europe: during the boom, people bought homes, and in many cases second homes and holiday homes. Eight-hundred-thousand houses have been built illegally without planning permission. House prices almost trebled within the decade from 1997 to 2008.

In the 2000s, Greece had the highest sales per capita of Porsche Cayennes. Between 2001 and 2006, sales of SUVs and luxury 4x4 vehicles doubled, despite rising petrol prices and a shrinking availability of parking space. The sales of sports utility vehicles soared from 4010 in 2001 to 9288 in 2005. Outstanding car loans in 2010 reached €8 billion, or 3.5% of GDP.

It was with the preparations for the 2004 Olympics that all semblance of budgetary control was thrown to the winds. Financial controls began to collapse, and extravagant expenditure on projects like the new Athens metro took off. All these grandiose infrastructure projects were built on the foundations of an economy still based on low value-added products such as tourism, shipping and agriculture. As one wag put it: "The Greeks were selling tomatoes to buy Louis Vuitton."

Euphoria over Greece's booming economy was not limited to Greek politicians. Bernanke, current chair of the US Federal Reserve, commented in 2004 that "economic shocks are becoming more minor and less frequent". The OECD reported in 2007 that "contrary to expectations of a post-Olympics slump, the economy has continued to grow briskly in 2005 and 2006 during a period of substantial fiscal consolidation".

The EU too deliberately turned a blind eye to all the evidence of growing economic chaos and dislocation until the crisis broke. As late as February 2009, the EU's economics commissioner Joaquin Almunia was still reporting that "the Greek economy is in better condition compared with the average condition in the eurozone, which is currently in recession".

There was one particular lobby within the dominant nations of the EU that had a special interest in indulging Greece: the armaments industry. Once within the euro from 2001 onwards, successive Greek governments, whether PASOK or New Democracy, indulged in borrowing and spending on a lavish scale, not only on day-to-day administrative corruption, but particularly on military hardware. French and German institutions had always been happy to promote Greek borrowing – provided that it meant orders for French and German manufacturers.

Greece has the highest level of defence expenditure as a percentage of GDP in the EU – higher even than the USA, and on a par with China. In 2003, Greece bought 170 Leopard tanks from Germany, and in 2007, 15 Mirage jets from France. Then, in 2010, Greece bought six frigates from a French company at a cost of €2.5 billion. Germany is the world's third-largest exporter of arms, after the USA and Russia, and its top two armaments customers are Turkey, which accounts for 14% of its sales, and Greece, which comes second with 13%. The fattest EU corporations have enriched themselves enormously from the continual clashes between Greece and Turkey in the Aegean, with recurrent complaints of alleged Turkish violations of Greek territorial waters and air space. Where does Greece's public-sector deficit come from? Largely from loans by French and German banks to finance these and similar purchases from French and German arms manufacturers.

While families are reduced to sleeping on the streets and scavenging from dustbins, frugality and austerity have not yet even marginally dented Greece's astronomical defence expenditure, which is still rapidly rising – mostly on new armaments from French and German manufacturers. The Greek economy has been grossly manhandled to suit the appetites of European big business. At over 3% of GDP, the Greek defence budget is actually one of the highest per capita in the world – more than, say, either France or Germany themselves.

And why were the European bankers so solicitous for the survival of Greece's membership of the eurozone and the EU, at such a heavy cost? Why extend such generous loans for the sake of their poor Greek neighbours? After all, once the crisis had first broken in 2009–10, a clean break from the euro and a quick return to a devalued drachma might well have led to a growth of tourism and agricultural exports. Given a little goodwill and aid for investment in reconstruction, it might have helped begin to save the Greek economy. However, such a solution would not at all have suited the European banks. They would have suffered losses far more drastic than the percentages shaved off their repayments under the bailout deal. Greece's creditors were sucking as hard as they could in anticipation of an ultimately inevitable default. It was a prime example of Charles Dickens' apt definition of a creditor's catastrophe: the death of the debtor.

Stereotyping

Historic conflicts always propagate convenient sneering stereotypes. The period of the Troubles in Northern Ireland, for instance, spawned a crop of jokes demeaning the Irish as stupid thugs.

While *Der Spiegel* disdainfully dismissed Greece as "a poor country at the far edge of the EU that has olive trees, blue skies, beaches... and not much else"[40], the mendacious caricature is universally peddled of the lazy, overpaid Greek worker. German politicians like Angela Merkel and Wolfgang Schauble mercilessly exploit this fabrication.

Merkel, for instance, used it to justify German intransigence:

> It is also about not being able to retire earlier in countries such as Greece... We can't have a common currency where some get lots of vacation time and others very little... We cannot simply show solidarity and say these countries should simply continue as before... Yes, Germany will help, but Germany will only help when the others try. And that must be clear.[41]

The truth, according to the OECD, is that the average Greek worker works longer hours than any other country in Europe, or any country in the world apart from South Korea. At 2017 hours per year, this is 40% more than the average German worker, who works 1408 hours a year – fewer than any other European workers except the Dutch.

As for their rates of pay, the average monthly salary of those Greeks lucky enough to have a full-time job is €1265; and 23.2% of private-sector workers earn less than €500 per month. Wages as a percentage of GDP are 35.2%, compared to 48.5% in Germany.

Conversely, Greek resentment of German bankers is hardly surprising. In February 2010, Deputy Prime Minister Pangalos reminded his compatriots that the Germans "took away the Greek gold that was in the Bank of Greece… and they never gave it back". When German politicians suggested that Greece should sell some of its islands as a step towards settling its debts, the popular response was: "What they didn't take militarily, they will take by economics."[42]

The troika have placed the entire blame for the crisis on Greece's notorious culture of corruption. Yet it is a corruption in which Germany and the EU had colluded up to the hilt.

What are regarded now as corrupt practices are well ingrained into Greek culture: the *fakelaki*, or small envelopes changing hands to speed up service; the *miza*, larger kickbacks or introduction fees. These lubricating costs amounted to an estimated total of €787 million in 2009. It was the Greek shipping tycoon Aristotle Onassis who once famously said: "Never trust anyone who won't accept a bribe." Actually, in world-corruption league tables, Greece comes out only as number 71 out of 180 countries, costing an estimated €20 billion a year (equivalent to 8% of GDP).

What's more, it is of course barefaced insolence for the banks and governments of Europe to dare to brand Greece as uniquely or conspicuously corrupt. No such strictures were made against the compliant and submissive ruling classes and parties of Ireland, Spain or Italy; nor against the governments of France and Germany which lied shamelessly to conceal their own budget deficits, nor against the banks throughout Europe, which gambled riotously with our own deposits on the speculative roulette wheels of financial derivatives and then squeezed billions out of the rest of us in reimbursement of the gambling debts on the grounds that they were "too big to fail", thus turning their own private debts into sovereign debts, for which we will all be paying for the rest of our lives, and those of our children, in cuts in our rights and living standards.

Resistance to taxation does have a legitimate place in Greek history. Double book-keeping had always been a traditional practice: a protection over the centuries against foreign plunder. Under Ottoman rule, it had been a matter of honour to avoid payment of the *haratzi* – an Islamic poll tax on Christians, compelling them to carry a certificate of payment of *jizya*, or face imprisonment. The Ottoman empire had even subjected them to what was called *devsirme* in Turkish (*paidomazoma* in Greek) – the abduction of one child in every five for conversion to Islam and service in the Ottoman army janissary infantry. In 1705 Greek rebels who resisted this levy were beheaded and their severed heads put on public display. At least one mother deliberately crippled her own child to save him from conscription. Since the time of the Ottomans, the state and the tax collector were the personification of rule successively by foreign kings, puppet dictators, Nazi tyranny, US domination, military dictatorship. Even after the end of the civil war, the population were still ruled by mercenary collaborators and all resistance was subject to merciless repression. It is only since 1974 that there has been even a credible semblance of parliamentary democracy.

Neither was the massaging of Greek budget data to accord with the Maastricht criteria such a dreadful secret: at worst, it was considered more the kind of unseemly social transgression tacitly overlooked in polite company. Greece was by no means the only member of the EU to have experienced difficulties in meeting the criteria laid down for membership of the euro, including France and Germany themselves, both of which had breached the Stability and Growth Pact. Portugal had breached the 3% budget-deficit limit in 2001, Germany and France in 2002,

Netherlands and Greece in 2003, and Italy in 2004 – all with impunity.

Greece's receipt of foreign aid likewise did not start with its accession to the EU. Since the establishment of the modern Greek state, Greece has been the recipient of regular infusions of foreign capital. There is nothing new about international creditor sharks circling around Greece. In fact, the Greek state was no sooner born in 1832 than it was faced with demands for immediate loan repayments. After the civil war, infrastructure bills like strategic roads and airports were paid for by the Marshall Plan or NATO; throughout the Cold War, Greece had been regarded as a major strategic constituent in the NATO alliance; and following the end of the Cold War, this practice continued through the EU.

One of the gains achieved in the aftermath of the fall of the junta was the granting of generous pensions to some state employees, equivalent to 96% of what were after all very modest salaries, starting at 58 years of age, a cost to the GDP of 13.5%, compared to an OECD average of 61% at 63, costing 10%.

Some anecdotal examples of fiddling and corruption include one census of public pensions which revealed 200,000 bogus disability and old-age pensioners, including 3423 who had been dead even before pension payments had started. Another survey found that a large proportion of recipients of state pensions were actually dead – 321 of them apparently aged over 100; that tens of thousands of people are estimated to be collecting their dead parents' pensions; that €30 million had been found in one doctor's bank account; that only 324 householders in Northern Athens had declared ownership of a private swimming pool in their tax returns, while 16,974 had been detected in that area by satellite photography; and that 30 civil servants were employed full-time – including a president and his full-time driver – to manage a lake that had actually been drained dry 53 years earlier. One official was found to have stashed away €9 million in his bank account. Another sat on 19 committees, each of which paid him a salary.

Quite apart from these historical factors, tax-evasion is rooted in the nature of the Greek economy. The main industry is shipping – and the shipping magnates pay no tax at all, other than a basic tonnage tax, and locate their companies in convenient jurisdictions offering the most lucrative tax havens.

Besides, Greece has the highest percentage of self-employed workers of any European country: by one estimate, 35.1% of the working population, compared with an OECD average of 15.8% (2007 figures). It is hardly unheard-of for self-employed tradesmen and professionals even in the most law-abiding countries to sometimes overlook the declaration of all their income. Some of the freelance journalists and broadcasters so indignant at Greek tax-evasion begin to sound a little like *Casablanca*'s Captain Renault, who, before collecting his winnings, is "shocked to find that gambling is going on in here".

In 2009 unreported income was estimated at €28 billion, depriving the state of revenues equivalent to 31% of the annual deficit. On average, it is reckoned that the real income of the self-employed is almost double their declared income.

The notorious Siemens case revealed that €200 million had been "laundered". Siemens' Greek branch was paying €15 million a year into a slush fund to pay "commissions" on contracts. To secure the €500-million OTE (Greek national telecoms) contract alone cost €35 million in *miza*. (A Chinese telecoms company had already bid for the order at half the cost, but was rejected.) Other German companies that were proved to have colluded in massive corruption were Ferrostaal and Daimler.

The prevalence of tax-evasion means that there were two parallel economies. Fewer than 5000 people declared an income of more than €100,000, while more than 60,000 households owned investments in cash and securities of more than €1 million. As one Finance Ministry official commented: "There are many people with a house, a cottage in the country, two cars and maybe a small boat who claim they are earning €12,000 a year. You couldn't heat the house or put gas in the car with that kind of income."

Along with other forms of corruption go election bribery and blatant nepotism. For instance, just before the 2009 election, 269 people were suddenly given jobs at the Ministry for Rural Development, including 18 of the minister's relatives. Most of the employees at the New Acropolis Museum were found to come from one village, Kalamata – the home base of the then prime minister Samaras, who had made these appointments when he was minister of culture in 2004.

Much of the state corruption is explicitly sanctioned. For instance, ministers are officially granted automatic immunity from prosecution. In 2003 a court ruled that bribes were not illegal provided they were not paid prior to the event; they could then be considered "gratitude gifts" rather than payment for services rendered. George Papandreou actually told European leaders that "Greece is corrupt to the bone". In 2010, Deputy Prime Minister Pangalos (whose grandfather, incidentally, had presided over a short-lived military dictatorship in the 1920s) made the startling admission to fellow MPs: "We all ate the money together."[43] This comment so enraged the starving demonstrators outside the parliament building that they threatened to seize this rather plump and conspicuously well-fed minister, slice him up for salami and "sell it for dinner".

European commentators have zeroed in spitefully on the reasonably generous pension rights won by state employees. (Many of them retire after 35 years' service on 95% pensions.) But they overlook Greek workers' subsistence-level wage rates and long hours, and, as usual, they exaggerate a few relatively trivial perks and then shut their eyes to bureaucratic embezzlement on an astronomical scale. It was discovered, for instance, that according to official statistics, expenditure on public-sector wages and bonuses comes to a total of €13 billion. If this were accurate, then that would give the public-sector workforce of 768,009 people – mostly humble and relatively low-paid employees – about €17 million per head! In fact, the minimum wage for a public employee is just €711, and 80% of workers earn somewhere between €1000 and €1500 a month.

After the fall of the dictatorship, the workers had won at last some leverage and trade-union bargaining power. The forces of repression were temporarily disarmed and disoriented. And given the seemingly limitless funding on offer from the EU and NATO, it was easier for governments, especially in the 1980s, to concede workers' demands and settle quickly, rather than risk confrontations they couldn't have any confidence in winning. Trade unions had been able to gain for themselves some protection against cowboy employers in the form of "closed shop" agreements, limiting for instance the employment of non-Greek crew on shipping lines, or securing the issuing of licences for electricians and taxi drivers – what the employers, with their armoury of favourable legal clauses, have the nerve to call "restrictive practices". Successive farmers' protests also won them subsidies more than double the EU average.

The money borrowed by the government had not been invested in research and development or technological capacity, but on a combination of corrupt handouts to cronies, on the one hand; but also, when necessary, to placate the demands of workers agitating quite justifiably for their share of the bonanza, in the form of long-overdue increases in wages and pensions – just recompense for the privations of the past.

But where previous governments had been understandably reluctant to confront the trade unions, under the new crisis conditions, a showdown could no longer be postponed. PASOK governments as well as New Democracy were now deploying troops to break strikes.

The cost of EU membership

There are far more profound reasons for the crisis in the Greek economy than mere accounting irregularities. Much has been written about how the Greeks have ruined Europe; but rather less about the damage done by EU membership to the Greeks. The foundations of the Greek economy are agriculture, tourism and shipping; all three have been devastated.

The Common Agricultural Policy bankrupted tens of thousands of Greek farmers, resulting in rural depopulation and the growth of urban poverty; and agriculture was later hit by a sudden reduction in EU subsidies following the accession to the EU of the poorer East European countries.

The tourism industry was crippled by entry into the euro. The maintenance of a strong euro pushed up prices by a differential of at least 25% above its nearest competitor Turkey, with its newly devalued lira, and the currencies of other neighbouring countries. Turkey and Egypt suddenly seemed more attractive destinations to Western holidaymakers.

Then the onset of the international recession cut shipping demand by a massive 90%.

The strength of the euro discouraged not only foreign visitors from spending their money in Greece, but also Greek shoppers in the northern regions who regularly slipped across the border to Macedonia (FYROM) or Bulgaria to buy petrol, household goods and vegetables at prices half those at home.

Alongside the lavish spending on modernisation – the creation of pedestrianised streets, the flourishing of street cafes, the Olympics, the super-modern public-transport system, etc. – are slums and overcrowding in the cities, especially Athens. It was the rich and upper-middle class who benefitted from EU membership. It is no accident that it was during the golden years of the 2000s that New Democracy governments were restored to power. Greece had enjoyed 14 years of continuous growth. Its economy had contracted in 2008, but only by 0.2%. It was only with the bursting of the euro-bubble and the onset of the economic crisis that PASOK returned to office.

When PASOK came back to power in October 2009 under the leadership of George Papandreou, son of Andreas, the new government promised to "open the books". A culture of statistical manipulation and double book-keeping by former governments was exposed. It was revealed that a secret arrangement had been concluded with Goldman Sachs to misrepresent the facts about the Greek economy. According to the government's revelations, previous statistics had seriously understated public borrowing requirements. Public debt as a proportion of GDP, it claimed, had soared: from 22% in 1980 to 175% in 2014. Greece's public debt-to-GDP ratio was 114%, and its budget deficit 12.7% of GDP; the deficit was not in fact 6%, as previously reported, but 12% of GDP, and was soon to rise to 15.4%.

What lay behind this announcement was a conspiracy with the EU to flagrantly distort the true explanation of the crisis. Most of the increase in public debt had arisen not from any alleged profligacy in public spending but from the widening gap between GDP and mounting interest rates on previously accumulated relatively modest debts (see chapter 11).

When the global financial crisis struck, the banks were rescued from a financial crisis which was the consequence of their own criminality by government bailouts, creating a sovereign debt crisis. In Greece, according to the report of the Debt Truth Commission, the government deliberately "falsified statistical data" to misrepresent what was fundamentally a banking crisis as a crisis of public spending. The government "illegally revised and increased both the public deficit and the debt" by inflating the liabilities of public hospitals and public corporations and manipulating the statistics relating to "swaps" with Goldman Sachs. As a result, it estimates, the budget deficit for 2009 was increased by 6-8 percentage points and the public debt by €28 billion." This was done in order to convince public opinion in Greece and Europe to support the bailout of the Greek economy, with all its catastrophic conditionalities for the Greek population."[44]

The effect of these revelations was a flight of capital from the banks, steep tax increases and a new austerity drive. Interest rates on government bonds soared, and the ratings agencies began a steep downgrading of government debts. The crisis was further aggravated by the Dubai property slump in November 2009.

George Papandreou sought support wherever he could, soliciting emergency loans from China and even pressurising GreekAmericans to lobby Obama, all in vain.

The writing was on the wall. Desmond Lachman of the *Financial Times* (who had earlier predicted Argentina's default) wrote in 2010: "Greece's euro membership will end with a bang."[45] The German economist Wilhelm Nolling wrote: "Greece faces the threat of state bankruptcy... The Greeks will have to leave the euro."[46] Nouriel Roubini wrote:

> Greece has long been an accident waiting to happen... But its problems are not unique. On their resolution rides the fate of its neighbours, the eurozone and perhaps the European Union itself.[47]

Under pressure from Europe's bankers on the one side and an angry Greek population on the other, successive deals were negotiated in 2010 and 2012, resulting in what were euphemistically called "bailouts". Actually, the very use of the word "bailout" is highly misleading. It was not the personal debts of the squeezed and starved Greek people, but the ledger balances of European bankers and corporate international creditors that were bailed out with a package of aid, loans and very partial debt write-offs, all administered under strict IMF supervision. They were really only further debts, advanced not to the suffering

Greek people, but to their rapacious foreign creditors – largely, in fact, to German arms manufacturers. The debts resemble a Ponzi scheme; the more debts are incurred, the more new ones are needed to meet the repayments on them. Under the blackmail of its vulture creditors, deals were imposed that ruthlessly stripped away even the formal trappings of governmental sovereignty.

But then, direct rule over Greece by foreign overlords was nothing new. Greece had suffered centuries of subjugation to the Ottoman Empire; and even after the first Greek territories had won their liberation, the British moved quickly to take control of its fate into their hands. They had foisted on Greece Bavarian and Danish kings, and a brace of aristocratic British warlords to command its naval and military forces respectively. Then again in the 1930s, control of the Greek economy had been subjected to oversight by an International Control Commission – a prelude to the imposition of the Metaxas dictatorship. The current troika (or "institutions") – the EU, the IMF and the ECB – are merely the latest manifestations of the same national humiliation.

The origins of the Western world's financial crisis lay in the global collapse in share-equity prices after 2000. Between 2000 and 2003 the Neumarkt fell by 98%, the NASDAQ by almost 80%, the Dow Jones by nearly 40% and the FTSE 100 more than halved. There was a growing flood of loose capital swilling around the markets, and for want of anywhere more useful, it poured into speculation on derivatives, securitised assets and other forms of increasingly bizarre and complex financial gambling. What had once been a productive enterprising class had rotted into little more than a parasitical kleptocracy. This in turn led to the sub-prime crisis of 2008, which triggered a colossal handout of funds by state governments to the failed banks in a rescue operation to save the system from collapse; and thus to a sovereign debt crisis. The burden of debt was transferred from the failed banks to state finances.

At its root, as the British Marxist economist Michael Roberts has explained[48], the drive for austerity is based not on ideological prejudice but on a real vital need to restore the profitability of productive capitalist investment. The swilling of vast sums of loose capital ballast had brought the world economy to shipwreck. The only way to restore the profitability of investment is to cut the share of surplus value going to the working class. This means cuts in wages and cuts in the social wage – i.e. in spending on pensions, schools, hospitals, etc. This was the remedy applied throughout the Western world, with immediate and draconian consequences from Iceland to Spain, and Ireland to Greece.

At first Greece had avoided direct exposure to the fall-out from the 2008 crisis. But now it was time to call in the stakes. More than 90% of the so-called bailout money granted to Greece in the following years went straight back into the Greek and European banking systems. The crisis of 2008 was "solved" by "nationalising" the banks' debts while leaving their profits untouched. It was this sleight of hand – not the famous "Greek lifestyle" – that created the sovereign debt crisis.

Chapter 9

Uprising

By 2008, life in Greece was transformed. The urban population had grown from 37% in 1950 to 59% by 1990. Life expectancy had risen from 68.9 years in 1960 to 78 in 2000. By 2013, 73% of the housing stock was owner-occupied compared to 22% that was rented, and 21% of the total were second homes. By 2008, GDP had grown over the previous decade at an annual rate of nearly 4%. Per capita GDP shot up from €826 in 1981 to a peak of €21,017 ($32,100) in 2008. Greece was among the 40 richest countries, and ranked 26th on the human-development index. This transformation was ascribed by most Greeks to admission to the European "club". Leaving aside the later punitive bailout deals, which clawed back these benefits with a vengeance, Greece was by 2013 the net recipient of €105 billion from the EU.

Even when the international financial crisis struck, funds initially kept flowing into Greece, which had stayed free from exposure to the toxic assets that had undermined the American banking system. But in 2009, the storm broke.

Following Greece's entry into the eurozone, it had been able to borrow cheap at generalised European rates. But once the credit crunch began to bite, the accumulated public debt sent Greece's cost of borrowing soaring. Sovereign bond yield spreads – a measure of interest rates payable on government bonds – exploded from 35 basis points in early 2008 to 300 in March 2009.

In October, with Greece on the brink of collapse, Costas Karamanlis called elections. His period in office had been one of vacillation, patronage and rampant corruption. PASOK swept back into power with 44% of the vote by an electorate repelled by New Democracy's record. They hoped that the departure of

Simitis with his Blairite ambitions and the return of a new scion of the Papandreou dynasty might justify renewed hopes of a restoration of the golden years of reform in the 1980s – all the more so in view of Papandreou's promise of a €3-billion stimulus package and the slogan: "There is money!"

Once the new government had dropped its bombshell, shamelessly manipulating the data to announce an upwards revision of the government deficit for 2009 from 3.7% to, eventually, 15.6% (five times the maximum allowed by the EU), the financial markets panicked. By January 2010 Greek bond spreads had risen to 380 basis points, and by May, to a staggering 1280. In April 2010, right on cue, the government turned to the eurozone countries and the IMF for rescue.

The paradox of the euro lay in the anomaly that it was a common currency without fiscal integration. The Maastricht treaty had imposed nominal limits on inflation rates, budget deficits, and gross government debt, which were further reinforced by the 1997 Stability and Growth Pact, but there was no legal obligation on the European Central Bank to support eurozone members that found themselves in trouble; they were left to their own discretion. There was no constraint on laxity, and no instrument on hand to counteract it. It was actually France and Germany that were the first to flout the guidelines. Acknowledging the incompatibility of such an arrangement, Helmut Kohl had predicted:

> One thing is certain. When this Europe... has a common currency... then no bureaucrat in Europe is going to be able to stop the process of political unification.[49]

Financial markets proceeded on the assumption that default was unthinkable, and this drove down borrowing costs in the peripheral economies, boosting spending. The loans financed the public-sector deficit in Greece and private-sector deficits in Spain and Ireland, especially in property assets. But this was not essentially a Greek problem: it was a crisis based on a systemic flaw in the European project.

There was no serious current-account deficit problem in Greece until the late 1990s, and even then, such was the apparent strength of the Greek economy that the government was not concerned about the risk of running a substantial deficit. By the time the world financial crisis had broken in 2008, it had reached nearly 13%. With the slowdown in the world economy, however, Greece was hit by a corresponding slump in its main industries, shipping and tourism, and the debt accumulated fast.

Bailouts

What was actually a banking crisis caused by a private debt bubble had been turned into a sovereign debt crisis (i.e. state bankruptcy). Since many European banks owned Greek bonds that would turn toxic in the event of default, this rang alarm bells. The EU improvised an ad hoc instrument to address this risk: the so-called troika, in which the European Commission and the European Central Bank enlisted the participation of the International Monetary Fund, in recognition of the IMF's long experience in dictating harsh terms to captive states, graphically emphasising the strict conditionality of any loan and its resolve to avoid "moral hazard".

On 23rd April, the Greek government requested the activation of a bailout package offered by the troika, and on 27th April, the credit-rating agency Standard & Poor lowered Greece's debt rating to BB+ ("junk" status). On 1st May, Papandreou announced a fourth round of unprecedented austerity measures, including further cuts in public-sector pay and pensions, new taxes and an increase in VAT. On 2nd May an immediate loan of €45 billion was duly approved, with additional loans in the pipeline amounting to €110 billion over three years.

The bailout came on savage terms. This first of the

Memoranda of Economic and Financial Policies imposed internal devaluation (a coy euphemism for cuts in living standards), cuts in public-sector wages and pensions, increases in VAT, a cut in the minimum wage, widespread privatisations and "fiscal consolidation" (general tax rises). Unemployment soared and many full-time workers had their wages cut to the minimum wage of €592 or less. At their expense, the deficit was initially reduced by more than €14 billion.

Draconic though these cuts were, the first round of austerity failed to stop the debt rising steadily and inexorably. In conditions of world crisis, markets panicked, investment dried up and exports stagnated. Greece was in a state of prolonged depression. On 29th June 2011, the Greek parliament passed a new set of swingeing austerity measures. The following day, the Office of the High Commissioner for Human Rights of the United Nations reported an independent expert's warning that the austerity measures could result in violations of the Greek people's human rights, including "rights to food, water, adequate housing and work under fair and equitable conditions".[50]

The years of political turmoil were beginning. In a poll published in May 2011, the two major parties between them were shown to be incapable of commanding a majority; even in the event that they formed a coalition, they couldn't form a government. There was a run on the banks; Greek banks lost liquidity equal to €1.5 billion after just two days of withdrawals.

The millions who had placed their hopes in Papandreou the third were disappointed. By October 2011 it was clear that a second "rescue package" would be needed. George Papandreou dithered, vacillated and grovelled to the bankers, surrendering to them all their demands. Then, on the point of signing the draconic memorandum, and dreading responsibility for its consequences, his nerve failed him. Overnight, in desperation, squeezed between two unyielding forces, almost as an afterthought George Papandreou proposed calling a referendum on the terms of the bailout, offloading responsibility onto the backs of the Greek electorate. Then, frightened by Merkel's furious reaction, he promptly dropped the idea and resigned. And that, in effect, was the inglorious end of PASOK.

It was then that the EU sprang its most insolent political experiment: a novel manifestation of colonial overlordship; not even proxy rule by the military this time, but direct personal rule by the bankers themselves. Why bother staging that extravagant electoral Punch-and-Judy show in which rival glove-puppets dressed in clashing colours perform elaborate pantomimes on the parliamentary stage while the real masters of the universe hide behind it? Why not simply install a real banker to administer direct rule by the European Central Bank? So the Karamanlises and Papandreous and Samarases were packed away in their boxes and in their place came the banker Papademos – faceless, unelected, unaccountable, unencumbered with the tiresome intrigues of parliamentary gamesmanship. The same ploy was simultaneously executed across the Adriatic in Italy, where the elected prime minister, Berlusconi, was arbitrarily elbowed aside – due in his case not to political impotence but to flagrant corruption – and replaced there too by an unelected grey-suited banker. It seemed a neat remedy for growing unrest in Greece and rampant sleaze in Italy respectively.

Under Papademos' administration, a second "rescue" package was put together, adding €164.5 billion and bringing the total bailout to €274.5 billion – far exceeding the €85 billion extended to Ireland in December 2010 and €78 billion to Portugal in May 2011. This time a token and derisory measure of debt-restructuring was built into the deal, with all payments due on the EU loans deferred until 2023.

The new package was approved on 12th February 2012, amidst strikes, occupations, riots and arson. Both major parties were rocked by defections; 43 MPs defied their leaders and were dismissed, and another dozen resigned.

The overall effect of these measures was catastrophic. Youth unemployment had hit at least 65%. Even workers still in jobs were living on half their former salaries. There were cases where workers in stable jobs but whose mortgages were attached to their wages were taking home no more than €200 a month. Most people could no longer heat their homes in winter – the forests surrounding Athens were getting cut down for firewood – or, often, even switch their lights on.

Personal incomes were by now reduced by a third; unemployment had reached 27%, and youth unemployment 60%; and the economy had shrunk by a quarter – a proportionate fall previously experienced only in the USA in the Great Depression. In four years, Greece had dropped from 40th to 56th place in the per-capita GDP league tables. Public debt reached €317 billion – over 175% of GDP. By the time of the second bailout, Greek bond yields had shot up to over 40%.

At the cost of swingeing tax increases, cuts in wages, pensions and benefits, and the loss of 150,000 jobs in the public sector alone, within five years Greece had turned a deficit of 10.6% of GDP into a primary surplus of 1.5%. Painfully and briefly, the package had shifted the current account into surplus. And yet at what cost? Overall, the package was a catastrophic failure. These drastic cuts had reduced unit labour costs by 22%; but in conditions of world recession, far from making Greek exports more competitive – as similar harsh measures had, marginally, in Ireland and Portugal – exports had actually fallen even faster than imports. Austerity had created a downward spiral, depressing demand, reducing tax revenues and swelling the debt burden to unsustainable levels. All that these draconian attacks on living standards had achieved was soaring poverty and unemployment.

Once Papademos had served his purpose, he was quickly returned to the obscurity of his desk at the bank, and normal political theatre was resumed. Two successive inconclusive elections were held, in May and again in June, and a humiliating coalition was finally put together consisting of two once formidable and now sadly reduced parties: a recycled New Democracy and the burned-out remnants of PASOK, both of which together still couldn't cobble a majority, plus a couple of ad hoc splinter groups to make up the numbers. This pantomime-horse government was made up of the head of Antonis Samaras – a wily New Democracy politician who had up to then nominally opposed the terms of both the first and second bailout packages – and the hindquarters of the last of the Papandreous, who had once promised the Greek people the earth.

Rage

Just as the savage austerity measures imposed throughout Western Europe were nothing less than a naked attempt by the ruling class to claw back all the gains in wages and social welfare of the post-war epoch, so too the even-more-vicious attacks on the living standards of the Greek people represented a delayed revenge for the concessions won following the fall of the junta.

The response of the population was the massive movement of 2010–12 and beyond, including some 800 sector strikes, countless smaller or local strikes, and no fewer than 40 one- or two-day general strikes.

This had already been foreshadowed by several warning signs: first, a wave of university student occupations in 2006–7, when hundreds of university departments were occupied in prolonged protests against proposals to introduce privatisation of higher education and to restrict access by poorer students; and then, a virtual youth uprising in 2008.

At around 9 pm on 6th December 2008, a police officer murdered Alexis Grigoropoulos, a 15-year-old schoolboy, without provocation and in cold blood, on the streets of the

Exarchia district of Athens. By midnight Athens was in flames. Across the city centre, shop windows were smashed and cars were torched. That same night, protests spread to 20 other cities. The next few weeks witnessed scenes reminiscent of the Polytechnic uprising that had spelled the beginning of the end of the dictatorship. This was a generalised youth uprising, more than just a protest triggered by the murder: an outpouring of youth despair and outrage at police brutality, unemployment, low wages and dead-end prospects. Students staged street protests, stormed out of their schools, marched on police stations, occupied university campuses, took over radio stations and even television studios; they torched police stations, banks, shops, cars, public buildings and even the Christmas tree on Syntagma Square. Riot police ran out of teargas and lost control of the streets, partially restrained by ministers nervous of the consequences of another fatality.

The youth riots were just a prelude to the mass fury that erupted in 2010–12: the sheet lightning before the storm of mass resistance to the troika. The one factor they hadn't counted on was the capacity of the Greek people to fight back. On "Ohi Day" (27th October, the solemn anniversary of Metaxas' reported retort to Mussolini's demand to station Italian troops on Greek soil in 1940) there were for the first time ever massive counter-demonstrations by Greek workers in Thessaloniki, in which the President was catcalled and branded a "traitor". Other slogans raised were "down with the plutokratia" and "nationalise the banks without compensation".

From 2010 onwards, there were massive mobilisations of the population – not just in the workplaces but above all in the public squares. Half a million people were on the march on 5th May 2010, the day of the first of the general strikes. On this occasion a tragic incident took place, possibly a premeditated provocation. A bank was attacked with Molotov cocktails and set on fire. Most of the employees escaped unharmed, but two women and a man were later found dead in the rubble, asphyxiated by toxic fumes when they found their escape from a roof exit blocked. Fire crews were impeded from reaching the scene by the crowds; the police accused "hooded youth", while demonstrators blamed the police for escalating the tension by their provocative use of pepper spray and tear gas. Significantly, the Greek Federation of Bank Employees' Unions placed responsibility for the tragedy on the bank management for its inadequate safety measures in the building.

By 2011, general strike followed general strike: on average, one every month and a half. Syntagma Square was occupied continuously for months, partially inspired by the contemporaneous occupations of Tahrir Square in Cairo and city squares throughout Spain by the indignados. The demonstrators included people of all ages and backgrounds, including one 102-year-old grandmother, who also spoke at the people's assembly. Teams of doctors and translators and food supplies were set up by the protesters at Syntagma Square.

The demonstrations soon spread from Athens to Thessaloniki, Larissa, Patras, Volos, Rethymno, Tripoli and Kalamata. Thousands of protesters occupied Thessaloniki's White Tower Square and Heraklion's Eleftherias Square for weeks on end.

Government ministries and public buildings were occupied. When the government imposed a universal property tax, with the threat to cut off the electricity supply of defaulters, workers occupied the electricity corporation's offices to prevent any disconnections. Later, when the public broadcasting corporation ERT was peremptorily shut down in June 2013, its employees not only occupied its studios but launched an innovative democratic broadcasting service involving a whole spectrum of creative talents and enlisting mass popular participation.

These indefinite, continuous occupations of public spaces embraced far wider strata than just the organised workers: they also drew in non-working women, the unemployed, self-employed, pensioners, small-business people, school and college students, immigrant communities... they became a modern manifestation of mass popular democratic assemblies, in which literally millions of people participated.

Among the improvised slogans seen on these demonstrations were:

Error 404, Democracy was not found.

I vote, you vote, he votes, she votes, we vote, you vote, they steal.

Greece, your turn has come, you have to stop burying your children.

The worst form of violence is poverty.

Adopt a new constitution, written by the people and not the members of parliament.

Refuse to pay the odious debt; cancellation of the memorandum; tax the rich.

The maid resisted. What do we do? (*A reference to the recent sex scandal involving former IMF director Dominique Strauss-Kahn.*)

A magical night, like in Argentina. Let's see who gets in the helicopter first! (*A reference to the escape by helicopter of Argentina's president from his palace in 2001.*)

Greece was rocked by almost continuous protests and strikes. May Day saw protest marches in Athens and Thessaloniki come under attack by riot police. Tents were erected in Syntagma Square and there were daily rallies of thousands. On 4th May, KKE members stormed the Acropolis and hung banners: "Peoples of Europe Rise Up!" A nationwide strike was called for 5th May. Airports, railways and ferry traffic in and out of the country came to a standstill. Schools, hospitals and businesses were closed. An estimated half a million people marched through Athens. Some demonstrators tried to storm the parliament building and scuffled with police, even chasing away the totemic

Evzones (ceremonial guards) from the Tomb of the Unknown Soldier. Protesters chanted "thieves" at the parliament building, and riot police hurled tear gas, flash bombs and smoke bombs at them. The finance ministry and other buildings were set on fire. Throughout Athens, demonstrators threw bottles and stones at the police, set rubbish bins on fire, broke windows, threw petrol bombs, set up barricades and burned cars.

Unlike in earlier periods of unrest, these demonstrations arose seemingly spontaneously, without any initiative or co-ordination from the official parties or trade unions. They were an outcry of universal fury at the demands of the EU and the IMF. Stung into action by the slogan heard from the indignados in the occupied squares of Spain – "Be quiet, the Greeks are sleeping!" – a banner was raised in reply in front of the Spanish embassy in Athens reading:

¡Estamos despiertos! ¿Que hora es? ¡Ya es hora de que se vayan! (*We've woken up! What time is it? It's time they left!*)

The next day, two new banners appeared – one in French:

Silence! Les Français dorment! Ils revent de '68! (*Silence! The French are sleeping! They're dreaming of '68!*)

And one in Italian:

Zitti, che svegliamo gli Italiani... (*Shush, you'll wake the Italians.*)

An information centre and a "book of ideas" were set up at Syntagma Square. In Thessaloniki, protesters hung a huge For Sale sign from the city's main landmark, the White Tower, as a protest against the government's wholesale denationalisation programme, which they condemned as "selling off our country's assets". There citizens were free to take the floor, voice their opinions and contribute their ideas. As the occupation continued, every day new demands were formulated, among them:

> Down with the corrupt politicians – send them home or to jail.
> We the people talk without fear; it's the politicians who feel fear.
> Their democracy gives us neither justice nor equality.
> Taxes aren't the same for rich and poor.
> Equal rights for everyone.
> Demonstrations every day at 6 pm, assemblies at 9 pm.

Demonstrators set up a gallows in front of the Greek parliament. On 31st May, one week into the protests, tens of thousands of demonstrators surrounded it, trapping the MPs inside. Huddled in the parliamentary chamber, MPs approved the proposed austerity measures, while Angela Merkel told the German parliament that "Europe's future is at stake". The next day they left early to avoid the blockade.

When the demonstrators were taunted by Greece's rotund vice-president, Theodoros Pangalos – the man who had admitted so elegantly that "we all ate the money" – they chanted back in response: "The country's sinking, Theodore, lose some weight!"

By 5th June, the crowd in Syntagma Square had swelled to half a million – the biggest demonstration since the 1980s. A Skype connection established direct links with the equally massive crowd in Madrid's Puerta del Sol. Demonstrations also took place in Thessaloniki, Patras and Heraklion, and other Greek cities. One of the most popular slogans of that day was:

> Bread! Education! Freedom! The dictatorship didn't fall in '74!

Demonstrations continued throughout June, in Athens and other cities across the country. At the end of the month, public-sector workers held a 48-hour general strike including civil servants, teachers, doctors and nurses. Journalists and others held solidarity strikes. Police tried to clear Syntagma and other public squares by driving through the crowds on motorbikes, throwing stun grenades and tear-gas canisters, including into nearby metro stations, storming neighbouring streets, randomly hitting passers-by and people eating at local tavernas, and hurling stones and blocks of marble at doctors in local makeshift infirmaries. Teachers' union leaders were among those beaten up. Around 270 people were injured on 28th June, and over 500 on 29th. Police blocked access to ambulances ferrying injured civilians to hospital. TV channels broadcast footage showing riot police co-operating with hooded neo-Nazis. For the first time since the massacre of December 1944 which sparked off the civil war, the five-star hotels on Syntagma Square had to evacuate their guests.

In the face of protests at police brutality from Amnesty International, Greek and foreign media, and even a few MPs from PASOK, the Minister for Citizen Protection, Christos Papoutsis, shrugged off all responsibility, claiming that "it's the police that operates, not the government", denying that the personnel shown in the video helping hooded neo-Nazi thugs were police, and even complaining that some of the demonstrators were "wearing better gas masks than the police".

The street protests were democracy in action. In a survey published by one TV channel, 95% of the respondents reported "positive impressions" of the protest movement, 86% supported it outright, and 35% said they had themselves personally participated in at least one protest.

In August the protests spread to the tourism sector. The Pan-Workers' Front staged a sit-in at some of Athens' most famous hotels on Syntagma Square and at the iconic Electra Palace Hotel in Thessaloniki, and the Federation of Tourism Workers held a 24-hour strike and a demonstration.

In September, teachers, doctors, taxi drivers, customs officials, tax collectors and refuse workers went on strike, and air-traffic controllers banned overtime. On 5th October there was another general strike. In October, seamen went on strike for 48 hours, shutting down the ferry services between the islands, and the customs officials who clear fuel-refinery deliveries held a 24-hour strike.

On 28 October – OHI day, a national holiday commemorating the national uprising against the Italian invasion threat – more protests erupted nationwide. For the first time ever, demonstrators physically prevented the staging of the traditional annual military parade in Thessaloniki, and the president of Greece was forced to abandon the ceremony, while, to the cheers of the crowd, the civilians' and conscripts' contingents on the parade marched as planned. At the Athens ceremony, participants in the annual student parade conspicuously turned their faces away from the Minister of Education and other bigwigs, and members of the Municipality of Athens brass band played with black ribbons fixed onto their instruments. Protesters in Heraklion threw eggs at the officials, and in Patras occupied the street where the scheduled parade was to take place. Politicians were heckled in cities across the country, including Trikala, Volos, Corfu, Serres, Veroia, Tripoli and Rhodes.

On 17th November, over 50,000 people marched in Athens, and on 6th December (the third anniversary of the murder of Alexis Grigoropoulos) thousands marched on the Parliament building, throwing Molotov cocktails at the police, who responded with tear gas.

Then, following yet another 24-hour general strike, as the newly installed bankers' prime minister Papademos introduced his package of austerity measures in Parliament on 12th February 2012, once again half a million protesters gathered in Syntagma Square. Police deployed tear gas and flash grenades, while sections of the crowd hurled back stones and Molotov cocktails.

Forty-five buildings were set ablaze.

On 5th April there was another huge demonstration after a pensioner had publicly shot himself rather than join in the daily scramble of scavengers picking through the garbage bins in search of food.

The fascist menace

Greece finds itself caught in a unique intersection of the two most acute inter-connected crises of the day: the collapse of the capitalist economy and the effect of endless wars, civil wars, "failed states" and a descent into virtual barbarism in huge swathes of the Middle East, Asia and Africa. Huge numbers of people fleeing starvation and war in Africa and parts of the Arab world and seeking refuge in Europe were arriving in Greece as their first port of call – a flood swelling to 800,000 within 2015 alone.

Racism had proved an irresistible tool for both the mainstream parties of the ruling Greek establishment. The PASOK minister Loverdos initiated an HIV scare to order mass arrests of so-called "immigrant prostitutes"; and New Democracy's minister for public order Dendias launched the indiscriminate arrest of thousands of immigrants.[51] The government ordered what amounted to a three-day racist pogrom in the Omonia district of Athens in May 2011. When the police launched Operation Xenios Zeus between August 2012 and June 2013, they arrested at random nearly 124,000 people of foreign origin; of these, only 6910 – 5.6% – were found to be illegal immigrants.

Amid the general current mood of courageous resistance, 15,000 immigrants staged a protest against the police raids. Other expressions of defiance included the heroic ongoing struggle by Bangladeshi strawberry pickers whose comrades had been shot down for demanding payment of their due wages, and the 595 sacked finance-ministry cleaners who went on strike and on one famous occasion physically chased visiting dignitaries from the troika down the street.

Meanwhile, the fascist monster was beginning to stir. The vote for the Nazi party, Golden Dawn, had soared from 19,636 (0.29%) in 2009 to 426,025 (nearly 7%) in June 2012. Raising flags bearing thinly disguised swastikas and banners with the slogan "Greece for the Greeks, blood, honour, Golden Dawn", and sheltered by its patrons in the police, half of whom they claimed as members, its thugs were beating up immigrants and anarchist students under the eyes of their allies in the police, and exploiting the crisis by offering to poor ethnic Greeks free food, blood and protection – all "for Greeks only".

And yet, for all the rabid ranting and thuggery of Golden Dawn, and the hardly-less-bigoted attacks by New Democracy and PASOK governments alike, what is remarkable, in the face of a constantly swelling influx of refugees arriving on Greece's shores, is the acceptance and even welcome with which they have been received by the Greek people. This is largely due to the principled stand of the SYRIZA government, one of whose first acts was to grant citizenship to the children of immigrants.

Fascism always drapes itself in the costume of its ancient national myths: Mussolini's Fascists in Roman togas, Caesarism and the Roman Empire; Hitler's Nazis in Aryan Nordic sagas; Franco's Falange in the Catholic Church and the Inquisition; the Indian RSS and Shiv Sena in Hindu gods, princes and the tales of Ramayana; ISIS/ISIL, Al-Qaeda, the Taliban and Jamaat-e-Islam in seventh-century Mecca and Medina and the early caliphates. Successive British fascist groups have cloaked themselves in the paraphernalia of the British Empire, and their American counterparts in the folklore of the American revolution, the frontier pioneers and the civil-war Confederate states.

Golden Dawn is naturally hell-bent on exploiting the glory of ancient classical Greece and, in the modern epoch, the war of independence. Given the popular attribution of democracy to the ancient Greeks (always rather sentimental and over-hyped), Golden Dawn insists on clarifying that

> Ancient Greece consisted of various city states or kingdoms... the only one of which that practised democracy was Ancient Athens... Athens was not representative of... the Greek people. Sparta, for example, was ruled by a King... Macedonia was also very far from being democratic, with Alexander the Great's empire being governed by military generals... Plato... spoke out against democracy as a political system... It is an indisputable fact that the vast majority of political life in Greece as a whole was not related to democracy at all...

Moreover, even in ancient Athens...

> only full blooded Athenian men who had served in the military and fought for the city state were permitted to vote. No immigrants, no slaves, nor even non-Athenian Greeks were permitted... The core ideals of Golden Dawn are based primarily on that of ancient Sparta, and to a lesser extent taking inspiration from more modern figures of our history such as... Kolokotronis [a military hero of the war of independence] and... Metaxas [Greece's 1930s fascist military dictator].[52]

Irrespective of their cultural disguises, what all fascist groups have in common is their racism, their thuggishness and above all their determination to destroy the labour movement.

Golden Dawn defines a Greek as:

> one who overwhelmingly carries the descent of the various ancient Greek tribes around the Mediterranean sea and the cultural legacy from them, through Orthodoxy up to the

present day.

Meanwhile, the much-publicised attempts by Golden Dawn activists to portray themselves as angels of charity – to pass themselves off as a Salvation Army rather than a bunch of storm troopers – have been exposed, among others by the website Jail Golden Dawn:

> The infamous photo of a Golden Dawner helping an old lady who 'was afraid of migrants' to go to the bank that hit the front pages a couple of years ago has now been exposed as nothing more than one of their leaders with his own mother! The 'soup kitchens' only for Greeks have been just clumsy photo opportunities out of their offices; nothing to do with any kind of solidarity network.[53]

An interesting insight into the services offered by Golden Dawn was revealed by a woman who had naively solicited their help in protecting her against a stalker, and duly received a visit from a party member.

> He made me an offer: he could break someone's arm and leg for €300 euros, set a car on fire for €1,000 euros, put someone in hospital for a month for €1,500 euros... Later he came back and told us not to say a word or he'd burn us alive.[54]

In late 2008, Golden Dawn had turned the Athens district Agios Panteleimonas into a local showcase as a prototype for its more ambitious nationwide project. For several years, its thug squads would patrol the streets, drive out migrants, attack mosques, shut down local playgrounds used by "foreign children" and refuse access to left activists or political campaigners. When their leader Michaloliakos was elected to the local council in 2010, he boasted that he would "turn the whole of Athens into an Agios

Panteleimonas".

By 2013, Golden Dawn felt confident enough to move on from xenophobia and mock charity work to direct attacks on the labour movement – for instance, boldly marching in military formation, armed with sticks and clubs, right into the Perama ship yards, beating up KKE trade-unionists and shouting slogans against the "communist-controlled union".

Their murder of the popular rapper Killah P (Pavlos Fyssos) in September 2013 aroused outrage, leading to the arrest of their leader and several MPs. In both the elections of 2015, though, they maintained an alarming share of the vote at around 7%.

Chapter 10

Hope

SYRIZA was a product of the spontaneous mobilisation of the Greek people over years, from riots to strikes to demonstrations to occupations to general strikes, eventually converging into a political front, a broad spectrum of protest. But its meteoric rise from obscurity to the biggest party – its share of the vote rising from 4.6% to 36.3% within six years – had an even more spectacular precedent in PASOK's phenomenal leap from nowhere in 1974 to 48% of the popular vote in 1981, and a clear overall parliamentary majority.

Like PASOK between 1974 and 1980, SYRIZA flew with lightning speed from nowhere to become the most popular party in Greece. Like PASOK originally, it inspired a new generation with radical slogans. The fate of PASOK was doomed once it had abandoned its initial radical slogans and tried to achieve the stability of a Western reformist party without enjoying the material base to sustain it. There was a lesson there too for SYRIZA. Unlike PASOK, though, it came to power in conditions of catastrophic crisis and desperate expectations.

SYRIZA started out not as a unified party with a coherent structure and discipline, but as a coalition of groupings. Under the dictatorship, younger KKE militants based in the Greek underground had broken loose from the "orthodox" Stalinist leadership based in exile, and followed a more flexible quasi-reformist line, parallel to that of the so-called "Eurocommunists" of Western Europe. Emerging from the shadows of the dictatorship in 1974, this faction, known as the KKE (Interior), soon found itself eclipsed by PASOK. However, the KKE (Interior) had retained some influence among the youth under the dictatorship and beyond, and morphed later into the *Synaspismos tis Aristeras*

(Coalition of the Left). This was eventually to form the main component of SYRIZA (Coalition of the Radical Left), though overall it was a hybrid gathering of 13 groups and independent politicians, including social-democrats, reformists, left patriots, feminists, anti-capitalists, environmentalists, Maoists, Trotskyists, Eurocommunists, Luxemburgists, Eurosceptics and dissident Orthodox Christians.

Only in 2013 did SYRIZA become a unitary party, although it still designated itself as a "United Social Front", encompassing a spectrum ranging from former dissident KKE members to left social-democrats to assorted radicals, united only in their resistance to the terms of the memorandum and their support for the mass protest movement; a coalition straddling a broad spectrum from Keynesians to Trotskyists, Stalinists to nationalists.

Born in the only country in Europe with a living memory of civil war, dictatorship and insurrection, SYRIZA started out on a higher political level than its counterparts elsewhere. PODEMOS, for instance, with which it is often compared, explicitly disclaims any link to the socialist traditions of the past and claims to be "neither left nor right". On the political spectrum it stands somewhere between SYRIZA and reactionary populist parties like the Italian Five-Star movement – with Deutsche Alternativ, UKIP and the openly racist Front National all pointing towards the more sinister alternatives ahead.

Like PASOK at its inception, SYRIZA was no stable traditional social-democratic party, matured over generations (not to say even somewhat rotted), like those of Germany, Scandinavia and Britain. It was not a revolutionary party, certainly, but neither was it a reformist party in the mould of the Labour Party, the SPD or PASOK once it had stabilised itself. The nature of a party is not determined solely by the illusions of its leaders. There is a significant contrast between a volatile party like SYRIZA, exploding into life from nowhere under the irresistible pressure of millions of workers and youth, and the established reformist parties, anchored in the old order by a heavily encrusted bureaucratic caste with a privileged stake in capitalist society. The era begun by the election of SYRIZA was vibrant with revolutionary potential, not only for Greece but for the whole of Europe. Stathis Kouvelakis commented perceptively that its victory was not comparable to "the election of François Hollande in 2012, or... the 'centre-left experiment' of Romano Prodi in Italy, or even like the case of François Mitterrand in 1981".

Its programme may have appeared relatively tame compared to those proclaimed even by the British Labour Party or the French Socialist Party in the 1970s – or, come to that, by PASOK at its inception. But today, in the aftermath of the great financial crash, what other social-democratic party even has on its "wishlist" the kind of reforms that SYRIZA initially tried to enact – moreover, in the context of a literally bankrupt economy, in the grip of a prolonged European recession, and against ferocious pressure and blackmail from its creditors? It began by defying a direct veto from the troika to provide free electricity and food stamps to the poor. What other social-democratic government even *threatened* to default on its debts to the bankers rather than on its promises to the electorate? If only Hollande or Miliband had even talked like SYRIZA.

The social-democratic parties had established a base in the labour movement precisely because they had in the past actually delivered tangible reforms. In its early years before the First World War, the SPD leadership had amassed enormous authority by securing benefits for the working class undreamed of by previous generations. In Britain, the Labour Party had earned in 1945–50 the loyalty of generations of workers by delivering a "welfare state", the NHS and nationalisation of major sections of the economy. It took betrayals, wars, civil wars and world wars to begin to undermine their credibility.

The communist parties, too, had traditionally thrived on the historic appeal of the Russian revolution and the sponsorship of the USSR, which had turned them into extensions of the Kremlin's diplomatic apparatus. The slow decay and eventual collapse of the Stalinist regimes had robbed these parties both of their political authority and their material sources.

SYRIZA resembled more closely those transient parties of the 1930s, like the ILP when it split from Labour in 1931, the German SAPD in 1931 and the Spanish POUM in 1935–6: dynamic, fluid, volatile formations. These parties were intrinsically unstable, in a process from the outset of flux and transition, representing a bridge between reformism and revolution, behaving almost like radioactive elements, with a limited half-life, fleetingly seeking out a stable foundation, and soon either subsiding into reformism, achieving a revolutionary mission or more probably fizzling out.

Trotsky made the following comment on the leftward-moving French Socialist Party in the revolutionary crisis of 1935-6. It could not be more scintillatingly relevant as a riposte to those sectarians who stood aside and scoffed haughtily at SYRIZA as a mere "reformist" party.

There can be no more devastating mistake in politics than to operate with ready-made conceptions that relate to yesterday and to yesterday's relationship of forces... A mistake of exactly the same kind is made by those comrades who, in appraising the Socialist Party, themselves operate with the ready-made formulas of yesterday: 'reformism', 'Second International', 'political support of the bourgeoisie'. Are these definitions correct? Yes and no. More no than yes... Naturally it would be a crude mistake to assert that 'nothing' has remained of reformism and patriotism in the party since this split. But it is no less a mistake to talk about it as about the social democracy in the old sense of the word. The impossibility of employing henceforward a simple, customary, fixed definition is precisely the flawless expression of the fact that what we have here is a centrist party, which, by virtue of a long protracted evolution of the country, still unites extreme polar contradictions. One must be a hopeless scholastic not to discern what is going on in reality under the label 'Second International'.

He concluded by urging his supporters

more deeply to penetrate the ranks of the Socialist workers, not in order to 'lecture' down to them from above as learned specialists in strategy, but in order to learn together with the advanced workers, shoulder to shoulder, on the basis of actual mass experience, which will inevitably lead the French proletariat on the road of revolutionary struggle.[55]

It was easy enough to criticise SYRIZA's programme; anyone with a bunch of old pamphlets could formulate a better one. But it was not a time for facile sloganising. There is no substitute for first-hand knowledge, participation and engagement. There was no existential threat; no immediate risk of military counter-revolution as in 1967, or in Chile in 1973 – something that remained a deadly but more distant future threat, but that at so premature a stage would be politically disastrous for the elite throughout Europe. To begin with, what lay ahead was a game of diplomatic Russian roulette between the EU and SYRIZA, involving threats and counter-threats, bluffs and blackmail, disguised concessions and stabs in the back. SYRIZA might wrest some minor concessions, or it might make a humiliating retreat; Governments might come and go; but the question of power would not be resolved in a matter of weeks. There could be several years first in which the opportunity was there either to consolidate a secure base for victory or to let slip the opportunity and pave the way for a bloody defeat. Ultimately the issue could not be resolved within the borders of Greece alone. It would be the workers of Spain, Portugal, Italy, France, Britain and Europe as a whole who together would determine the final outcome.

Trotsky had used the term "centrist" to label those fluid parties of the 1930s; and yet that term too is only an approximation transplanted from a different epoch. It originally referred to those parties in the early 1920s that had vacillated between the two poles of the Second and Third internationals (the so-called "2½ international"), and was later borrowed by Trotsky to refer to those parties repelled by both traditions but still hesitating to commit themselves to what on the eve of a new world war seemed the only viable alternative: the creation of a new international. Today these allusions are obsolete.

Like these shooting stars of the past, SYRIZA was born out of a sudden historic shock: the overnight pauperisation of Greek society. But there was a recent precedent in Greece for SYRIZA's meteoric spurt of growth. PASOK too had suddenly materialised apparently from nowhere, impelled to power by the shock of the military dictatorship and the vitality of the popular uprising that had overthrown it. A confluence of accidental factors had then lent PASOK a couple of decades of unexpected stability during its golden years of patronage and social recuperation, before vanishing into thin air just as suddenly as it had materialised. SYRIZA too could disappear just as fast.

Trotsky in his day could be scathing in his criticisms of Fenner Brockway or Andres Nin, leaders respectively of the ILP and the POUM; but his tone in correcting their mistakes was very different from his denunciation of the betrayals by the reformist and Stalinist leaders. At times he showed exasperation at their blunders, but his aim was not to undermine or denounce them but to win them, and those who had faith in them, to a clearer and sharper standpoint.And, after all, he was Trotsky. He had the authority of three decades in the spotlight of history, as the leader of the Petersburg Soviet in 1905, the organiser of the October insurrection in 1917, the founder of the Red Army, the creator of the Left Opposition, the mainspring of efforts to found a new international. Fellow campaigners today lacking such credentials need to contribute their ideas with a humility commensurate with their own rather more modest records.

SYRIZA was not weighed down with the ballast of the old social-democratic parties of Europe, facing the same slow laborious stages of development. It is not just a question of tempo. All strands of opinion were put to the test. Charlatans, chancers and other accidental figures can have shallow roots in these parties and a precarious hold over their membership, but their ranks are from the outset alive with debate. Marxist ideas could not prevail unchallenged. Just as in the days of Marx and Engels, there would inevitably be an explosion of rival ideas. Conflicting ideas must be countered with arguments that are measured, well-founded and grounded in a proper study of history and context, avoiding hasty and impressionistic slogans, or any suspicion of lying in wait ready to pounce triumphantly on any mistake. The outlook was rich with revolutionary potential, not only for Greece but for the whole of Europe.

Power

On 25th January 2015, the election victory of SYRIZA opened a new chapter in the story of European resistance against austerity. After years of magnificent but impotent protest, the Greek population had turned in its frustration from direct protest on the streets and squares back to the polling booth and the political plane. It seemed that a new era was beginning.

SYRIZA had gained the trust of the electorate in its intention to try to secure tolerable living standards, against the efforts of the troika to inflict on Greece the same punishment it had already visited on the peoples of Bosnia, Romania, Bulgaria and Hungary, as a further step towards the imposition of Victorian-era pauperism throughout Europe. This stood in sharp contrast to the social-democratic practices of PASOK in its last years. It was the duty of fellow campaigners against austerity to criticise its policies as allies, respecting their good faith, warning of the pitfalls ahead.

SYRIZA's victory was a living monument to five years of struggle on the picket lines and of intense debate among the crowds occupying the public squares. At the 2009 elections, PASOK had won 45% of the votes, and SYRIZA 4%. By the elections of January 2015, SYRIZA's voting percentage had *doubled* since 2012 and increased *eightfold* since 2009.

At the double elections of 2012, PASOK's support had collapsed and New Democracy had suffered heavy losses. The first of that year's elections was inconclusive. No party exceeded 20% of the vote; even in coalition together, the two main parties could not scrabble together enough seats to form a majority. SYRIZA's share of the vote had quadrupled from 4.6% in 2009 to 16.8% – just 2% behind New Democracy. With no mandate for government, new elections were held a month later. This time, SYRIZA's share of the vote had soared again to 26.9% – within a hair's breadth of first place. Within three years, its share of the vote had shot up sixfold. Under Greek electoral law, the marginal plurality achieved by New Democracy gave it a statutory 50-seat bonus, which just enabled Samaras to cobble together a coalition government with the support of PASOK and its minor offshoot DEMAR.

Then, after three years of turmoil and street protests, Samaras finally cut his losses. The outgoing coalition had lost momentum, and Samaras almost wilfully courted parliamentary defeat by provoking an unnecessary crisis over the election of a new president. His government disintegrated and departed the scene almost as incongruously as the fleeing junta in 1974. For his part, Papandreou deserted the sinking ship of PASOK by splitting to form a new mini-party.

By now, SYRIZA was a fully-fledged party with a consti-tution, a new programme and all the authority of a government-in-waiting. There was a huge human tidal wave amassing behind it: or rather, a confluence of two waves of protest: by workers at the slashing of their livelihoods, and by youth at the robbery of their future. That was all that capitalism had to offer; the surge of support for SYRIZA was a revolt against capitalism.

Where six years previously, SYRIZA had still been just one of a number of supernumary extras on the sidelines, now, amid a surge of renewed hope and excitement, SYRIZA swept to power, winning 36.4% of the vote and securing 149 seats. Its share of the vote had grown eightfold in six years. It came within a hair's breadth of an absolute majority, propelled into responsibility for the lives and livelihoods of the Greek population.

Tsipras put his finger on the real meaning of the election as a landmark in the history of the continent. "Greece is on the cusp of a historic change. SYRIZA is no longer just a hope for Greece and the Greek people. It is also an expectation of a change of course for the whole of Europe." SYRIZA's victory was greeted throughout Europe as a potentially pivotal turning point – the product of a groundswell of workers' resistance, the beginning at last of a decisive fightback. Its programme was riddled with lacunae and ambiguities, but its election represented a historic opportunity. The immediate threat to its success seemed to be the danger of traps, slips, errors of judgement, rather than outright betrayal.

The main beneficiaries of popular rejection of the old ruling parties were neither Greece's age-old traditional opposition the KKE, nor the explicitly revolutionary ANTARSYA, but new parties: SYRIZA on the left and – a sinister warning for the future – the fascist Golden Dawn (Chrysi Avgi) on the right.

How was it that the party embodying the rich historical traditions of Greek resistance had found itself bypassed? The KKE had put forward an abstractly left programme ("the workers must take power") but throughout the events of the last few years it had consistently refused to participate in any united front or joint struggles along with other sections of the movement. It had sullenly stood aside from the youth uprising of 2008-9, denouncing the youth as anarchists and hooligans and jeering at SYRIZA for "patting the hooded rioters on the back", and boasting (improbably) that "in our revolution, not a pane of glass will be broken". Throughout the years of mass protest, it had held separate rival strikes and demonstrations, and boycotted any general strikes, demonstrations, occupations of public spaces, etc. organised by other parties or trade-union federations. It had then shrugged aside the crucial elections of 2012 as "an establishment trick". The KKE had practised the grossest ultra-left sectarianism, reminiscent of the Stalinist parties in the early 1930s, who had thwarted all attempts to form united fronts against fascism and shunned social-democrats as "social fascists".

The KKE leaders boasted that they had maintained their level of support intact in the elections and even slightly increased it over that of the previous election, having scored 5.5% this time compared to 4.5% in June 2012. What they were slyly glossing over was the fact that overall their vote had slumped disastrously since winning 8.5% in the elections of May 2012, to say nothing of the long haemorrhage of support for the KKE since their high point of 13.1% in the June 1989 elections. At a time of economic crisis and social catastrophe, this loss of support was just punishment for their stubborn sectarian refusal of all co-operation with other left parties.

The other left grouping ANTARSYA had likewise failed to gain any impetus from the growing tide of protest. Throughout a period that witnessed the movement of millions in waves of general strikes and demonstrations, this coalition of small left groups with its explicitly revolutionary programme had failed to establish more than the narrowest of bases. By January 2015, its already miniscule vote had halved since May 2012 – to 0.64%.

Meanwhile, SYRIZA had stood in solidarity with every antigovernment protest, strike and demonstration, from the youth uprising to the public-square occupations, and rose to the challenge of contesting for power even before it had formulated a programme or established a party structure. This was to prove its ultimate weakness as well as a strength.

Forming a government

SYRIZA's first task was to form a government. Finding itself just two seats short of an overall majority, it seemed reasonable to seek an alliance first with the only other anti-austerity party represented in parliament with a working-class base: the KKE, an elementary choice as an ally against the right. Tsipras duly phoned the KKE's general secretary Koutsoumbas on the night of the election; but Koutsoumbas refused point-blank to meet with him, and rejected out of hand any form of collaboration with SYRIZA – not even to the extent of passively supporting it in a vote of confidence.

On the very first day of SYRIZA's election campaign in January, Tsipras had proposed a government of the left: explicitly, a government of SYRIZA, the KKE and ANTARSYA. The KKE's refusal of support to a SYRIZA-led government – a stance tantamount to strikebreaking – had been asserted publicly many times in the course of the election campaign and justified on the basis of "ideological and political differences". It was not prepared even to open negotiations and place before Tsipras a programme of minimum conditions as a bargaining counter for co-operation, which might have guaranteed some safeguarding of workers' interests and inroads into the power of capital. It would at least have removed any possible justification or pretext to turn elsewhere for support. How could the KKE justify refusing to join a coalition – a united front of the left against the troika? It would be an act of treachery to vote with the capitalist parties to bring it down, or to abstain to the same effect, when it represented the hopes of millions of workers, and SYRIZA should have been able to count on its support, rather than find itself driven into an unsavoury deal with the right. It was a decision incomprehensible to working-class Greeks desperate to fight against the troika; a betrayal of the hopes of activists throughout Europe for a united fightback against austerity.

SYRIZA consequently formed a coalition government with the populist right-wing nationalist party ANEL (Independent Greeks), a split-off from New Democracy. It was an ominous step; but the KKE bore primary responsibility for the failure to establish a government of the left. To spurn the spectacular mandate SYRIZA had only just won and refuse to grasp the challenge for want of an overall majority would have meant gambling with the electorate and risking a downward spiral of popular confidence. It would have been seen by the electorate as a cop-out, a betrayal of the trust they had placed in their desperate need for relief.

SYRIZA should first have shamed the KKE by a public appeal, ideally to form a straight coalition with it, but if not, then at least to allow it to form a minority government by pledging support for it in any confidence vote. The KKE was not even prepared to promise abstention. If public pressure was still not enough to budge the KKE from its sectarian obstinacy, then the only option was to accept under protest the token inclusion of ANEL's leader Kammenos as a minor coalition partner, carry through some immediate dramatic reforms, and then be ready the very first time that it was blocked on a clear issue of principle – something which could be clearly understood as such on the streets – to go back to the electorate and appeal for a renewed vote of confidence and a decisive overall mandate. Once that moment was there, it must lose no time in dislodging ANEL from the defence ministry.

ANEL's insistence, as a precondition of participation in the coalition, on being awarded the defence portfolio was ascribed merely to a wish to mollify its patriotic voters, but it had ominous overtones. No one was expecting an imminent military coup at that point – even the military top brass had surely learned something from the fiasco of 1967–74 – but the posting of ANEL at the ministry was still significant in that it would forestall any risk that SYRIZA might try to purge the officer caste of its most reckless reactionaries. By assuming responsibility for the choice of top officer personnel, it was locking into place guaranteed access to an ultimate safety mechanism, to be kept in reserve for future contingencies.

One shameful consequence was the almost immediate conclusion of a special defence deal by Kammenos with the Israeli government – a pact matched only by a similar agreement between Israel and the USA – providing for joint training by their defence forces on each other's respective territory and awarding special mutual legal exemptions. This was a flagrant provocation to the ranks of SYRIZA, who were committed to solidarity with the Palestinian people and some of whom had personally been victims of the Israeli assault on the peace flotilla in 2010.

What's more, the inclusion of ANEL as a minor partner in the coalition was not the only warning sign of what was to come. In addition to appointing Kammenos defence minister, with a solemn promise to exempt the massive defence budget from cuts, Tsipras also made plainly gratuitous concessions to the right. He appointed as Interior Minister Yiannis Panoussis, a former member of the pro-memorandum Democratic Left party, who was soon conniving in brutal police attacks, abusing prison hunger-strikers, violating the sanctity of university asylum for the first time since the 1973 Polytechnic uprising, and ranting against the left, youth and trade-unionists. The new foreign minister Kotzias adopted a pro-Israeli and Islamophobic approach and turned a blind eye to provocative public parades by the Army special-forces unit shouting warmongering anti-Turkish slogans; the Central Bank governor retained from New Democracy days effectively undermined SYRIZA's economic policies. Dimitris Mardas was appointed deputy minister of Finance just days after making a vitriolic attack on named SYRIZA MPs. Tsipras later appointed the controversial media-establishment figure Lambis Tagmatarchis as director of the restored public broadcasting company ERT, and – most disturbingly of all – New Democracy's Prokopis Pavlopoulos as president of the republic.

For all these misgivings, at the outset no principled line had yet been crossed. On the contrary, the new government's defiant decision the very next day to grant automatic citizenship to all children of immigrants born in Greece, along with the creation of a Ministry of Immigration with a mandate to protect their human rights, was a deliberate snub and a delicious provocation to ANEL. This decision was agreed on the new government's very first day in office, when it also committed itself to a raft of demonstrative reforms, including restoration of the minimum wage to its 2009 level and immediate enactment of emergency measures to address the humanitarian disaster: food stamps; reconnection of electricity supplies; transport and medical coverage for everyone; restoration of labour legislation; abolition of unfair taxes on land; a tax reform to make the rich pay; reinstatement of all public employees who had been sacked; an end to the privileges granted to private media; reconstitution of the state radio and television network ERT; a halt to privatisation of the ports, infrastructure and energy; and an end to police repression of popular demonstrations. The new government also alleviated the private debt of poor citizens to the state; ruled that no one owing less than €50,000 could be arrested for non-payment of debts and taxes; and protected primary residences with a taxable value of up to €300,000 from foreclosure.

Dignity

On 5th February, thousands of people attended a spontaneous demonstration organised through social media in support of the government. An opinion poll reported that 76% of the population were positive about the government's overall performance, and put support for SYRIZA at 47.6% compared to New Democracy's 20.7%.

Stathis Kouvelakis described the popular mood in those days:

An atmosphere of effervescence is spreading, a sense of newfound dignity, of determination both to support the government in the face of blackmail and to exert pressure to prevent any retreat...[56]

These measures were in full accord with SYRIZA's programme. While preparing for the impending elections, SYRIZA had drawn up the so-called Thessaloniki programme, which included among others the following points:

- write-off the greater part of the public debt's nominal value (as with Germany in 1953);
- a 'European New Deal' of public investment financed by the European Investment Bank;
- a socially viable solution to Greece's debt problem... to pay off the remaining debt from the creation of new wealth and not from primary surpluses;
- immediate increase in public investment by at least €4 billion;
- rebuilding the welfare state, restoring the rule of law and creating a meritocratic state;
- a National Reconstruction Plan to replace the Memorandum;
- free electricity to 300,000 households currently under the poverty line;
- programme of meal subsidies to 300,000 families without income;
- free medical and pharmaceutical care for the uninsured

unemployed;
- special public transport card for the long-term unemployed and those under the poverty line;
- reducing the price of heating fuel for households;
- restitution of the €12,000 annual income tax threshold;
- progressive taxation;
- restoration of the minimum wage;
- a net increase in jobs by 300,000 in all sectors of the economy;
- restitution of protection of employment rights;
- restitution of collective agreements;
- re-establishment of public radio and television.

It estimated the total cost of these reforms at €11,382 billion – within its expected total revenues of €12 billion.

When we look at the terms of the Thessaloniki Programme, they are hardly more radical than those of any of the European social-democratic parties in the post-war period up to around the 1970s. In the context of the neoliberal era of cutbacks and austerity, however, they stand out as an expression either of sheer delusion or of wilful defiance.

First, however, there was the little matter of the debt to deal with.

Chapter 11

Debt

It is an outright lie that the Greek debt crisis is the result of successive governments' irresponsible profligacy in spending. The truth, as the Debt Truth Commission revealed[57], is that Greece's public expenditure was actually lower than that of other countries in the Eurozone... with the exception of one item: defence expenditure, which accounted for €40 billion of the debt (largely owed to German arms manufacturers, much of it for fraudulently mis-sold redundant weaponry). When Greece joined the EU in 1981 its public debt represented only 25% of GDP. Fully two thirds of the increase in its debt by 2007 is a result of the "snowball effect" caused by the shortfall between GDP nominal growth and the implicit interest rate on the accumulated debt. The majority of the Greek debt to foreign banks (55%) came not from the public but the private sector.

The Greek debt currently stands at around €315 billion. This is the equivalent of almost €30,000 for every man, woman and child in Greece! Let's look at that figure again: every baby born in Greece today starts life with a €30,000 debt burden around its neck! Over how many lifetimes are the Greek people expected to pay off this so-called debt? How much spare cash does the troika imagine the Greek people have got stashed away, starved and pauperised as they are already, to even begin? The EU insistence of the troika that it be paid back bears no relation to real life: it is a declaration of imperial slavery. In 2015, Greece paid back almost €22 billion, amounting to a staggering 10% of GDP.

The American Keynesian Brad de Long, supporting the advice of Paul Krugman and Joseph Stiglitz that Grexit would have been preferable, expressed surprise at the Europeans' "irrational" insistence on austerity when it was clearly not working. "The eurozone is making the mistakes of the 1930s once again... in a more brutal, more exaggerated, and more persistent form."

With their high "exposure" to the Greek banking system, German and French banks were desperate to prop them up to prevent "contagion". So who was really bailed out? As an American economic historian explains:

German banks, led by the troubled Commerzbank, held some 17 billion Euros of Greek debt. The exposure of the German private sector, including pension funds, insurance companies and thrifty burghers searching for yield, came to as much as 25 billion Euros, a considerable fraction of what the Greek government owed. What was at stake, in other words, was not just the solvency of the Greek government but the stability of the German financial system.[58]

In 2012, in view of the staggering burden of debt, the EU leaders had agreed with Samaras that, while trapping Greece still deeper in debt obligations, private creditors would take a "haircut" in what was owed them. In other words, French and German creditors exchanged Greek government bonds of dubious value for new ones nominally worth a little less, but guaranteed by the European Stability Fund. At the same time, punitive new austerity measures were imposed. The target was to reduce Greek government debt from its current level of 165% to 120% of GDP by 2020. Actually, groaning under the weight of the debt, the Greek economy fell victim to a further deflationary spiral. The IMF had predicted that Greece would grow as the result of its aid package in 2010. Instead, the economy had shrunk by 25%. By 2015, the Greek debt ratio had grown to 175%. It is now expected to reach 200% by 2020.

By January 2015, GDP had collapsed by more than 30% since its peak before the crisis: a decline comparable only to that seen in the USA during the Great Depression. And, as in the USA, so in Greece it was the weakest who shouldered the heaviest burden. According to one study, in the four years since the start of the crisis...

- the nominal gross income of Greek households decreased by almost a quarter;
- nearly half the decline was the direct result of wages cuts;
- the increased tax burden cut net income still further by almost 9 percent;
- it was low- and middle-income households which were the most severely affected;
- public-sector employees lost around a quarter of their income;
- in the private sector, wages and salaries declined by 19% between 2009 and 2013;
- unemployment surged from 7.3% in 2008 to 26.6% in 2014;
- youth unemployment reached almost 60% – a figure which would have been substantially higher if it had not been for a flood of youth emigration. Since 2008, 200,000 young people had emigrated.[59]

In 2014, 73.5% of Greece's unemployed had been out of work for more than a year, compared with 67.1% in 2013. Attiki, which includes Athens and Piraeus, has the highest proportion of long-term unemployment of any region in Europe: 77.3%.

The average annual pre-tax income of all Greek households had fallen from €23,100 in 2008 to just below €17,900 in 2012 – a loss of nearly 23%. But that was before taxes were taken into account. Direct taxes increased by nearly 53%, and indirect taxes by 22%. The tax base was actually extended "downwards" so that still more of the very lowest paid were hit. Poorer households paid disproportionately far more in taxes. The tax burden on those on lower incomes rose by 37%; on upper incomes, by only 9%. The poorest households lost nearly 86% of their income; the richest, at worst less than 20%.

Almost one in three Greek households had an annual income below €7000. Forty percent of the population were living below the poverty line, with wages and pensions often halved and benefits slashed, and many Greeks too poor to heat their homes or even switch their lights on. It was reported by the Organisation for Economic Co-operation and Development that nearly 20% of Greeks "lacked sufficient funds to meet daily food expenses".

By 2015, every day 59 businesses were closing, costing 613 jobs and €22 million every 24 hours. Infant mortality had risen by 40%, and the rate of suicides by 45%. The director of a funeral parlour reported that some families could no longer afford to even bury their dead. Bodies were lying unclaimed at public hospitals for the local municipality to bury them. There were even reports of maternity wards holding new-born babies hostage until their mothers could scrape together the money to pay their bills. Since the crisis began in 2008, over 10,000 suicides have taken place.

Meanwhile, incidentally, €120 billion was being held abroad by Greeks oligarchs, often hidden in London properties or Swiss bank accounts.

Both PASOK and New Democracy governments had made empty boasts that Greece was on the road to recovery. But the troika's pilot experiment to squeeze Greek wages and benefits to Chinese levels had hardly begun. Greece was undergoing an experience that can best be described as the vivisection of an entire population: a laboratory experiment conducted on the living body of the Greek nation to test out how far it could withstand the trauma of ever more drastic surgical amputation.

Fatal concessions

How did SYRIZA propose to bring about the social-democratic utopia envisaged in the Thessaloniki programme in a country crippled with debt? By taxing the rich? These include world-famous shipping magnates – notorious tax-evaders with assets that are by definition highly portable – and the owners of such enterprises as energy and construction groups and football clubs. The greed of the Greek oligarchs long predates the crisis. These plutocrats had avoided paying tax through the Metaxas dicta-torship, the Nazi occupation, the civil war and the colonels' regime. They had no intention of starting to pay taxes now, merely at the request of some passing government. That is why, when in 2010 the troika began belatedly to insist that Greece balance the books, the entire weight of that responsibility fell upon the only people who were already paying taxes, because they had no chance of avoiding them: that poor minority of Greeks locked into the PAYE system, whose tax payments were deducted at source – a workforce of 3.5 million wage-earners that very quickly shrank, as a direct result of the cuts imposed at the dictates of the troika itself, to just 2.5 million.

Tsipras imagined that he could reason with the creditors. The fact is that SYRIZA's ministers had no strategy to solve the crisis; just a portable emergency kit of assorted tactics. They put all their faith into their powers of rational persuasion to coax, cajole, charm or shame the bankers into a reasonable compromise. They tried to "convince" their "partners" to "understand" the "justice" of Greece's position. But bankers are predators. You don't reason with a tiger; it doesn't recognise electoral mandates.

Nasos Iliopoulos, a member of the political secretariat of SYRIZA's central committee – and not a member of the Left Platform – reflected later, after the troika's victory in imposing a humiliating defeat on SYRIZA, on the lessons of its mistaken approach...

Our enemy took us seriously. Our enemy believed that we truly are a systemic danger... We did not take ourselves that seriously. We never prepared ourselves for a real battle. What brought us to this point is the ease with which our strategy was planned on the basis of a best-case scenario: we were going to reach a good agreement which would include debt reconstruction and financial support and therefore we would be able to put our political programme into operation, perhaps with some minor setbacks. The numerous concerns about the enemies' plan... never sparked off the preparation of the upcoming battle. During this period we provided our enemies with the space that they needed... There was a clear message for us... that humiliation of our left government would be a goal pursued at any cost... All of our efforts and methods employed during these past few months may have been suitable for a quiet, peaceful period of bourgeois parliamentarism but certainly not for the current state of emergency.... Sadly, the bourgeois way of doing politics and the culture of parliamentary cretinism have deep roots within us...[60]

SYRIZA's first finance minister was the outspoken leather-jacketed motor-cyclist Yanis Varoufakis. Sometimes, the more daringly unconventional a politician's style and persona, the more prudent and circumspect his policies. Varoufakis started out from the premise that the time is not ripe for socialist demands, and that in the age of neoliberalism, to propose Keynesian reforms constitutes a more realistic challenge to the prevailing orthodoxy. So polarised had society become, and so far had socialist traditions dimmed, that Keynesianism was now considered subversive, a "left" ideology.

Varoufakis argued that it was "necessary to rescue European capitalism from itself". He characterised the 2008 crisis as capitalism's "second global spasm" since the Great Depression.

Should we welcome this crisis of European capitalism as an opportunity to replace it with a better system? Or should we be so worried about it as to embark upon a campaign for stabilising European capitalism? To me, the answer is clear. Europe's crisis is far less likely to give birth to a better alternative to capitalism than it is to unleash dangerously regressive forces that have the capacity to cause a humanitarian bloodbath, while extinguishing the hope for any progressive moves for generations to come... I am sad that I shall probably not be around to see a more radical agenda being adopted.

Varoufakis' argument is an expression of frustration. He had previously accepted the post of economic adviser to George Papandreou in the hope that he could "help stem the return to power of a resurgent right wing that wanted to push Greece towards xenophobia", but soon realised that

Papandreou's party not only failed to stem xenophobia but, in the end, presided over the most virulent neoliberal macroeconomic policies that spearheaded the eurozone's so-called bailouts – thus unwittingly causing the return of Nazis to the streets of Athens.

His conclusion was that

it is we, the suitably erratic Marxists, who must try to save European capitalism from itself... not out of love for European capitalism, for the eurozone, for Brussels, or for the European Central Bank, but just because we want to minimise the unnecessary human toll from this crisis.[61]

Varoufakis was not the first socialist to have drawn back from the challenge. There is never a prior guarantee that bold radical measures will succeed, and there are always comforting arguments that caution and moderation are more prudent. At the outbreak of the First World War, the German social-democrats rationalised their vote for the Kaiser's war credits by the argument that the first task was to rescue "civilisation"; while their French counterparts provided a mirror-image justification for "resisting German militarism". It was Rosa Luxemburg who posed the ultimate choice before humanity as "socialism or barbarism". Who could deny that there are elements of sheer barbarism today in Greece – starvation, homelessness, suicide, the rise of Golden Dawn – and within the confines of capitalism, no hope of escape from it?

Actually, the idea that the creditors might be persuaded to relax their stranglehold did not at first sight seem implausible. It was not inconceivable that some factions within the EU might agree to token concessions. After all, it is not as if anyone had the illusion that the Greek debt could ever be paid back. The troika's very programme of accumulating austerity cuts was seeing to that. Every year the Greek economy was plunging deeper into the swamp; the ratio of the debt burden to GDP was swelling year by year.

But bank loans are not like personal loans between friends. The very last thing creditors want is their money back. Debts do not appear in the ledgers on the deficit side of the page: they are highly lucrative assets. The deeper the debt, the more interest to be scooped up, guaranteed into infinity. Moreover, in 2012 they had still been dealing with one of their own: their fellow European Central Bank director Papademos – unelected, unaccountable, imposed by blackmail on the Greek people. They could afford to reach a private "gentleman's agreement" to help him lubricate passage through parliament of its draconic provisions. They were hardly inclined to accommodate a radical left government in full view of the eyes of workers and anti-austerity campaigners throughout the continent. Even the most trivial adjustment of the debt would immediately be seized upon as a precedent, risking a spread of defiance to Spain and the rest of

Europe. The creditors might be persuaded to whittle down Greece's €300-billion debt if they could be confident that that would end the crisis and restore stability to Europe. But if Greece won a respite, then what would happen to the whole chain of European debt? What about Portugal and Ireland – each obediently servicing their debts of €200 billion each? What about Spain, with its trillion-euro debt, or Italy, whose debt now stands at a colossal €2.25 trillion?

Overnight, the bankers could find themselves confronted by a continental united front of angry anti-capitalist governments, swept into power by a tidal wave of protesting, marching, striking populations. And even if the bankers themselves were not fearful of the consequences, then what about the current governments of these countries, all of them virtual stooges obediently enforcing their austerity programmes? If Greece were to succeed, they would be facing certain overthrow tomorrow. Once one card flips, the whole house of cards comes crashing down.

No matter how clever the debating points of Greece's negotiators, once the decision had been taken by Tsipras to throw away his sole trump card by unilaterally suspending debt repayments, then all the power was in the hands of the bankers. And on 20th February they set the traps which would assure them of success. Tsipras and Varoufakis signed away fatal concessions. It was not Varoufakis but the troika which showed the cunning and expertise to win the tactical game hands down. It locked the government into months of helpless paralysis, trapped by its pledge to take "no unilateral action" to pre-empt a settlement. This meant guarantees that there would be no bank nationalisations, no capital controls, no default on repayments.

$7.2 billion of the bailout from the second memorandum was still outstanding, payment of which was contingent on periodic "reviews"; it would not be released until a new memorandum was signed. It restricted the government from issuing treasury bills (short-term IOUs) and prevented Greek banks from buying these treasury bills (lending to the government). By promising not to take "unilateral action" to curb, control or nationalise the banks (and thus the power of the ECB to regulate their lending), SYRIZA had handed over whatever defensive power they might have had.

Among the SYRIZA parliamentarians denouncing the deal was the 93-year-old MEP Manolis Glezos, the legendary hero who on 30th May 1941 had torn down the Nazi swastika flying over Athens from the Acropolis; the revolutionary prisoner and torture victim sentenced to death in turn by the Germans, the Italians and the Greek government forces in the civil war. Later Tsakalotos and even Tsipras, who had initially welcomed it as a "victory", admitted it was a grave mistake.

Somehow the government did manage to enact some humanitarian relief measures, but only a tenth of what had been promised. And yet it still concluded a deal worth half a billion euros with Lockheed Martin to upgrade planes for the navy.

Claims on Germany

One of the planks of SYRIZA's platform was a proposal to claim compensation from Germany for Nazi war crimes against the Greek people, which could amount to €341 billion – more than enough to cancel Greece's debt. In 1960, in a bilateral out-of-court, state-to-state agreement, Germany did pay Greece DM115 million (€57.5m) in damages, and Germany argued that the issue of war reparations was now closed. Then, after Germany's reunification in 1990, the issue of war reparations was considered to have expired.

In 1997, a Greek district court upheld the right to file a claim for compensation to survivors and relatives of victims of one of the most notorious atrocities of the occupation: the Distomo massacre in 1944, in which SS forces murdered 214 villagers, bayoneting babies in their cribs, stabbing pregnant women and beheading the village priest. The supreme court ordered seizure of German assets in Greece for this purpose, but no justice minister has ever enforced that order; and in 2012 the International Court of Justice at The Hague ruled in Germany's favour that governments have immunity from foreign court judgments in cases brought by individuals.

It was recently brought to light by the German Die Linke MP Andrei Hunko that the same German government that is withholding compensation from the Greek wartime victims of the Wehrmacht is still today paying war pensions to the Wehrmacht's Spanish fascist allies of Franco's Blue Division who fought together with the Wehrmacht at Stalingrad.[62]

Quite apart from compensation for the slaughter of thousands and the systematic starvation of hundreds of thousands of Greeks during the Nazi occupation, Greece believes it also has a legitimate claim on Germany for reimbursement of the forced "loan" levied by the Nazis on the Greek Central Bank. This amounted to 476-million reichsmarks or, according to Greek estimates, €11 billion today – one sixth of the €65 billion that Greece today owes towards Germany's share of the bail-out. In the 1960s, the then chancellor Ludwig Erhard promised that Germany would repay the loan once it reunified, probably assuming that this would never happen. (For more information, see http://cadtm.org/The-cancellation-of-German-debt-in?debut_articles_auteur=120 and http://cadtm.org/In-February-1953-the-allied-powers.)

Greece has also reminded Germany that at the 1953 Conference of London, to which Greece was among the signatories, creditor countries agreed to forgive West Germany's massive debt, thus laying the ground for the country's economic miracle.

In view of the intransigence of the ECB and the EU in rejecting the Greek claim as redundant and provocative, it never amounted to much more than a debating point. However, several SPD and Green Party politicians spoke out in favour of repayment of the forced loan. One German tourist couple even calculated their own personal share of what was owed and donated it to the town hall of the Greek island where they were staying on holiday.

Nevertheless, SYRIZA's indecision on the issue gave it the worst of both worlds. When confronted by a hungry tiger, you have various practical choices: throwing it some scraps, killing it, running for your life, etc. Thumbing your nose and sticking your tongue out at it is not generally considered a good idea.

Sometimes appeasement is unavoidable. If you don't have favourable conditions or resources, then temporary subterfuges to placate it are permissible; but they won't help for long; they will only feed the appetite of the beast. Jeers, however, will only enrage it. SYRIZA's intermittent taunts – its supporters' depictions of Merkel and Schauble as Nazis, its empty threats to take over German embassy buildings in Athens, etc. – fall into that category.

The Truth Commission

As the months of deadlock dragged on, ever greater attention was focusing on the root causes of the crisis and the very legitimacy of the debt.

Soon after the election, with approval from Tsipras, an-official commission was set up by Zoi Konstantopoulou, president of the Hellenic parliament, to audit the public debt, in collaboration with the Committee to Abolish Third-World Debt, an international network of social movements established in 1990. Organisations from over 40 different countries are members: 18 in Latin America and the Caribbean, 15 in Africa, eight in Europe and four in Asia. It participated in the anti-globalisation movement and the World Social Forum, and its purpose is to identify "illegal, illegitimate, unsustainable or odious debt". Composed of 30 experts – half from Greece and half from outside – the Greek commission examined the debts contracted by Greece since the mid-1990s. Its main creditor, representing 80%

of its public debt, is the conglomerate known colloquially as the "troika", which was the collective name for the European Central Bank, the EU (itself comprising the European Commission, the European Stability Fund and 14 individual European countries) and the IMF. Most of the remaining 20% of the Greek public debt is owed largely to Greek banks, with the other 3–4% to various vulture funds, hedge funds and investment funds.

The Commission reported back in June:

> The largest part of Greece's post-2009 debt was in fact private debt that had been converted into sovereign debt... The odious, illegal and illegitimate nature of the Greek debt as a whole (particularly the conversion of private into public debt)... The loans disbursed to Greece since 2010... were used almost entirely (almost 92%) in order to repay capital and interest to creditors... Since February 2015, following the ascent to power of SYRIZA, the forms of coercion and intervention were mostly direct and threats were not limited to the government but also to the Greek people...

The report denounced the debt as "a direct infringement on the fundamental human rights of the residents of Greece" and called it "illegal, illegitimate, and odious". It showed that "the unsustainability of the Greek public debt was evident from the outset to the international creditors, the Greek authorities, and the corporate media"; that "the increase in debt was... due to the payment of extremely high rates of interest to creditors, excessive and unjustified military spending, loss of tax revenues due to illicit capital outflows, state recapitalization of private banks, and the international imbalances created via the flaws in the design of the Monetary Union itself"; and that "the Greek public debt can be considered as totally unsustainable at present". It concluded that "people's dignity is worth more than illegal, illegitimate, odious and unsustainable debt" and expressed its hope that it would be "a useful tool for those who want to... stand up for what is endangered today: human rights, democracy, peoples' dignity, and the future of generations to come". Announcing its findings, Zoi Konstantopoulou declared: "The Greek people have a right to say: we don't want to pay back an illegal or an illegitimate debt."

The Commission precisely defined these descriptions. It might be argued that "illegality" means little in international relations; where treaties and protocols are violated, all the pompous pretensions of the United Nations etc. are houses of cards blown down by the strongest predators. But the purpose of the Truth Commission is not to make pious appeals to the gangsters but, firstly, to educate the victims, restore their dignity and build the only force that can offer resistance: the solidarity of the people; and secondly, to equip governments with the necessary cast-iron arguments to justify unilateral acts of self-defence to protect their citizens, as Ecuador did in 2008.

When the new Memorandum of Understanding was signed, the Truth Commission followed up with an excoriating analysis of its content. "The stance of the ECB and its financial coercion of Greece and its people was not only direct but wholly unveiled and extremely hostile", it declared, citing "the decision of the ECB to limit the provision of additional liquidity to the Greek banking system, which effectively brought about the imposition of capital controls, contravened its mandate and core responsibilities". It quoted a Barclays Research paper which estimated that "Greek banks could have accessed" (in other words, were thus deprived of) "an additional 27 billion in emergency funding". This was a case of direct coercion devised with the express purpose of influencing the outcome of the referendum.

Noting that following the July capitulation, Greece had abstained from voting on a United Nations resolution about sovereign-debt restructuring, it concluded that "Greece's position on this matter can only be the result of pressure from its

creditors, as its abstention is wholly against national interests".
It added:

> Direct statements against the NO vote and the calamities that
> would befall the Greek people were moreover made by
> powerful officials of the EU, in clear defiance of democracy...
> All of the above were designed and meant to instil fear in the
> Greek people and hence to sway its vote in favour of the YES
> option, and additionally to coerce the Greek government into
> accepting the terms of its creditors.[63]

It noted that under the new MoU, "any bill that comes before
parliament must receive the approval of the creditors before
being adopted", and added that the new Code of Civil Procedure
even dictates that if any enterprise becomes insolvent, "private
banks will always carry the status of preferential creditors, above
and beyond the state".

The statements of the Truth Commission amount to a devastating proclamation, in the historic tradition of the Ecuador
report. While harbouring no illusions that appeals to justice and
law could count for anything among the beasts of the capitalist
jungle, the Commission lived up to its mission: to lay bare for all
to see the truth about the origins of the Greek debt, and to justify
a unilateral and sovereign act of defiance and self-defence.

Of course, the bankers weren't too concerned about the Greek
people's "fundamental human rights"; they gobbled up odious
debts every day for breakfast. Around the conference table in
Brussels, they continued to sit stony-faced in haughty disregard
for all Tsipras' eloquence, wit, charm and pleas for clemency. For
them, the only items on the agenda were to cut wages and
pensions, scrap workers' job-protection, raise taxes and sell off
cheap the country's assets. It was a direct tug-of-war between the
workers of Greece and the bankers of Europe, with SYRIZA as the
increasingly threadbare rope.

At one point in the negotiations in February 2015, one solution suggested by the troika delegation was to stop paying wages and pensions! According to Elena Panariti, a member of the Greek team, "when we say that we have liquidity problems, they tell us to make no payment of salaries and pensions for one or two months". Varoufakis denounced this insolent suggestion as "shameful".

As the standoff with the moneylenders dragged on, the Greek government was struggling to pay its wages and pensions bills. The cash was running dry. In May the government was forced to delay settling bills and paying wages, and soon it was reduced to scraping out the children's piggy banks, so to speak: sequestering the meagre current-account balances of government departments, public corporations, local government budgets, etc. – whatever cash balances were left. The Athens prefecture alone handed over €80 million. It couldn't even guarantee that the money scraped together would go towards wages and public expenditure rather than to the IMF or the ECB.

The clock was ticking and the deadline for the next payment to the IMF was fast approaching. "We have met them three-quarters of the way", said Varoufakis. "They need to meet us one-quarter of the way." SYRIZA's Nikos Filis warned: "Now is the moment of truth, on June 5th. If there is no deal by then... they won't get any money." And, sure enough, the day soon came. Interior Minister Nikos Voutsis announced on television: "This money will not be given and is not there to be given."

Default on due payment to the IMF is almost unheard of. Up to then, the only countries in living memory ever to have dared do that were Somalia, Sudan and Zimbabwe (and, in the distant past, Cambodia, Honduras, Argentina under Peron and Indonesia under Sukarno, who withdrew from the IMF and was promptly overthrown by a CIA-orchestrated coup). In 2008, Ecuador had suspended repayments on debts to Western governments and private creditors because they were based on "corruption, lack of transparency and shady deals", and Iceland had opted not to settle debts claimed by the United Kingdom and the Netherlands. In the end, Greece's failure to pay up on time didn't technically quite meet the definition of an outright default. Sensing the government's wavering resolve, the IMF discreetly extended the deadline, and, having made its gesture, Greece soon paid up its due instalment of €2.05 billion. Days later, it also paid another €4.2 billion to the European Central Bank.

However, Greece's insolvency was reaching crisis point. The banks were haemorrhaging cash – literally running out of banknotes – and were barely capable of covering even weekly pensions and benefits payments of €120 each. Worried that capital controls may be only hours away, panic-stricken depositors rushed to ATMs to withdraw their savings. Queues quickly formed outside banks around the capital. The banks shut down indefinitely, and restricted account-holders to withdrawals of a maximum of €60 a day. Companies were down to their last stocks of raw materials; factories had cut shifts and were ready to shut down operations; tourist bookings had crashed. There was a risk that imported food stocks would run out. And the European Central Bank tightened its squeeze with an unprecedented decision to freeze ELA (emergency liquidity assistance) at €89 billion – a flagrant breach of its legal obligation to uphold financial stability. Meanwhile the demands of the creditors became increasingly insolent. The bankers were enjoying sweet revenge for six months of radical bluster and the threat of default. As Varoufakis commented, this was a coup no less brutal than that of the colonels in 1967, but one imposed by banks instead of tanks. "Why did they force us to close the banks? To instil fear in people. And spreading fear is called terrorism…"

The noose was tightening…

Chapter 12

From Defiance to Surrender

With negotiations deadlocked after five months of futile confrontation, backed up against the wall, without a single bargaining chip in his pocket (once he had discarded suspension of repayments or outright default), Tsipras turned heel and stormed out. He had one last grand gesture left: to submit for direct ratification by the Greek people the price demanded by the creditors. Let the people speak!

On 27th June, Tsipras announced a referendum putting directly to the people the creditors' "unbearable" demands, which he described as:

an ultimatum towards Greek democracy and the Greek people... blackmail for the acceptance on our part of severe and humiliating austerity without end and without the prospect of ever prospering socially and economically... These proposals, which clearly violate the European rules and the basic rights to work, equality and dignity, show that the purpose of some of the partners and institutions was not a viable agreement for all parties, but possibly the humiliation of an entire people.

Ministers denounced the "barbaric measures" being demanded. Konstantinos Chrysogonos, a SYRIZA MEP, told the BBC:

It's obvious that the deal creditors are proposing to the Greek government is beyond the popular mandate this government has... There was probably no other way but to submit the demands of the creditors to a referendum.[64]

Echoing that sentiment, Varoufakis tweeted: "Democracy deserved a boost... We just delivered it. Let the people decide. (Funny how radical this concept sounds!)"

Lafazanis, energy minister and leader of the Left Platform, called for a NO vote against measures which had resulted in widespread "misery and pillaging":

> It is a democratic decision and the Greek people are being called to give a democratic answer. And that answer is going to be a resounding NO... If the Greek people say a big NO, it is going to be impossible for those who wield power not to take note, unless democracy no longer exists.[65]

In words that should come to haunt him, Tsipras made a solemn promise to the Greek people: "I personally pledge that I will respect the result of your democratic choice, whatever that may be."

What was behind his flamboyant gesture? In the light of subsequent events, it is hard to say. Was Tsipras naïve enough to trust in the fundamental decency of the creditors in honouring the will of the Greek people? Did he expect them to yield gracefully? Did he genuinely think that a NO vote would "strengthen his hand in negotiations"? Or at least open the way to an honourable compromise? Or was he counting on a YES vote, which might offer him a pretext to relinquish responsibility and either resign, leaving his successors to bear the disgrace, or capitulate without dishonour on the basis of a spurious democratic pretext?

Maybe he himself could not have answered that question. At any rate, having made a strangely subdued and perfunctory call for a NO vote, Tsipras remained uncharacteristically quiet. This referendum was an unprecedented assertion of real popular democracy, pitting an oppressed people against the world's billionaire bankers. And yet there was nothing remotely approaching the kind of full-blooded crusading campaign that was called for.

Throughout referendum week, the outcome was unpredictable. Early indications suggested a hesitant or finely balanced result. But then the people spoke – and their voice was deafening. By a margin of almost two to one, the Greek people cried NO! 61.3% of the population rejected the troika's blackmail. Practically every single demographic category of voters voted NO – whether classified by age, gender, occupation, income, economic status or level of education. Among 18–24 year-olds, 85% voted NO; the NO vote among all but one of the other age groups ranged between 60% and 72%. People at all levels of income voted NO, from those "facing great financial difficulty" (63.1%) at one end of the spectrum to those "living comfortably" (52.3%) at the other. Even 56.7% of "company owners" voted NO. The sole technical borderline exceptions were the over-65s, the pensioners and the professionals – but even among these categories, the NO vote lost only by wafer-thin majorities: 45% of the over-65s voted NO, 48% of pensioners, and 49.9% of professionals! It was an unmistakable mandate for throwing the deal back into the faces of Greece's tormentors.

In retrospect, it seems that it was the people's stubborn resistance to the shrill and virulent media campaign that had been let loose on them to stampede them into a YES vote that emboldened the electorate and elicited from them this overwhelming NO.

Reports from local correspondents and comments on the internet illustrate the exhilaration especially of the youth…

No one in Athens knows what will happen next. No one. But everyone agrees that the referendum signifies a radical rupture. All we can report on for now is what people are discussing, what is happening at the moment, while we are here: listening, talking, laughing, cheering… On the one hand, there is Sunday's overwhelming OXI ("No"), a powerful articulation against austerity, false compromises, old elites; a rejection even stronger than left optimists dared to hope for. On the other, there is also the drama of closed banks and the threat of state bankruptcy... What if the government can no longer pay our wages? What if even the meagre 60 euros per day can no longer be withdrawn from ATMs?

The Greek people said NO to the dictatorship of the fiscal order and gave new energy to their government's mandate... The government provoked a political earthquake – and seems to be surprised by the strength of this disruption...

Revolution in the air? Yes and no... People have proven that they can lose fear... The people are willing to take a risk and fight... The hundreds of thousands at Syntagma Square in the days before the referendum signalled but one clear message: we accept the declaration of war... The people did not succumb to a fear of the terror of closed banks...

SYRIZA actually was able to mobilize far beyond its own electorate, to reach people long said to have lost any connection to politics... The excluded, the poor, the invisible, the superfluous – they took the stage and showed their willingness to take on the uncertainty of OXI...

The government no longer needs to accept a deal at any price, because the people have agreed to back this path... For the moment, people have conquered fear... Listening to the talk yesterday evening had the momentary impression of being part of a discussion on the eve of revolution.

Lapavitsas, of the Left Platform, wrote:

This is one of those moments when it does feel good to be Greek... This week has been an extraordinary week... They said NO. They basically stood their ground and said no, we're not going to have it. We're not going to accept the old ways.

We want something different... And the most dramatic thing was that actually this was said by the youth... That's the first time they've spoken since the beginning of the crisis, and they said no...

Just after the referendum, Lapavitsas wrote:

The Greeks have shown... yesterday that they are ready to face up to whatever will come their way from the lenders. The lenders must not forget that... SYRIZA needs to take radical measures quickly. It needs to put the knife in... It's completely unacceptable that a few oligarchs can run the mass media in this country, wage war against the government, and still owe the state enormous amounts of money. Enough of that. The Greek people don't want any more... And then action is also needed with regard to big business. This country is run in the interests of a small group of very powerful, very rich, and very corrupt people. The Greek people are up in arms about that... SYRIZA has been delinquent in this respect, very slow. We need action quickly. So all these things... have to start happening in the next few days. And... the country needs to deal in a decisive way with the lenders. Enough is enough. If this means devising new ways of creating liquidity, then we will devise new ways of creating liquidity... The country's running out of Euros, but the state can issue [means] of payment in Euros... Print IOUs, for instance... Greece will not be blackmailed... People are very, very angry...[66]

Thanassis Petrakos, another prominent member of the Left Platform, declared:

The NO of the referendum was a radical and a class NO... We should prepare exiting the eurozone and say that clearly to the people... The first steps are the public control of the banks and of the Greek central bank and a crackdown on oligarchy.[67]

Back to Brussels

In his memoirs, a member of the British Trade Union Congress recalls a meeting at 10 Downing Street during the general strike in 1926, when the prime minister reminded him that any power challenging the state must also be prepared to take on the functions of the state. "Gentlemen", he concluded, "are you ready to take power?" "At that point", the writer reported, "I knew that we had lost." Tsipras must have had similar feelings after the victory of the NO campaign in the referendum.

Much to his own surprise, he returned to Brussels with a ringing mandate to defy the bankers... and absolutely no idea how he was going to honour his undertaking to the Greek people to respect their decision. And, in a craven display of deference to those he persisted in calling his "partners", he was accompanied this time not by the irritating and sarcastic Varoufakis – on whose dismissal they had insisted – but by the more malleable Tsakalotos.

Tsipras and Tsakalatos timidly proposed a modification of the terms of the troika's pre-referendum ultimatum. The German response was to demand not just capitulation by Greece, but abject surrender. *The Guardian*'s Larry Elliott called it a Carthaginian peace – a reference to a response by the ancient Romans to an earlier negotiating gambit: "a brutal settlement, burning down Carthage and enslaving those inhabitants it did not massacre."[68]

Rather than offer concessions which risked setting ablaze a continental forest fire, the troika methodically applied a policy of unqualified brutality. The intransigence of the European institutions had nothing to do with any wish to restore Greece to solvency. It was a matter of straight political blackmail.

Far from strengthening Tsipras' hand, without a clear alternative strategy all that the referendum had achieved was to enrage his interlocutors. At the final negotiations, for two days and nights, Tsipras was subjected to treatment at the hands of his tormentors that was described by one participant as "mental waterboarding". Another senior official summed up his ordeal differently: "They crucified Tsipras in there." The outcome was never in doubt. The best that Tsipras and Tsakalatos could do was to wheedle for nominal cosmetic concessions – and the troika were in no mood to grant even these.

By dawn on the Monday morning, after 14 hours of continuous bargaining, Tsipras and Merkel decided that they had reached a dead end, and that Greek withdrawal from the eurozone was the only realistic option. It was later revealed that a German finance ministry paper dated 11th July had "called for Greece to be expelled from the Eurozone for a minimum of five years".

At this point Tusk intervened; he physically stood in the doorway and told them: "Sorry, but there is no way you are leaving this room."[69]

The final and apparently unassailable obstacle to agreement turned out to be something quite inconsequential: the nature and designation of the new privatisation fund to be created on the proceeds of sequestered Greek assets. In an act of gratuitous humiliation, Merkel had insisted that it be not only controlled but physically located outside of Greece's borders, and that its commandeered loot of €50 billion from sales of Greek public property – public assets to be stolen from the Greek people and worth almost a third of their national income – be allocated exclusively to appeasing the greed of the creditors, i.e. devoted to debt repayments. Tsipras' last whimper was a quibble for a smaller fund, the proceeds of which would be reinvested in Greece.

The meeting had broken up for the night only after hours of furious wrangling, in which all parties heeded the French finance minister's advice to everyone to "get it all out and tell one another the truth". According to eyewitnesses, the Finnish finance minister shouted at Tsakalotos like a naughty schoolboy; the Slovenian prime minister wagged his finger at Tsipras; the Italian prime minister rebuked him; and the German finance minister Schäuble yelled at Draghi, chairman of the European Central Bank, that he was "not an idiot". By this point, all the parties had taken it for granted that Greece was about to leave the eurozone, and Schäuble for one was enthusiastically pursuing that outcome.

Finally, François Hollande took Merkel and Tsipras aside into Tusk's office to suggest a compromise over the location of the proposed privatisation fund. Rather belatedly, he appealed for Greece's "sovereignty" to be honoured. "Nothing would have been worse than humiliating Greece. Greece didn't seek charity, but solidarity from the eurozone." He also insisted on the removal from the final document of any reference to Schäuble's preferred option of a "temporary" Greek exit from the eurozone.

Clutching at these cosmetic concessions, Tsipras meekly agreed. For all Hollande's blandishments, there was nothing honourable about this agreement. The truth of what had happened was unmistakable.

Capitulation

Following the referendum, on 11th July only two members of SYRIZA's Left Platform had voted against giving Tsipras authority to negotiate a new deal. Two days later, Tsipras negotiated the framework of a deal that betrayed everything the party had stood for in the 25th January election – a blatant repudiation of the mandate given him by the referendum. Tsipras lamely indicated that he would "try to limit the bailout's negative impact... We have no other choice but to implement it, looking for a way to gradually disengage from the bailout and foreign monitors."

No Central Committee of SYRIZA was called to discuss the

deal, even though a majority of the CC opposed it. Their views were simply ignored.

The deal stamped out all the reforms enacted by SYRIZA since its election. It was a national humiliation comparable to the Versailles Treaty, the Munich betrayal or the degradation of Czechoslovakia in 1968, when Dubcek was sent home in disgrace from Moscow to appear on television, with tears literally rolling down his face, to announce the reversal of all the reforms of the "Prague Spring".

The terms of the agreed memorandum were more draconic than those of 2010 and 2012; even more so than those rejected so decisively by the Greek people only the previous week. They involved swingeing wages and pensions cuts, tax increases and the establishment of a humiliating wholesale privatisation fund, to be directly administered by the troika.

Tsipras had accepted a brutal austerity package to repay a debt that can never be repaid. The EU has demanded that £50 billion be raised from privatisation. Yet, against the backdrop of a stock market crash of 40% over the last five years, only £3 billion has been raised from the privatisations in the preceding two bailouts!

The seizure of Greek assets is a repeat of the treatment handed out by the International Committee for Greek Debt Management after Greece went bankrupt in 1898. A conglomerate of six European powers led by Britain impounded customs duties in the port of Piraeus and seized revenues from stamp duty, tobacco, salt, kerosene and other goods.

The compulsion on Greece to tighten austerity still further will deepen the depression and ensure that budget targets are missed yet again and the deficit will continue to swell – just as happened with the last two bailout packages.

The Nobel economist Paul Krugman commented "This goes beyond harsh into pure vindictiveness, complete destruction of national sovereignty, and no hope of relief",[70] and Simon Schama called it "the beginning of the end of the EU".[71]

Tsipras was not granted even the token fig-leaf of debt relief. This was refused by the EU even in the face of pressure from the IMF and the USA.

Greece had suffered six years of economic catastrophe, a lost decade of investment, massive youth unemployment, a "brain drain" and a banking system in ruins. The accusation that this was the result of SYRIZA's failure to observe the terms of the memorandum was a lie. The troika had denied Greece a viable debt-restructuring agreement in 2010 because it feared "contagion" to Portugal, Spain and Italy. More and more debt was heaped on to Greece in 2010 and again in 2012 to save the European banking system.

The deal left Greece trapped in a debt imposed by blackmail and almost guaranteed to crash once there is a new global downturn.

Already, only 49.4% of the population aged 15–64 had a job by the end of 2014, and those still in work had suffered an 18% drop in real wages since 2007. Now there would be further cuts in social welfare and pensions as well as further attacks on labour rights. Pensions had already been cut 12 times since 2009, and now further cuts were demanded. An increase in VAT from 13% to 23% would raise average Greek household expenses by an estimated further €650 a year. Neither would small businesses be spared; new business deregulations would ruin small shops, endangering many of the 15,000 local bakeries and the 11,000 pharmacies.

At the same time, the common heritage of the Greek people had been stolen from them. Wholesale privatisation of the country's assets was a key element in the deal, selling vast swathes of its resources to foreign corporations. Public assets worth €50 billion were to be handed over to a new privatisation trust fund. In short, the whole country was up for sale, and the government was in effect to relinquish power. The sole concession won by Tsipras was that the €50-billion fund of plundered privatised assets – assets previously commonly owned by the Greek people – would be physically located in Athens, rather than Luxembourg, though still administered directly by representatives of the troika. Alongside Greece's airports, energy, oil, water, highways, the postal service and telecommunications, the fund would even include the houses of people unable to keep up with their mortgage repayments; people whose homes had previously been protected would be thrown onto the streets by the ECB.

The deal meant almost total surrender of authority to the creditors, reducing Greece to colonial status, and giving them total oversight over the imposition of their programme, with quarterly reviews scheduled to enforce its goal of converting the current primary deficit of 1.5% to a projected primary surplus of 0.25% of GDP this year, and 3.5% in future years. This involved rushing through parliament no less than 40 pieces of legislation enacting 57 specific measures to give a quasi-legal façade to a process of brutal plunder.

In his annotated copy of these "terms of Greece's surrender", Varoufakis paraphrased the text as follows:

> The Greek government must introduce new stringent austerity directed at the weakest Greeks that have already suffered grossly... for a new extend-and-pretend loan... Greece must subject itself to fiscal waterboarding, even before any financing is offered... The SYRIZA government must be humiliated to the extent that it is asked to impose harsh austerity upon itself as a first step towards requesting another toxic bailout loan... The SYRIZA government must accept the lie that it, and not the asphyxiation tactics of the creditors, caused the sharp economic deterioration of the past six months; the victim is being asked to take the blame on behalf of the villain... The Greek government needs to formally

commit to strengthening their proposals (i.e. to make them more regressive and more inhuman)... The Greek government... must commit to further, automated austerity as a result of the troika's newest failures.[72]

He summarised the effect of each clause of the agreement as follows:

- to deal a major blow at the only Greek growth industry – tourism;
- to reduce the lowest of the low of pensions;
- complete control by the troika of the way Greece's budget balance is computed, with a view to controlling fully the magnitude of austerity it imposes on the government;
- foreclosures, evictions and liquidation of thousands of homes and businesses;
- to cut by 85% the secondary pensions that the SYRIZA government fought tooth and nail to preserve over the past five months;
- to make sure that no collective bargaining is allowed, industrial action to be banned and collective dismissals allowed at the employers' whim; there should be no mechanisms that waged labour can use to extract better conditions from employers;
- a tsunami of foreclosures;
- an East German-like Treuhand to sell off all public property, but without the equivalent large investments that West Germany put into East Germany in compensation;
- public property to be sold off and the pitiful sums to go toward servicing an unserviceable debt – with precisely nothing left over for public or private investments;
- to turn Greece into a democracy-free zone modelled on Brussels, a form of supposedly technocratic government, politically toxic and macro-economically inept;

- to reduce the lowest wages;
- the troika strikes back and demands that the Greek government invite it to return to Athens as conqueror – the Carthaginian peace in all its glory;
- the Greek Parliament must, again, after five months of short-lived independence, become an appendage of the troika – passing translated legislation mechanistically;
- in addition to promising that it will no longer legislate autonomously, the Greek government will retrospectively annul all the bills it passed over the past five months.

By its demonstrative humiliation of SYRIZA, Europe's bankers had deliberately demolished its credibility, and dealt a devastating public blow to its naivety in having deluded itself that its mix of charm and guile could ever have trumped them in the first place.

The IMF

The National Institute of Economic and Social Research estimates that by next year the economy will have shrunk by 30% since 2010. It warns of a permanent recession, concluding that a debt write-off of at least 55% is necessary to avert such a disaster.

Even the IMF – hardly noted for undue squeamishness – recoiled from this act of brigandage. According to its own terms of reference, it is prohibited from extending loans that will plunge its victims into unsustainable levels of debt – and for good reason, since it was never conceived as a charity. The IMF guidelines state that loans can only be advanced where there is a clear path back to debt sustainability, usually defined as borrowings of less than 120% of GDP. Having already twice overstepped this requirement and bent its own rules by participating in the previous two bailouts of Greece, later confessing that its economic projections had been "overly optimistic", it was not prepared to compound its mistake. It drew the line at placing its resources into still further jeopardy by contributing to this latest deal, and insisted on an "explicit and concrete agreement" on debt relief. Naturally, the IMF's unexpected profession of solicitude for the Greek people did not extend to any commitment to relief of that portion of Greece's debt which was owed to the IMF itself; it was only pressing the EU and ECB to agree to a reduction of its own share.

The IMF revised its earlier prediction of a fall in output of 5.5%, followed by recovery, to a catastrophic fall of 17%; expressed its disbelief at the unattainable target Greece had been set of a constant primary budget surplus of 3.5% extending for "several decades" into the future; and announced that "Greece's debt can now only be made sustainable through debt relief measures that go far beyond what Europe has been willing to consider so far". Christine Lagarde personally remarked: "I remain firmly of the view that Greece's debt has become unsustainable and that Greece cannot restore debt sustainability solely through actions on its own."[73]

A key factor behind its belated concern for Greece's future was its dependence on US dollars. It reflects the diplomatic and strategic concerns of the USA for Greece's stability and even its continued commitment to NATO in a highly volatile region, in the context of aggravated tension with Russia; rivalry with China; war in the Ukraine; civil war in Syria; failed states in Iraq, Libya and Yemen; an Islamic insurgency; instability in Turkey; renewed war with the Kurds; and the occupation of huge swathes of territory by ISIS; to say nothing of the recurrent wars between Israel and the Palestinians. To add to this mix yet another element of instability in a Greece driven by desperation to seek potential alternative allies in Russia and China seemed hardly prudent.

Prompted by all these considerations, the IMF report stated bluntly that "Greece's public debt has become highly unsustainable". It predicted that Greece's debts will reach "close to 200% of GDP in the next two years". Even the European institutions, which had initially expected the debt to account for 160% by 2022, came to agree with this prognosis, predicting more precisely that they will come to 201% in 2016. The IMF therefore called for "deep upfront haircuts" (outright write-offs of a portion of the debt), and/or "debt relief through maturity extension... a very dramatic extension with grace periods of, say, 30 years on the entire stock of European debt".

To devote 15% of its GDP every year from now until 2045 to pay off its €320-billion debt "would require primary surpluses of 4+% of GDP per year, and decisive and full implementation of structural reforms that delivers steady state growth of 2% per year (with the best productivity growth in the euro area) and privatization". Yet previous governments led by New Democracy and PASOK each in turn fell precisely because they were incapable of delivering either the annual 4% surpluses required to service the debt or the "structural reforms" everyone agreed were necessary: an end to the age-old problems of red tape, corruption and tax-evasion.

The IMF insisted that Greece needed an extra €50 billion immediately and unconditionally; a 20-year debt-repayment holiday; and a substantial straight write-off of the debt equivalent to 30% of GDP. Without at least a substantial compromise on these demands, including crucially a debt write-off, the IMF would not contribute its proposed €15–20-billion share of the €85-billion settlement.

And yet a straight debt write-off is something that the EU governments will resist to the last. Germany and its fellow hard-liners Estonia, Finland and Lithuania fear that a straight debt write-off would set a dangerous precedent for Spain, Portugal and Italy. At best it could accept a discreet adjustment of interest rates and repayment schedules.

Chapter 13

Outrage

The SYRIZA government had embarked on a modest anti-austerity programme and found itself beset by traps, manipulated into fatal concessions which brought it to a choice: between defiance and martyrdom on the one hand, or humiliation and capitulation on the other. It had flirted with the first option, then scuttled into the second.

SYRIZA's fatal weakness had been its naive assumption that it could outsmart or sweet-talk the troika into agreeing softer terms. As Maria Pentarakis put it:

The leadership of the Greek government believed that change is possible through debate and good-will negotiations... It aspired to achieve emancipation through reason... The class approach was missing from the Greek government's negotiations; it thought it was facing 'European partners' rather than class opponents...[74]

It was pointless patiently explaining to the creditors that, after all, they could never hope to get their loans repaid, and that a compromise deal would actually be in their best interests. Perhaps Tsipras and Varoufakis hadn't heard the ancient fable of the frog and the scorpion. The scorpion asks the frog for a lift across the river on his back, and persuades him that there is no danger that he will sting him, because in that case they would both drown. When they are halfway across the river, the scorpion stings the frog anyway, and explains in response to the indignant frog's reproaches as they both sink to their watery graves: "but that's my nature." The bankers behave like bankers because, since they feed off the perpetual source of interest involved and count the borrower's debt as an asset, the last thing they want is their money back.

In pursuit of the mirage of a happy compromise satisfactory to all parties, SYRIZA had zig-zagged tactically from one elegant negotiating ploy to another: from intransigence in January, to concessions in February, from compliance to defiance and back again over the next few months. It had an impressive array of tactics at its disposal, but no overall strategic plan. Its mistake was to trust in the honour and good faith of the enemy. This stance may have been adopted initially as a negotiating ploy or a double bluff; but it came to look like breathtaking gullibility, disarming the front-line negotiators and demobilising the back-up troops. At its high point, the SYRIZA government finally dared to do exactly what it should; something that no previous government could ever have dreamed of doing: it consulted the people. And then, the very next day... it ignored their answer. Perhaps Tsipras and Tsakalotos had reviewed the troops on parade and concluded, like the Duke of Wellington: "I don't know what effect these men will have upon the enemy, but, by God, they frighten me." And so with a flourish they brought out their final tactic: abject surrender.

And yet... in that case, what was SYRIZA for? If the people had wanted a government that was going to hand over to the bankers whatever they wanted, they'd already had two perfectly good compliant stooge governments with plenty of practice at collaboration, without needing a new one.

Tsipras' capitulation threatened to undermine the whole purpose of SYRIZA's existence and put its future at risk. The *Financial Times* goaded Tsipras to violate his mandate still further, gloating:

Tsipras... was forced by the creditors to eat his words and accept a bailout programme that is far tougher on Greeks than he could have achieved if he had adopted a more accommodating line immediately after he took power in January. His political somersault, known as a 'kolotoumba' in Greek, is a little like the U-turn that Mitterrand undertook in 1983, abandoning most of the socialist economic programme on which he had won the French presidency two years earlier and aligning France more closely with Germany. Mitterrand's change of policies was so remarkable, and so effective, that he held power for two seven-year terms and paved the way for France's co-launch of the euro in 1999. But to this day debate persists about the extent to which he was really a socialist. Will the same be said one day about Tsipras? Or will he fall from power, sooner rather than later, because – unlike Mitterrand – he will not make a serious attempt at implementing the economic reforms implied by his 'kolotoumba'?[75]

Shock

Tsipras's capitulation to the troika aroused shock and outrage. Just as Papandreou had been elected on a promise to raise living standards... and then signed the first memorandum; just as Samaras had nominally opposed that memorandum... and then went on to implement the second; now Tsipras, elected on an explicitly anti-austerity platform... was imposing a third memorandum, even more vicious.

A general strike was called by the Federation of Public Sector Unions for 15th July – the same day that the Hellenic Parliament voted on the agreement. In the chamber, 39 SYRIZA MPs voted no or abstained, and Tsipras had to rely on the votes of the pro-austerity parties. Almost one third of SYRIZA MPs voted against the final terms of the bailout, leaving Tsipras short of the 120 votes needed to win a confidence vote (two fifths of the 300-seat assembly).

Playing on nationalist sentiments, the right-wing tabloid Dimokratia reported it under the headline: "Greece in Auschwitz: Schauble attempts eurozone holocaust". Among the long-suffering working class, where historical memories run deep, many saw the memorandum as another Varkiza (the treaty that the Greek Communist Party had been tricked into signing with the British in 1945 to disband the resistance forces), and invoked the memory of the guerrilla hero Aris Velouchiotis, who had shown the courage and foresight to refuse to disarm. The traditions of the resistance, the civil war and the popular uprising that brought down the colonels live on. Eleni Portaliou, SYRIZA's former mayoral candidate for Athens, called for the formation of a "social EAM" (referring to the wartime resistance movement).

To quote again the leading SYRIZA activist Maria Pentaraki: "For the first time in my 35 years of political, progressive campaigning, I cried. The struggle though continues..." She quoted Brecht, who asked "what is the robbing of a bank compared to the founding of a bank?", and Jefferson, who warned that "the banks and corporations... will deprive the people of all property until their children will wake up homeless on the continent their fathers occupied... The banking institutions having the issuing power of money are more dangerous to liberty than standing armies."[76]

One of the deal's most outspoken critics was Varoufakis, who immediately after the referendum had been forced to resign, having been personally blackballed by the troika from admission to the negotiations. He drew a direct analogy with the colonels' coup:

A new Versailles treaty is haunting Europe... The Euro summit statement... is purely and simply a manifestation of the politics of humiliation in action... The Eurogroup's list of demands represents a major departure from decency and reason... The crucial question is: Does the Greek economy stand any chance of recovery under these terms?... The recent Euro summit is indeed nothing short of the culmination of a coup. In 1967 it was the tanks that foreign powers used to end Greek democracy... In 2015 another coup was staged by foreign powers using, instead of tanks, Greece's banks... The Euro summit statement of yesterday morning reads like a document committing to paper Greece's terms of surrender. It is meant as a statement confirming that Greece acquiesces to becoming a vassal of the Eurogroup.[77]

Criticisms also came from more orthodox sources. In advance of the deal, the German economist Walter Munchau had been warning against the imposition of a further austerity package:

It was the unsustainability of the previous agreement between Greece, its European creditors and the International Monetary Fund that brought SYRIZA to power... The creditors are responsible for the current mess by insisting on an economically illiterate adjustment programme... The key to a Greek economic revival has to be an end to austerity... Athens should have been allowed to default... I am sceptical about another round of extend-and-pretend dishonesty where governments or banks grant loans in the full knowledge that they will never be repaid...[78]

On 15th July, 109 of the 201 members of the Central Committee of SYRIZA issued a statement condemning the new memorandum's "onerous and humiliating terms", calling on the government "not to succumb to the extortionate ultimatums of the creditors" and warning that the agreement is "not compatible with the ideas and the principles of the left". It also demanded that Tsipras keep to his promise to hold a Central Committee meeting before submitting the proposed agreement to a parliamentary vote. (The Political Secretariat's earlier unanimous vote to convene a Central Committee meeting had been ignored.) The statement continued:

On 12 July, a coup was carried out in Brussels... a coup that takes aim at any notion of democracy and popular sovereignty. The agreement with the 'institutions' was the result of the blackmailing of the country through economic strangulation. It is a new memorandum, with onerous and humiliating terms of supervision, disastrous for the country and our people. We realize that suffocating pressure was put on the Greek side in the negotiations, but nevertheless, we believe that the people's proud no vote in the referendum must forbid the government from succumbing to the extortionate ultimatums of the creditors. This agreement... is not compatible with the needs of the working class and the popular masses. This proposal cannot be accepted by the members and the cadres of SYRIZA.[79]

Stathis Kouvelakis called it "the theatre of the absurd":

How else could one characterise the total reversal of the meaning of an event as amazing as the July 5 referendum, only hours after its conclusion, by those that called for a NO vote to begin with?... How is it possible for a devastating NO to memorandum austerity policies to be interpreted as a green light for a new memorandum?... What was the point of the referendum and the struggle to achieve victory in it?... All of this is unfolding before our eyes as if nothing has happened, as if the referendum were something like a collective hallucination... Last Sunday, the Greek people staggered Europe and the world, responding en masse to the government's call and, in conditions unprecedented by the postwar standards of any European country, overwhelmingly voted NO to the extortionate and humiliating proposals of the lenders. Both the extent of the NO vote and its qualitative composition, with its enormous lead among workers and youth, testify to the depth of the transformations that have...

crystallized in such a short time, in Greek society... But from Monday morning, before the victory cries in the country's public squares had even fully died away, the theatre of the absurd began... The public, still in the joyful haze of Sunday, watches as the representative of the 62% subordinated to the 38% in the immediate aftermath of a resounding victory for democracy and popular sovereignty. On Tuesday, the government, with no new 'proposal' to make, transfers its operations to Brussels... and, as is absolutely logical, finds itself confronted with a new and even harsher ultimatum... The government has achieved nothing other than a full return to previous entrapment, from a much more unfavourable position, under the pressure of even more relentless economic asphyxiation. It has managed to squander the powerful injection of political capital from the referendum in record time, following at all points the line of those who had opposed it and who have every reason to feel vindicated, despite being trounced at the ballot box. But the referendum happened. It wasn't a hallucination from which everyone has now recovered.[80]

Zoi Konstantopoulou, the courageous fighter and highly respected president of the Greek parliament, told the Greek parliament on 11th July:

For five months the government... has been waging an unequal battle within a regime of suffocation and blackmail... inside a Europe that is turning into a nightmarish prison for its peoples... The Greek people honoured the government that entrusted them, and the parliament that allowed them the right to take their lives and fates in their own hands. With bravery and pride they announced: NO to blackmail! NO to ultimatums! NO to the Memoranda of servitude! NO to the repayment of a debt they did not create and that is not attributable to them! NO to new measures of impoverishment and exhaustion! The lenders have stubbornly insisted on transforming this NO into a YES, and they have found allies who gleefully collaborate with them... This NO of the people transcends all of us and compels us to defend their right to fight for their lives. To wrestle. Not to live a half-life or a life on our knees.[81]

Kouvelakis talked of "post-traumatic shock... disillusion, anger, and profound unease" and called for a "political consolidation and articulation" of the aspirations of the 62% that had voted NO in the referendum.

Yorgos Mitralias – a leading figure in the Truth Commission – noted that the youth organisation, the trade-union fraction of SYRIZA and 39 MPs had all condemned the "monstrous" Brussels agreement and promised to fight to the end, including in the streets, against the agreement and the government. Mitralias called 13th July 2015 "Black Monday" and drew chilling parallels with "August 4th, 1914, when the German Social-Democratic Party in the Berlin Reichstag spelled the beginning of the tragedy of the twentieth century". He declared that "our fine bureaucrats" had turned themselves into "good loyal managers of the capitalist system and its barbarism". In an allusion to the treacherous Social-Democratic Minister in Germany from 1918 who had mobilised the proto-Nazi Freikorps battalions that went on to smash the workers' councils and murder the revolutionaries Rosa Luxemburg and Karl Liebknecht, he warned that some of the "bureaucratic mediocrities within the government and SYRIZA" were already busy "preparing their credentials for the role of modern clones of Noske the bloodhound... No one can dare say that history isn't repeating itself."[82]

Days later, Mitralias wrote of the new disposition of forces. The "Tsipras tendency" of SYRIZA was now going to "take charge of a new government that would govern the country with the absolutely decisive collaboration of all the neoliberal parties (New Democracy, PASOK, Potami)"; it would receive implicit support from Golden Dawn and the KKE, which are "in the words of their leaders, lately in agreement with the Tsipras government that Greece must remain faithful to the Euro" while "the main opposition force" was now to be found "first and foremost in the left wing of SYRIZA".

Mitralias again compared the capitulation of SYRIZA to that of the German SPD and the Socialist International, which had "negated their whole reason for existence by voting for war credits for the slaughter of the First World War". He wrote that in both cases the "worm of betrayal" had been long buried within those parties, and predicted that "the present capitulation of SYRIZA... will have the same or even worse consequences in Greece" – but also far beyond Greece.

> From all corners of Europe, but also beyond, we are confronted by an avalanche of messages reporting a feeling of deep disappointment, anxiety or even despair that is spreading among millions of citizens in and outside Europe, who believed that under the leadership of SYRIZA, they could finally fight together successfully against austerity and the debt-system... SYRIZA's betrayal comes at a very critical historical moment, when the racist extreme right is advancing almost everywhere in our continent.

Tsipras bore "downright criminal responsibility in creating this dangerous situation":

> Hundreds of [SYRIZA's] key workers, deputies, members of the Political Bureau of the Central Committee, youth leaders, trade union fraction and other party organs slam the door and walk out, violently denouncing the 'treason' of the Tsipras government... a collapse of SYRIZA in the polls and... resur-

rection of the traditional right wing New Democracy...
Popular Unity do not seem to be any kind of inspiration either
to the disappointed crowds... General demoralisation... is
forcing an important part of the people... to turn their backs
on politics... The Greek Communist Party (KKE) has made
Popular Unity... its main enemy which it attacks day and
night with... exceptional violence... Golden Dawn [is]
already well established, ready and waiting... in this Greek
society which has been looking for a long time like... the
dying Weimar Republic... The current extreme fragmentation
of the radical left forces is equivalent to a veritable act of...
suicide which lays the ground for the neo-Nazi far right.[83]

Elections

Having trampled underfoot the overwhelming mandate handed
him by the referendum before the ink was even dry, and accepted
every one of the punitive conditions of the troika, Tsipras
elbowed aside the party's Central Committee and hurriedly
called elections, in effect soliciting an instant endorsement from
the electorate over the heads of the authorised structures of his
own party.

At 56.6%, turnout was the lowest at any election for decades
– a significant drop from the numbers who had voted in the
January elections (63.23%) and the referendum held only weeks
previously (62.5%). The fall in the overall vote – an abstention
rate of 43.4% – reflected an understandable ballot fatigue among
the electors. It was the third time this year that they had been
called upon to vote; and since Greeks are required to vote
wherever they were first registered, or alternatively undergo a
complicated bureaucratic re-registration procedure, voting often
entails travel, expense and disruption. But, above all, the consequences of the recent referendum had irrefutably confirmed to
most Greeks the pointlessness of voting. They had only just
made unmistakeably clear in the referendum their own

preference for an end to austerity; and their wishes had been ignored. If matters were to be determined over their heads in Brussels in flagrant disregard of their democratic decision, then what was the point of registering yet again what at best could only amount to a futile protest?

What is surprising in the circumstances is that well over half the electorate nevertheless did vote, and that SYRIZA held on to its decisive lead, winning 1,925,904 votes, compared to 2,245,978 in January. If we add to these the 155,242 votes for Popular Unity – the left breakaway from SYRIZA – the overall drop in the combined vote for both wings of SYRIZA was only 164,832. Nearly 2.5 million people – 2,428,874, or 44.72% of those voting – still voted for the left parties (SYRIZA, Popular Unity, the KKE and Antarsya).

Finding himself once again short of a parliamentary majority – this time by six seats – Tsipras chose as before to form a coalition with the vaudeville bigots of ANEL (Independent Greeks), whom he considered the least threatening of potential rivals, and the least brazenly compromised in Greece's dirty past political culture – primarily due to their unfortunate lack of prior opportunity.

The September 2015 election result showed that, in spite of Tsipras' outright capitulation, the electorate still preferred a government that had for five months shown at least nominal resistance to the demands of the troika, rather than deliver themselves back into the hands of its eager former accomplices. We should remember, though, that this was a hastily called snap election, held – prudently, from Tsipras' point of view – before the savage measures agreed under the new Memorandum of Understanding had been fully understood, let alone actually imposed and begun to bite. It did not take long before even one or two members of Tsipras' newly hand-picked parliamentary party had shrunk from enforcing some of the new bailout conditions, reducing SYRIZA's majority to a hair's breadth.

Was capitulation inevitable? Was there any viable alternative? Tsipras shrugged off his surrender with the standard cliché of all defeated generals. In a feeble attempt to deflect blame, he quoted the famous comment of King Pyrrhus of Epirus after a battle in which several thousand of his soldiers had died – "one more such victory and we are undone" – and described the outcome as "a Pyrrhic victory against the Greek people". It is true that to win this battle, the troika had been compelled to tear off its mask of benevolence, at future risk to its credibility; but it is hardly regretting its victory or lamenting its humiliation of SYRIZA.

Equally predictably, Tsipras glibly borrowed off-the-shelf rationalisations from Lenin:

> Lenin is the first to speak of compromise... He devotes several pages to explaining that compromise is part of revolutionary tactics. In one passage, he gives the example of a bandit pointing a pistol at you and saying 'your money or your life'. What is a revolutionary supposed to do? Give his life? No, he has to give the money in order to claim his right to live and continue to struggle.[84]

The question remains: is Tsipras continuing to struggle, except against those who continue to resist? In the same chapter, Lenin also makes a distinction between

> a compromise enforced by objective conditions... a compromise which in no way diminishes the revolutionary devotion and readiness for further struggle on the part of workers who have agreed such a compromise, and a compromise by traitors who try to ascribe to outside causes their own selfishness, cowardice, desire to toady to the capitalists.[85]

We will leave to others an answer to the delicate question of how

Lenin might have characterised Tsipras' compromise. In any case, rather than quote mere hypothetical ripostes from a polemical pamphlet, Tsipras could have cited real momentous historical sacrifices that Lenin actually did concede in the face of superior brute force: the forfeit of territory and surrender of populations at the Brest-Litovsk peace talks with Germany; or the abandonment of huge swathes of state property and authority under the New Economic Policy.

But can we conceive of any circumstances in which Lenin might have signed this memorandum? True, under compelling circumstances Lenin did not shrink from making equally painful concessions. But the single mission of SYRIZA was, not to magically square the circle of restoring to the Greek people decent conditions of life while simultaneously keeping the creditors happy; but to demonstrate graphically to the people the real forces that they were up against, and how to gather around them the power to prevail over them. Experience is a great teacher, and even without much guidance from SYRIZA, the people proved at the referendum their grasp of the issues and their determination to fight. How much more tragic, then, that their answer was so arrogantly brushed aside on the morning of 6th July.

It was not wrong for SYRIZA to use every possible device to exploit splits within the enemy ranks and wrest concessions from the bankers. Negotiations with the class enemy are sometimes obligatory. The Bolsheviks knew precisely when to negotiate (for instance, at Brest-Litovsk), when to resist by force (during the civil war) and when to concede (with the introduction of the New Economic Policy). A deal with the enemy must never be a substitute for a programme for victory, but SYRIZA had a mandate and it could not back down from this confrontation.

At its very first cabinet meeting, the SYRIZA government had taken exemplary action to safeguard wages, pensions, job security, and protection of the poor – a model to anti-austerity campaigners throughout Europe. And yet, by the judgement of one member of the political secretariat of SYRIZA's central committee – not a dissident, let alone a member of the Left Platform – Nasos Iliopoulos, whom we have already quoted previously, these shining reforms were undermined by the failure to take elementary measures at the outset to tackle the source of the enemy's power; by the absence of any moves to impose capital controls, nationalise the banks, levy new taxes or strengthen collective bargaining rights.

> How could we believe that we were preparing ourselves for the battlefield when we were not putting even the minimum of efforts to restrict the power of our enemy's main weapons: banks and the mass media? It is outrageous that during all these months we have not passed through the parliament our own tax legislation… It is outrageous that we have not voted for the reinstatement of collective bargaining which would have provided working people with the means to fight for democracy and dignity at their workplaces.[86]

To Tsipras' argument that the mandate SYRIZA had received from the electorate ruled out abandoning the euro, Iliopoulos replied:

> It is true that SYRIZA's programme was not pro-drachma. But it was not pro-MoU either. How did we reach this point of being left with two choices of which none is compatible with our programme?

Iliopoulos' conclusion, however, reflects a general (and under-standable) feeling of impotence:

> We have reached a dead end… Every alternative strategy that we could have followed has already failed too. Additionally,

we have to make another horrific admission... The weight of power relations... are, more clearly now than ever before, in favour of the imperialistic forces. Because fights are not won by those who are right but instead by those who are powerful. We must avoid pursuing a different strategy that will result in the same mistakes. This is the strategy of an 'agreed exit' which would reincarnate just the same illusion of hope as our former insistence on the certainty of a 'mutually beneficial agreement'. There is no apparent reason why the forces that want to see SYRIZA fall apart will suddenly change their minds and offer a beneficial 'agreed exit'... We need to plot another strategy as soon as possible.

While the Tsipras wing of SYRIZA had been guilty of an irresponsible degree of improvisation and eclecticism, the left too was not without blame. In describing the reaction of "all those who vested hopes in the prospects of a SYRIZA government" as one of "post-traumatic shock", Stathis Kouvelakis has accepted that, "however much events vindicated our perspective", as a member of SYRIZA's central committee for the previous three years, he and his fellow Left Platform CC members too bore "a part of collective responsibility for this debacle". He correctly explains that the outcome was not simply due to a "secret plan to 'sell out'"; it was the result of "the total bankruptcy of a specific strategy".

Kouvelakis argued that the left should have challenged this approach from the start.

The choice of focusing on negotiations with the troika with a view to reaching a mutually acceptable solution... didn't just tie the hands of the SYRIZA government, opening the way for the capitulation that followed. Its first and most immediate consequence was to paralyze the mobilization and destroy the optimism and militancy that prevailed in the first weeks after the January 25th electoral victory.[87]

This choice had led to "appeasement of the centre of economic power" and of the "oligarchy", and "continuity of the repressive mechanisms of the state". As examples of this he pointed to the appointment of reactionary establishment figures to the key posts of president of the republic, deputy prime minister, defence minister, minister of public order and director of the public broadcasting company.

We might also add to Kouvelakis' list the ultimate humiliation, conceded by Tsipras within hours of the referendum result: to let the enemy pick his own chief negotiator – in this case by substituting Tsakalotos for Varoufakis. As Varoufakis observed: "They are unanimous in their hatred of me, and I welcome their hatred… I shall wear the creditors' loathing with pride."[88]

Alongside the political mistakes came organisational failures. Kouvelakis described the effect on life inside SYRIZA:

> Even before assuming office, SYRIZA had tended to become less and less democratic as a party… The process went entirely out of control when SYRIZA went into government. From that time on, the high circles of the government and the key centres of political decision-making acquired absolute autonomy from the party.

He complained that the central committee had only met three times between January, when SYRIZA had come to power, and the signing of the new memorandum in July; and that the Thessaloniki Programme had soon come into conflict with government policy to the point where, in his words, it rapidly became taboo even to mention it within the ranks of the government, or even within the party.

Chapter 14

Alternatives

Tsipras' July coup had presented the ranks of SYRIZA with a *fait accompli*: rejection of the democratic outcome of the referendum; complicity in a third and still-more-vicious Memorandum of Understanding; a purge of the SYRIZA parliamentary party; an ultimatist electoral plebiscite. These measures had all the elements of a putsch.

The Left Platform, including 25 former SYRIZA MPs, immediately proclaimed the foundation of a new party, Popular Unity, to resist the new memorandum. It called for mass mobilisations, stood by the Thessaloniki programme, opposed the capitulation of Tsipras to the EU and the collaboration of the Tsipras government with Israel, and called for a return to the drachma and an exit from NATO. Lafazanis declared: "We no longer have a democracy... but a Eurozone dictatorship."[89]

Some considered the split a tactically questionable step, given that over half of SYRIZA's central committee had opposed the deal, and that there was still opposition to Tsipras within SYRIZA. The party's previously loyal general secretary Koronakis resigned, complaining that the central committee's decision to hold a party congress in September had been ignored. The former deputy finance minister Nadia Valavani opposed the deal and later joined Popular Unity. The MP Iro Dioti refused to stand, saying that the bailout deal is

> not financially viable and deepens the recession as well as social inequality... A party congress would have allowed SYRIZA to craft a plan to help Greece get rid of bailouts in the future... As far as I'm concerned, I cannot serve this plan.[90]

Even some members of the formerly "moderate" 53+ faction, which had previously supported Tsipras, accused him of undermining the party's interests for the sake of holding on to power, and demanded that he make a commitment to implementing social policies in line with SYRIZA's values. That being so, wasn't a split premature?

And yet, in the event of new elections, even with a still-confused alternative programme, could the left have let slip the opportunity to present an electoral challenge to Tsipras, thereby leaving the electorate no outlet to voice their protest? Wasn't it crucial to offer a left alternative to help cut across the danger of a resurgence of Golden Dawn? According to Yorgos Mitralias:

> the political climate is one of a real 'civil war'... Tsipras and his friends are... the Noskes at the top of the government... The only thing left to do with these cynical traitors is to fight against them by all means in order to save what can be saved of the honour of the left. Otherwise we will see Golden Dawn exploiting the anger of the poor people and turning the Greek drama into a European nightmare.[91]

As it turned out, Popular Unity won just 155,242 votes – 2.86% of the vote – and failed even to cross the threshold to gain representation in parliament. Making every allowance for the handicaps it suffered – the headlong rush to precipitate new elections before the new party could establish itself, the clampdown on debate within SYRIZA, the triumphalist jeering of the media, etc. – nevertheless the election result for Popular Unity was bitterly disappointing.

Only 11 weeks prior to the election, 3.5 million Greeks had voted a decisive NO to austerity. Fewer than one in 20 of these voted at the general election for Popular Unity. Why then did they show so little enthusiasm at the election for the only party committed to standing by the result of that referendum? (To its shame, let us remember, the KKE had called for a spoiled ballot – in effect, abstention: a boycott.)

The very low vote for Popular Unity could be interpreted as an expression of exhaustion, demoralisation, despair. It could represent a perfectly understandable sense of helplessness and resignation. And yet in that case why had SYRIZA itself, the prime source of their disappointment, not also been swept away by this mood, as might have been expected? It is necessary to undertake a critical examination of the alternative programme offered by the left.

The euro and the drachma

What had previously operated as SYRIZA's Left Platform, and now presented itself as an independent force under the name Popular Unity, stood for rejection of fiscal austerity, default on debt repayments, exit from the eurozone and restoration of a sovereign currency: a return to the drachma.

Left Platform members like Lafazanis argued that it is better to be outside the eurozone than to remain trapped within its straitjacket. Even Varoufakis, who was opposed to voluntary withdrawal from the eurozone, had prudently prepared a "plan B", as he was duty-bound: an alternative transitional arrangement for a return to the drachma in the event of expulsion from the euro. (For even contemplating this back-up reserve plan, he was threatened with impeachment for treason!)

It is not difficult to appreciate why most Greeks found unthinkable the prospect of ejection from the eurozone, and consequently almost certainly from Europe. Entry into the EU in 1981, and its apparently irreversible consolidation through admission to the eurozone in 2001, had marked in popular consciousness a turning-point in Greek history – a respite at last from Greece's saga of wars, coups, dictatorships, occupations and civil wars. As in Spain and Portugal, the EU and the euro represented a promising future: democracy, welfare, opportunity, acceptance into a community of progress. Among the youth, they stood for opportunity and freedom to travel. The euro had come to symbolise their attainment of stability and, for many, relative affluence. It signified the readmission at last of Greek civilisation from its outer fringes into the heart of a Europe of peace and prosperity.

Conversely, the drachma was not just a symbolic memento of the privations of the past; it was a highly dubious gamble for the future, too. To entrust their fate to a restored drachma seemed to most Greeks a reckless leap into the void and, at worst, a catastrophe. Without any secure guarantee of stability, an improvised currency rolling off the printing presses of a bankrupt country could rapidly plummet in value.

This fear was entirely rational. The monster of hyper-inflation had been by no means laid to rest in Germany in 1923, the classic textbook case with which everyone is familiar, when inflation was running at 2,000,000,000% a year. Even this was not the worst example. In Hungary in 1945–6, the daily rate of inflation reached more than 200% – prices were *trebling every day*; and in China in 1947–9, they were doubling every five days. And hyper-inflation was not just a matter of history; within living memory, similar rates of hyper-inflation had struck Argentina, Mexico, Nicaragua, Brazil, Serbia... The most recent case was Zimbabwe in 2007–9. Prices were doubling every day; a loaf of bread ended up costing 35-million Zimbabwe dollars. This currency is only now to be formally demonetised, and banks are offering to buy up all accounts ranging anywhere up to *175-quadrillion* Zimbabwe dollars – that's 175 followed by 15 zeros! – for a flat price of five US dollars. (Prior to the onset of the crisis, the value of the Zimbabwean dollar had been pegged at parity with the US dollar: an exchange rate of 1:1.)

Greeks have ample reason of their own to be haunted by the folk memory of hyper-inflation. During the wartime occupation and especially in its aftermath, inflation had soared to 13,800%

per annum, with prices doubling every 4.3 days. By 1944, banknotes were circulating with a denomination of 100-trillion drachma. There was plenty of justification for modern-day Greeks' insecurity and unwillingness to risk their subsistence on so flimsy a footing.

Meanwhile, there was one faction of European bankers who were only too eager for Greece to walk out of the eurozone, the most prominent being Greece's arch-enemy Wolfgang Schauble, who was offering financial inducements to tempt Greece into what was euphemistically disguised as a "five-year holiday" from the eurozone. The right-wing British paper *The Telegraph* even taunted SYRIZA in an article headed: "Another bout of hyperinflation may be just what's needed to bring Greeks to their senses."[92]

The only safeguard against a restored drachma flying into freefall would have been to secure a fixed exchange rate with an external "hard" currency which could guarantee its parity. Tsipras did explore this option, but could find no access anywhere to the necessary hard-currency reserves on which to shore it up. He had seriously contemplated seeking a deal with Putin to secure backing for the drachma from the Russian rouble, and high-level meetings were held between officials in Athens and Moscow in the first months after SYRIZA was elected; but he met with a blank refusal. Since the civil war in Ukraine and the annexation of the Crimea, Russia was already smarting from the effects of European trade sanctions, and had absolutely nothing to gain out of provoking further friction by indulging in what would have been a mere quixotic gesture of solidarity with a negligible Balkan state. And any hope of rescue by Russia was definitively demolished by the fact that it had not even offered a bailout to Cyprus, where it had billions of its own money invested, when the banking system of that country had collapsed under EU pressure. According to Kammenos of ANEL, "we were sold down the river by everyone who said they would help. We had no roubles... to put up as collateral... nor any other foreign currency."[93]

Popular Unity called for nationalisation of the banking system, a comprehensive system of capital controls, exit from the eurozone and adoption of a new currency. This was essential if the government was to be anything but a helpless catspaw for the bankers. It went on to claim that on this basis it would be possible to "effectively address the humanitarian crisis, cover social needs, reconstruct the social state... take the economy out of the vicious circle of recession" and constitute "the first step in a process of social change, of recovery of national sovereignty and of economic progress combining growth and social justice". But was such an outcome guaranteed? Wasn't it even naïve to expect it? And perhaps all the more so, to borrow the fading social-democratic reputations of Sweden and Denmark as evidence that such a course would not make Greece any "less European"?

Popular Unity had not managed to reassure Greeks that withdrawal from the common currency and a return to the drachma was a safe alternative option. They despised the memory of the drachma and were justified in fearing that any new currency would inevitably plunge in value, thus massively increasing the burden of debt, payable in euros at a rapidly depreciating exchange rate. Default would of course be inevitable, but this in turn would block access to international credit. Devaluation would push up the cost of imported goods and services, and the absence of either a credible currency or access to credit could result in catastrophic shortages of food, energy and medical supplies. It is true that for a few years after 2001, Argentina had survived the consequences of its own default, but without Argentina's substantial export markets, the principal economic asset that Greece could rely on would be tourism – which would itself in such circumstances be highly vulnerable to the effects of a probable shortage of imported energy and to a general scenario rocked by political and social turmoil.

The Left Platform's Costas Lapavitsas nevertheless argued that "to beat austerity, Greece must break free from the euro". He advocated an approach to the troika for a 50% write-off of the debt, a new currency devalued by just 20%, and protection of the new Greek currency with liquidity from the ECB.

The British Marxist economist Michael Roberts commented:

Even if the Troika were to agree to such a 'negotiated exit', which is a moot point; and even if the new Greek drachma only depreciated by 20% (extremely unlikely), the Greek economy would still be on its knees, unable to restore living standards for the majority. Devaluation and rising prices would eat into any gains made from cheaper exports... Greek capitalism is no position to turn things round with its own currency... The alternative to the troika should not be posed as 'leaving the euro', but rather 'breaking with capitalism'...It won't be able to export enough to stop the economy dropping even further into an abyss and taking its people with it. Grexit also means not just leaving the euro but also the EU, and without any reciprocal trade arrangements that Switzerland has, for example... The issue for SYRIZA and the Greek labour movement... is not whether to break with the euro as such, but whether to break with capitalist policies and implement socialist measures to reverse austerity and launch a pan-European campaign for change.[94]

To quote Themos Demetriou:

Falling back on a 'return to the drachma' ticket emasculated all the internationalist and revolutionary implications of the anti-austerity politics SYRIZA stood for. Popular Unity was just offering another elusive capitalist way out of the Greek crisis.[95]

Other voices

Besides Popular Unity, there were other voices promoting alternative platforms.

The KKE had maintained throughout the crisis a consistently sectarian and abstentionist standpoint. To the question "What would you have done if you had been in the place of the SYRIZA government?", the KKE paper *Rizospastis* replied, with characteristically evasive bluster:

> If we, the KKE, were in the 'place' of SYRIZA... if we were in the 'place' of taking over a government that is a tool of the power of monopolies... if we were in the 'place' of negotiating on behalf of Greek capitalism... if we were in that 'place,' we would not do anything more or less than what SYRIZA is already doing... But if we were in that 'place', we would no longer be a Communist Party... But let us turn the question around: What would have happened if... we had a real workers' and people's government... in which communists would of course play a decisive role? Such a governmental power would not be trapped in the dead ends of an anti-people negotiation with the imperialist organizations of the EU, the ECB, and the IMF. It would not even start the kind of process we have lived through in the past five months... It would not acknowledge the entire existing institutional and legislative anti-people and anti-labour framework... It would abolish all of them; it would overturn them. It would also not recognize commitments to the EU, the ECB, the IMF, and the NATO... It would put an end to the participation of the country in these imperialist groups... Such a power and government would immediately sign mutually beneficial international agreements with other states, to import medicine, food, energy, precisely because it would not have the commitment to participate in imperialist organizations like the EU, the NATO, etc...[96]

Spyros Marketos of Antarsya wrote:

> Tsipras had betrayed the people even before the referendum...
> The leading group, the traitors, as the rest of the Left already
> calls them, don't have the majority in the Central Committee
> of SYRIZA. In the parliament they cannot pass the measures
> without the support of the right-wing deputies of New
> Democracy, Potomai, and PASOK...The social reaction will be
> huge... They will create a social explosion...We must call a
> spade a spade and a treason a treason. And not give them the
> benefit of the doubt. They betrayed everything they stood for
> until yesterday... Now we're entering the stage of the IMF
> riots, as they are called. But these IMF riots will be against
> SYRIZA, it is quite probable that it will send the government
> to the helicopters, they will flee...This memorandum has
> horrible consequences for the people in Greece, for the Left
> and for the Left internationally. It is a betrayal, pure and
> simple...[97]

Maria Pentarakis wrote:

> The European creditors, like other loan sharks, threatened
> Greece with an exit from the Eurozone if it implemented any
> of its anti-austerity policies... The Greek economy was being
> squeezed to death by its creditors as they progressively
> refused to accept Greek bonds and stopped emergency
> funding...The balance of power during the negotiations of the
> Greek government with the European Union, European
> Central Bank and Eurogroup made impossible any other
> outcome than defeat and subsequent enforced acceptance of
> further austerity... Public debt has been used as a means of
> redistributing resources from people to financial capital insti-
> tutions. Resources have been taken away from the welfare
> state and transferred to the banks... Greece was crushed

because it attempted to challenge the predominance of neoliberal policies and hence it had to be subjugated and humiliated in order to serve as a warning to other progressive parties and social movements in Europe... The 'oxi' mandate is still alive and fighting. One thing is sure – the anti-austerity struggles continue either within party politics or beyond.[98]

The former "Communist Tendency" of SYRIZA, now allied with Popular Unity, commented:

Having mobilized the masses and won a huge victory, the leaders of SYRIZA immediately waved the white flag of surrender and gave in to all the demands of the European creditors... This shameful capitulation has caused widespread disappointment... The initial mood of shock and disorientation has turned to fury... Tsipras thought he could use the referendum result as 'leverage' to get a better deal. In the end he got an even worse deal than the one that had been resoundingly rejected by the people of Greece in July... Now the government that was elected to oppose austerity is preparing to carry out savage cuts. This has inevitably plunged both Greece and SYRIZA into a deep crisis... It is necessary to expropriate the bankers, shipping magnates and the rest of the parasitic oligarchy that really rules Greece.[99]

And the socialist group XEKINIMA wrote:

Had Tsipras been prepared to reject the deal, say no to austerity and explain that Greece was being expelled from the euro because of this, while offering a bold revolutionary socialist alternative, he would have rallied the support of millions. Had he put himself at the head of a determined campaign on that basis, the mass of the Greek working class, the youth, big layers of the middle class and small farmers would have responded enthusiastically. Moreover, an appeal for solidarity to the working class and youth of Spain, Portugal, Italy, Ireland and the rest of the EU would have brought millions on to the streets demanding an end to austerity. The surge in support for Jeremy Corbyn in the Labour Party leadership contest in Britain indicates the potential backing Tsipras could have won internationally. Even in Germany, Die Linke (The Left) was compelled to vote against the latest deal, unlike previously. 250 demonstrations in support of Greece took place throughout the EU at the time of the referendum, a small glimpse of the support that could have been rallied. Equally, socialists are opposed to the workers of Germany, Finland or anywhere else paying for this crisis – as right-wing politicians in these countries try to claim would be the result of concessions to Greece. An appeal by Tsipras to the workers in these countries would also have received a warm response.[100]

These assertions may sound sweeping. Would Tsipras really not have been blamed for the appalling consequences of expulsion from the euro? Had the millions demonstrating already in the streets of Europe against austerity been enough up to now to restrain the troika? Can we be sure that workers in Germany and Finland would really have seen so easily through the divisive propaganda of their governments and offered the Greek people a "warm response"? The terrible threats ahead should not be glossed over...

And yet what other alternative was there to Tsipras' supine capitulation? How else could the vicious circle be broken?

Chapter 15

The International Dimension

The real motive for the troika's determination to crush SYRIZA was spelt out in unmistakeable language by Donald Tusk, current president of the European Council:

> I am really afraid of this ideological or political contagion, not financial contagion, of this Greek crisis... The febrile rhetoric from far left leaders, coupled with high youth unemployment in several countries, could be an explosive combination. For me, the atmosphere is a little similar to the time after 1968 in Europe. I can feel, maybe not a revolutionary mood, but something like widespread impatience. When impatience becomes not an individual but a social experience of feeling, this is the introduction for revolutions.[101]

Tusk is right. Something is stirring. There is a restlessness in the air. It started at the turn of the millennium with the anti-globalisation demonstrations in Seattle, Prague, Gothenburg and Genoa, and gathered pace with the worldwide protests at the impending Iraq War. Then came left electoral victories in Latin America, the Arab Spring; the Occupy movement; the Marikana miners' strike; the Greek protest movement; the Spanish indignados; strikes and rallies throughout Europe and worldwide; the overnight rise of new parties, both right and left; the election of a nominally anti-austerity coalition in Portugal; Black Lives Matter and the Sanders phenomenon in the USA; and the Corbyn surge in Britain... After decades of setbacks, the first stirrings of a new awakening were beginning to shake the ground.

The purpose of this chapter is to place the Greek experience in this context.

SYRIZA relied almost exclusively on its negotiating skills. But what happens at the negotiating table is determined by the objective balance of forces on the ground. As Ronald Reagan's secretary of state George Shultz once said, "negotiations are a euphemism for capitulation, if the shadow of power is not cast across the bargaining table".[102]

Shadows, of course, don't just hover haphazardly in the air, nor can they be conjured up at random. A shadow can only be cast by a real material substance. Towering over the table loomed the monstrous shadow of the real, tangible, incontrovertible power of the banks. The objective balance of power was weighted crushingly, overwhelmingly, towards the European bankers.

Mobilisation

What material counterweight could SYRIZA throw into the scales to offset their power? Debating points? Lectures in economics? Appeals for leniency? Only the force that had propelled it into office: the will of the population of Greece. That had been displayed over years of public protest, and – most recently and irrefutably – at the referendum.

Was that enough? The Greek workers can hardly be accused of passivity. For keyboard agitators around the world, mobilised in their ones at their computer terminals and occupying nothing more than their swivel chairs, calls for the mobilisation of the working class and the occupation of the workplaces are easy. In general they are right; but generalities are not enough.

Mobilise? No working class has mobilised like the Greeks for the last five years: in strikes, demonstrations and occupations of public squares. The solidarity they have shown, in general strike after general strike – *42 general strikes in five years*, at the last count! – is almost without precedent.

Ah, say the critics, but these were just street protests; why didn't they occupy their workplaces?

Greece has the highest rate of unemployment (26%); the

highest rate of self-employment (30–35%); and the lowest average concentration of employment in the EU. Small businesses employing fewer than ten workers account for 46% of employees, 58% of the total number of enterprises and 32% of value added. Greece also has the lowest proportion in Europe of companies with more than 250 employees – and even these are mostly banks or chain stores, whose workers are scattered in local branches around the country.

Certainly, those workers concentrated in sufficient numbers did successfully occupy banks, government ministries, public buildings – some of them for weeks or months: the electricity-corporation employees who occupied its premises to halt the disconnection of property-tax defaulters; the employees of the public broadcasting corporation ERT who took over its headquarters in defiance of closure orders.

But let's look at those figures again. More than a quarter of the Greek workforce are unemployed; one third of those still working are self-employed; and nearly half of those with jobs work in enterprises employing just a handful of workers. More than four fifths of Greek workers are either unemployed jobseekers, self-employed tradesmen or labourers scattered in small-scale workshops. Where are these workers meant to mobilise? What workplaces are they supposed to occupy?

There is only one only major "industry" in Greece: shipping. Greek shipowners operate almost 20% of the global fleet of merchant ships, and more than half of the European Union's fleet. The industry accounts for 7.5% of the Greek economy and employs around 200,000 people, including around 50,000 Filipino seamen. The shipowners' predominant share of the global shipping industry largely depends on the fact that they pay no taxes on profits from shipping operations, and no taxes on ship sales, just a simple flat-rate "tonnage tax". So far the Greek shipping tycoons have resisted tempting offers from Britain, Ireland and Cyprus to boost their own shrinking national shipping registries, but their response to all proposals to levy fair taxes is to threaten to set up operations in London, Singapore and Dubai. "I am in Greece because I love my country, but I won't stay around to see my business ruined", said one tanker-fleet owner. Since most investment in shipping is by definition portable, imposing taxes would only drive it out of the country. The ships would have to be commandeered – expropriated. That would require a massive international campaign similar to that mobilised by the Liverpool dockers in the 1990s, to blockade all access to fugitive shipping; and that presupposes a continental-wide co-ordination of protest.

It was the streets, the squares, the public spaces that became the site of occupations. The mass of humanity crowding into the public squares, inspired by the examples of Tahrir Square and the Spanish indignados, more than made up in inclusivity and breadth of composition what they lacked in access and proximity to the levers of production. They drew into joint struggle and mutual dialogue workers, pensioners, the unemployed, housewives, students, youth, small entrepreneurs, veterans and – crucially – migrants and refugees. The mass occupation of the city squares was the most eloquent, striking, public manifestation conceivable of popular outrage; an assertion in the flesh of the common popular solidarity of the 99%, stretching across the entire mass of the oppressed and deprived population. The effects of this were graphically illustrated in the demographic breakdown of voting in the July referendum.

The expression of resistance was resourceful, creative, spontaneous. The phenomenon of street protests and mass occupations of public spaces is no mere passing fad, but a manifestation of contemporary resistance and solidarity worldwide: from Tienanmen Square, Palace Square and Wenceslas Square in 1989 through to Tahrir Square, Puerta del Sol, Placa de Catalunya, Zuccotti Park, Causeway Bay, Symphony Way, Oaxaca, Madison and many more protracted assemblies of protest, including

Syntagma[103]. Reclaiming the streets and squares is an assertion of democratic rights not just within the confines of an under-industrialised Greece, but universally in the context of globalisation and modern production techniques in the era of the internet, 3D printing and zero marginal cost.

Along with this expression of rising consciousness came a creative outpouring of autonomous self-organisation. As always, while politics plays out its moves in the stratosphere, people on the ground improvise their own strategies for survival. In the communities the embryo of a new society was germinating. Experimentally, by trial and error, elements of an alternative "solidarity economy" were springing up, combining age-old community traditions of the bartering of goods and services with modern interactive networking systems, bypassing monetary transactions altogether.

In the "Athens Time Bank", members exchanged credits for services measured by hours of working time, including plumbers, mechanics, electricians, teachers, hairdressers, doctors, dentists, even yoga teachers and – significantly – psychotherapists. Also in Athens, the Helleniki clinic served more than 100 people a day, using voluntary services and donated supplies. Communes, direct farmer-to-buyer sales groups and non-profit enterprises were launched. In some neighbourhoods, alternative local currencies were devised, including the *votsalo* (pebble) and *tem* currencies. Thousands of Greeks participated in the parallel market: nationwide "solidarity economy" projects in which buyers were linked directly with producers of food and daily household necessities, bypassing the supermarkets. There were annual "festivals of solidarity" in which thousands of people gathered each autumn for discussions, concerts and workshops. These all helped maintain the requirements of civilised life and drew upon the pooled skills of redundant workers in all fields.

This came together in the magnificent institution of popular self-help, Solidarity for All, which provides social pharmacies, social medical clinics, social kitchens, social groceries, "markets without middlemen", a social collective of mental-health professionals, social solidarity drop in centres, time banks (sharing skills and time), olive-oil collectives, and the highly organised "potato movement" whereby farmers trade directly with consumers, cutting out the wholesalers and the supermarkets. There are dozens of volunteer clinics in Athens and all over Greece. For example, in Kalamata, around 60 doctors volunteer their services. In Piraeus and elsewhere, the trades of the unemployed are registered, and in return for food and services, they are all obligated to render four hours' service per week. A virtual currency is in operation.

To cater for the needs of the thousands of migrants arriving on the islands, Solidarity for All provides welcome committees, medical aid, water, food, and advice. A superabundance of clothes for the use of arriving migrants been received from collections in Germany. Schools, clinics and therapy centres have been set up for their benefit. SYRIZA's MPs donate a substantial proportion of their parliamentary salaries to this solidarity campaign.

Here too, the humanity and decency of the Greek working class collide with the demands of the rulers of Europe. Not content with having already bled Greece dry in revenge for a financial crisis of its own making, the EU is now also heaping on to it the impossible burden of containing the flood of refugees fleeing from Middle Eastern wars that are themselves a direct consequence of US and European meddling. By geographical chance, Greece happens to be their first port of call in Europe; but rather than congratulating Greece on its civilised reception of migrants, the EU is threatening to punish it for alleged administrative oversights in the registration process, by excluding Greece from the Schengen agreement, thus cutting off Greece's own young citizens' last remaining lifeline of employment in Europe.

Even while crushed under the heel of Europe's bankers, the Greek people opted to stay in Europe. Now in return they face captivity within a national cage. A razor-wire fence has been erected inside the Former Yugoslav Republic of Macedonia to seal Greece's border. European bureaucrats are currently considering a range of previously unthinkable options, including criminalising the NGOs that are helping to settle arriving refugees; and even demanding that the Greeks sink their inflatable boats en route from Turkey. It would be a policy, as Paul Mason says, of "forcing Greece to drown migrants and turning it into a quarantined prison camp if it refuses."[104]

Revolution?

The focus on electing a government pledged to resist austerity was not a step back but the mark of a leap in consciousness: a recognition that mere demonstrations and even strikes are not enough; that what is required is a political offensive. SYRIZA had a rare opportunity to channel this inexhaustible supply of spontaneous initiative and improvisation into a comprehensive programme for a new society. There was no solution to the debt crisis within the existing system.

Capital controls could have been imposed as soon as SYRIZA came to power in January; as it was, they were belatedly introduced only in July – and even then, at the instigation of the creditors themselves. The banks could have been nationalised straight away; even the US and British governments had nationalised large sections of the banking sector under the impact of the 2008 crash. The government could have announced immediate default on the unpayable debt. Companies laying off workers or withholding payment of wages could have been taken over. Flowing from this, other strategic enterprises could have been nationalised, especially the shipping fleets. An emergency programme could have been launched to rebuild the infrastructure. Neighbourhood committees could have taken over administrative functions. Such a programme was already implicit in the situation.

These policies make up in outline the only rational solution to the crisis. But they would certainly not offer an easy way out. On the contrary, remorseless attacks and sabotage would be inflicted by the bankers and capitalists and their political institutions, bringing in their wake violence, starvation and chaos.

Negotiations between adversaries have a place in every struggle. SYRIZA had a mandate and it could not back down from the challenge. However, its overriding obligation was to evaluate every step it took by one single criterion: its effectiveness in demonstrating to the population what they were up against. In passing from scattered strikes and impotent riots to general strikes and mass occupations, the Greek people had taken a giant step towards class unity and solidarity; by passing beyond these street protests to the projection of their aspirations onto the political plane, they had taken a further leap forward. Every step that SYRIZA took had to be measured by its capacity to raise the level of understanding throughout society of the tasks they faced in common. The need to replace capitalism and carry through a socialist programme was not a sectarian fantasy arbitrarily grafted onto reality; it sprang inescapably from the very needs of human society. Its necessity would be posed more and more sharply in the course of these events. Workers, women and youth would be intently monitoring each twist and turn, meeting, debating, improvising, demanding... Every obstacle placed in their path by the troika would come under their scrutiny. The population was on its feet.

The only realistic strategy was to rally the mass of the population and appeal for solidarity across Europe. It would be mandatory for a socialist government to take full control of the economy, nationalise the banks and the dominant corporations, strip the capitalists of their power to rule, and develop the structures for democratic administration by the mass of the population, the true creators of wealth. But within the confines of Greece, there would be limited scope for such a regime to hold out. These are general slogans, nebulous broad-brush formulations, and in the thick of a battle abstractions are not enough.

In an opinion poll in 2011, 33% of the Greek population opted for "revolution". Did the conditions really exist in Greece for revolution? Someone who should know is Lenin, who summed them up as follows:

> For a revolution to take place, it is not enough for the exploited and oppressed masses to realise the impossibility of living in the old way, and demand changes; for a revolution to take place it is essential that the exploiters should not be able to live and rule in the old way. It is only when the 'lower classes' do not want to live in the old way and the 'upper classes' cannot carry on in the old way that the revolution can triumph. This truth can be expressed in other words: revolution is impossible without a nationwide crisis (affecting both the exploited and the exploiters).[105]

No one will deny that Greece was in the grip of an almost unprecedented nationwide crisis; nor that the "upper classes" were unable to live and rule in the old way, and that the "lower classes" found it impossible to live in the old way.

Lenin continued:

> It follows that, for a revolution to take place, it is essential, first, that a majority of the workers (or at least a majority of the class-conscious, thinking, and politically active workers) should fully realise that revolution is necessary, and that they should be prepared to die for it; second, that the ruling classes should be going through a governmental crisis, which draws even the most backward masses into politics (symptomatic of any genuine revolution is a rapid, tenfold and even

hundredfold increase in the size of the working and oppressed masses – hitherto apathetic – who are capable of waging the political struggle), weakens the government, and makes it possible for the revolutionaries to rapidly overthrow it.

Again, no one can reasonably question the exponential increase – certainly "tenfold", if not "hundredfold" – in the number of people from all levels of society who had been drawn into active political struggle. Let us remember the remarkable finding of one survey which reported that more than one third of respondents – 35%! – had personally taken part in at least one street protest. And if proof is needed of the demonstrators' awareness of the international character of the movement against austerity, it is necessary to look no further than the banners they were flying, written not just in Greek but in English, Spanish, French, Italian and German. They were consciously and explicitly rallying the working people of Europe to join together with them in a continental-wide uprising. Finally, the referendum proved in hard incontrovertible arithmetic that almost two thirds of the population were ready to defy the bankers, at no matter what cost.

Were a majority of politically active workers ready to risk their lives for the sake of the revolution? Given a leadership ready to match the defiant mood of the people, who can say how far they would be prepared to go?

From a logistical point of view, Greece would not be the first choice of countries to lead a continental-wide struggle against capitalism. It has a scattered working class, no large centres of mass production, a relatively "closed" economy, peasant traditions of guerrilla rebellion... But then, who would have chosen Russia either? It is a law of history as well as physics that a system collapses first at its weakest point: the chain snaps at its weakest link. Greece was the most vulnerable to the pressures of the financial crisis, and it was the first to buckle under the strain.

The only effective bargaining counter available on the Greek side of the table was the force of example and the spread of resistance throughout Europe. But if Tsipras could frighten the bankers with the spectre of a spread of the campaign westward, then conversely the only conceivable response of the bankers had to be: no concessions, on the contrary even more exemplary public punishment for all to see. And that is the meaning of Tusk's comment. The European Union crushed Greece for fear of revolution throughout Europe.

The riposte of the Greek people to the attacks on their rights, their livelihoods and dignity by Europe's bankers was admirable; but they have paid the price of being a little ahead of the rest of us. They could not undertake this task alone; they must spread the appeal to the workers of Europe to follow their cue. They stepped forward to confront the enemy, but found themselves isolated and exposed.

A historical comparison

Driven beyond breaking-point by slaughter at the front and hunger at home, in 1917 the Russian workers, soldiers and peasants had overthrown their oppressors. If they had foreseen the tribulations ahead of them in 1917, would they have launched their revolution? Perhaps not. Their country was already steeped in age-old backwardness, with only pockets of industry, low productivity, long hours, mass illiteracy and a per-capita income about one tenth of that of the USA; but by the time they emerged from three years of civil war and foreign armed intervention, Russia was plagued with mass starvation, deadly epidemics, a desperate scarcity of finance, technical expertise and spare parts. Seven-million homeless orphans roamed the country, cannibalism was rife, industrial production was down to *one ninth* of the 1913 figure, and agricultural produce had fallen well below the pre-1900 level.

However, history had not granted them the luxury of contemplation; they were impelled by the immediate duress of slaughter at the front and hunger at home. And above all, it was their isolation in conditions now of virtual barbarism that was responsible for their suffering – the failure of the revolution elsewhere, not their victory at home – that had doomed them to the privations ahead.

It was not at all fanciful or outlandish for the Russian workers to count on their brothers and sisters throughout Europe to come to their rescue. It was an absolutely reasonable, practical and almost commonplace assumption that had led them to view their struggle firmly in the context of a Europe-wide revolution. After all, as late as in November 1912, meeting at an Extraordinary International Socialist Congress at Basel, the Socialist International – not a sect but the established voice of millions of organised workers throughout Europe and beyond – had unanimously warned the ruling classes of Europe:

Let the governments remember that… they cannot unleash a war without danger to themselves. Let them remember that the Franco-German War was followed by the revolutionary outbreak of the Commune, that the Russo-Japanese War set into motion the revolutionary energies of the peoples of the Russian Empire, that the competition in military and naval armaments gave the class conflicts in England and on the Continent an unheard-of sharpness, and unleashed an enormous wave of strikes. It would be insanity for the governments not to realize that the very idea of the monstrosity of a world war would inevitably call forth the indignation and the revolt of the working class. The proletarians consider it a crime to fire at each other for the profits of the capitalists, the ambitions of dynasties, or the greater glory of secret diplomatic treaties.[106]

And in actual fact, within months of their own uprising, revolution really was raging throughout Germany, Austria, Hungary, Poland, Italy, France and elsewhere. The royal dynasties of Europe were rudely dethroned, as the Hohenzollerns and Habsburgs followed the Romanovs into oblivion. In Britain, growing militancy was expressed in the general strike on the Clyde, the great mutinies among the British forces in France, the Triple Alliance of trade unions, the adoption by the young Labour Party of a socialist programme (the famous Clause Four which was to define the party's socialist aspirations for the next 80 years) and the mass Councils of Action which sprang up expressly to defend the Russian revolution and impede the intervention; councils which Lenin called "Soviets, in essence if not in name".

The mass of participants in the Russian revolution understood that they were part of an international phenomenon. On the very day of the October revolution, the resolution of the Petrograd Soviet affirmed its conviction that "the proletariat of the countries of Western Europe will aid us in conducting the cause of socialism to a real and lasting victory". In his classic eyewitness account, the American journalist John Reed recorded the common thoughts of working-class Petrograd insurgents on the streets: "Now there was all great Russia to win – and then the world!"

The historic proclamation made the next day to the Congress of Soviets ended with an explicit call to the workers of Britain, France and Germany to "help us to bring to a successful conclusion... the cause of the liberation of the exploited working masses from all slavery and exploitation". Lenin addressed the delegates with the hope that "revolution will soon break out in all the belligerent countries", and Trotsky warned that "if Europe continues to be ruled by the imperialist bourgeoisie, revolutionary Russia will inevitably be lost... Either the Russian revolution will create a revolutionary moment in Europe, or the

European powers will destroy the Russian revolution." Reed reports that "they greeted him with an immense crusading acclaim".[107]

He gives ample evidence of the extent to which these internationalist ideas had percolated through to the working population. He quotes a Red Guard who "plied me with questions about America... Are the American workers ready to throw over the capitalists?" He also quotes a soldier fresh from the front: "We will hold the fort with all our strength until the peoples of the world arise", who then addresses Reed directly: "Tell the American workers to rise and fight for the social revolution!"

Reed continued:

Something was kindled in these men. One spoke of 'the coming world revolution, of which we are the advance guard'; another of 'the new age of brotherhood, when all the peoples will become one great family'.

Even the peasants – illiterate, superstitious, steeped for centuries in veneration of Tsarism and Russian orthodoxy – became inspired. Their heroine Maria Spiridonova addressed their congress days after the October revolution:

The present movement is international, and that is why it is invincible. There is no force in the world which can put out the fire of the revolution. The old world crumbles down, the new world begins.

The Russian workers, soldiers and peasants understood that their revolution was doomed without the solidarity of the workers of the world. The world's capitalists, too, understood that the October revolution constituted a mortal threat to their own survival. Suddenly the warring powers joined together in combined attack on their common enemy. British naval forces landed in Murmansk, on the pretext of "helping to defend the revolution against Germany"; within days they were marching south on Petrograd, disarming the workers and shooting local Bolsheviks. The Japanese landed at Vladivostok and set up a dictatorship under the Tsarist Admiral Kolchak; Germany occupied the Ukraine in collusion with White Guards Krasnov and Wrangel. While the Allies screamed that Lenin and Trotsky were "German agents", Germany countered that "in the Bolshevist movement... the hand of England is seen".[108]

The Bolsheviks knew that ultimately their only strength lay in the common class interest of workers everywhere. Their supreme task was the foundation in 1919 of the Communist International, the world party of socialist revolution. They granted autonomy and the rights of secession to all the nations of the former Great Russian Empire. They chose to suffer the humiliating terms of the Brest-Litovsk peace treaty with Germany, ceding large areas of territory and provoking crises within the party and a government split with their Left SR allies, rather than break the faith of the people and allow them to drift into the clutches of the White terror. They made open appeals for peace, renounced all claim to booty and annexations and published the secret treaties, to expose to the workers the real interests of the capitalist governments.

In the emergency debate in 1918 over whether or not to seek a peace treaty with Germany, Lenin had even said:

> If the German movement is capable of developing at once in the event of peace negotiations... we ought to sacrifice ourselves, since the German revolution will be far more powerful than ours... It is not open to the slightest doubt that the final victory of our revolution if it were to remain alone, if there were no revolutionary movements in other countries, would be hopeless... Our salvation from all these difficulties... is an all-European revolution.[109]

Twenty-one foreign armies had poured into Russia in a concerted attempt to crush the revolution in its cradle. Once the intervention had begun, the Bolsheviks greeted the enemy soldiers with leaflets printed in all their languages, explaining that they had been sent by their bosses to crush a workers' republic, reporting the news of the revolution raging throughout Europe, and appealing for active help. This had an immediate effect on the foreign war-weary workers in uniform. It was the invincible power of workers' internationalism that saved the Russian Revolution. At one point, only a small area surrounding Moscow and extending barely to Petrograd had been in the hands of the Red Army. Russia was starved of arms. But mutinies in the French fleet stationed off Odessa, in the British, German, Czechoslovak and other armies, came to the rescue. In Britain, the main contributor to the intervention, the TUC condemned the Siberian occupation in September 1919 – and Siberia was evacuated within days. General Golovin reported on his negotiations with Winston Churchill in May 1919 as follows: "The question of giving armed support was for him the most difficult one; the reason for this was the opposition of the British working class to armed intervention..."[110] Councils of Action had sprung up throughout Britain to defend the Russian revolution. In May 1920 the men in London's East India Docks refused to load the "Jolly George" ship with hidden cachements of arms for Poland: mass demonstrations were held throughout the country, and a joint meeting of the TUC, the Labour Party NEC and the Parliamentary Labour Party threatened a general strike unless the intervention was called off. The intervention stopped most abruptly and the Red Army had no difficulty in clearing up the native Tsarist relics within a few weeks. At indescribable cost, for the moment the revolution survived.

International solidarity

Human solidarity is a natural feature of civilised society and especially of modern working-class culture, the elementary building block of trade-unionism. Greeks above all are aware of the vital part played by European supporters and volunteers in their own war of independence. Workers' solidarity was shown on a global scale in the worldwide boycott of South Africa which helped bring down the apartheid regime. It reached its fullest expression in the Spanish civil war in the 1930s, when no fewer than 35,000 volunteers travelled to Spain to form an international brigade and enlist in the republican armies fighting fascism, with another 10,000 participating in an auxiliary non-combatant role. Up to 25,000 of these ended up sacrificing their lives for the cause of workers' solidarity.

Activists throughout Europe were following keenly events in Greece, but sympathy alone could not affect the outcome. Not only were there no longer the vast networks of support and solidarity available to past generations, in the form of mass parties and internationals; above all, there was no common agreed programme to solve the austerity crisis. That is the key to a solution.

Could a bolder policy have offered the Greek people any respite? Within the borders of a single country – all the more so in Greece, one of the weakest economies in Europe – there could be no such guarantee.

Active propaganda to convince first the Greek people and then those of Europe as a whole should have been paramount on the agenda of the SYRIZA leadership. SYRIZA was under siege; it was defeated. It had no way out other than as part of a broader Europe-wide struggle. Victory in Greece depended on solidarity and relief from the growing movements throughout the continent, and especially in southern Europe, and the campaign for an alternative socialist Europe.

There was no shortage of calls for international solidarity: appeals, rallies, tributes, collections, petitions. In Britain the Greece Solidarity Campaign held countless conferences and rallies. 250 demonstrations in support of Greece took place throughout the EU during the week of the referendum campaign alone; and at the opening of a new €1-billion ECB headquarters in Frankfurt, 20,000 people held a demonstration with banners proclaiming "solidarity with Greece". On one memorable occasion, a Colombian office-cleaner was flown from London to Athens with a donation of £500 collected by her workmates for the striking female cleaners of Athens. These 595 women, sacked from their jobs cleaning Finance Ministry offices throughout Greece among a total of 3900 laid-off government workers, spent 20 months camping out on the street in a public vigil in one of the longest, most militant and most popular strikes in Greek history. All the sacked government workers were rehired by the SYRIZA government on enhanced contracts.

Among active anti-austerity campaigners, awareness of the ritual humiliation of the Greek people and awe at their spirit of defiance fed into the growing tide of resistance. The election of SYRIZA had given an initial impetus to PODEMOS in Spain; it encouraged 80,000 water-charge protesters on to the streets of Dublin, many of them waving Greek flags in solidarity; it helped inspire a surge of over a quarter of a million people behind the Corbyn campaign to reclaim the Labour Party for the working class; and it found an echo in the election of a left coalition government in Portugal. Nevertheless, the limited scale of explicit solidarity action reflects the early stage of resistance in most countries.

The crisis in Greece is just one symptom of the international crisis that began with the financial crash of 2008. As the Cypriot Marxist Themos Demetriou says,

It cannot be resolved on a national level; any resolution will have to be international... The present battle in Greece has been lost. That the capitulation of Tsipras is the defining act of this loss cannot be questioned, but in all probability this battle would be lost a little further down the road. Tsipras could see this and he chose to throw in the towel rather than take further punishment. The war however is being fought on the wider fields of Europe... Instead of promising wonders from a severing of the oppressive link with the Euro and the EU, I would much prefer a call for a change in Europe. It should be clear by now that the old Europe is dying and the new Europe is fighting to be born... The hour of judgement is nigh... The worst crime at this instant is not to recognise the epoch whose first sign was SYRIZA's rise to power. If Europe misses this opportunity and sinks back to politics as usual, the future may be truly bleak...[111]

Today's concerted assault by global capital on the fragile hard-won rights of working people the world over can no more be resisted for long on their own by the Greeks, no matter how determined, as could previous attacks on a national scale in Britain in the 1980s, for instance, by the Militant Labour councillors of Liverpool City Council. What they did, however, is raise a flag of defiance. It is the defiant voice of Greece's referendum majority, not the white flag prudently raised by Tsipras, that will inspire the next phase of the struggle.

Revolutions unfold through ebbs and flows over prolonged periods. In pre-war Spain, for instance, it took eight years from the overthrow of the Primo de Rivera regime in 1931, through to the high point of the Barcelona insurrection of 1937, before its final bloody defeat at Franco's hands in 1939.

In Greece a crucial chapter is finished; but resistance is by no means crushed. The re-election of an albeit-emasculated SYRIZA in September is confirmation of that. The massive general strike of 12th November 2015 – a strike which even SYRIZA had to support –proved beyond question that the story is far from over. On 21st January 2016, farmers, ferry crews, lawyers, doctors, engineers and pensioners took to the streets. Then came yet another huge general strike on 4th February 2016 - *the 42nd general strike* in about five years of turmoil hardly paralleled in postwar European history. The Greeks were first to face the enemy; it's time for the rest of us to catch up.

A workers' international

In a reference to the historic gathering of socialist internationalists that had gathered under the shadow of the World War in 1916, Yorgos Mitralias called for "a new Zimmerwald" – in other words, the preparation for a new workers' international:

> It is imposed upon us by the terrible dangers of our times, by the black clouds of the neo-fascist menace that are gathering over Europe, by the current arrogance and boundless insolence of triumphalist capitalism which can promise nothing but disaster to humanity.[112]

The building of a new workers' international is a matter not of life and death, but of the very survival of the human species. The alternative is staring us all in the face right now: endless wars, racism, terrorism, repression, mass migration, fascism.

The original champions of democracy had to confront the feudal lords by building national movements of revolt; the pioneers of socialism had to build worldwide networks. Capitalism is sucking the whole world into a single vortex, and the working class has no option but to operate accordingly. In political awareness and organisational cohesion, the co-ordination of the working class may have receded; but objectively, its latent power and fusion has grown exponentially, through its massive growth in China, Asia, Africa and Latin America; the worldwide proletarianisation of women, who now make up at least half of the world's workforce; the heightened awareness and integration of workers and youth worldwide through migration, modern telecommunications and social networks. For the first time ever, the working class makes up a majority of the world population, and its centre of gravity is rapidly shifting away from Europe and America. For every worker in the old metropolitan countries, there are now five spread across the globe. China has twice as many industrial workers as all the G7 countries put together. [113] While the socialist consciousness of the old proletariat has faded, that of the new proletariat has yet to flourish.

Events in Greece are just a miniature foreshadowing of the drama to come. Europe is still on the brink of a gigantic explosion which will shake society to its foundations, and this too is only a prelude to the entry of the working class of Asia, Africa and Latin America, not to mention North America and Australia, onto the world stage.

The current underground strike wave in China recalls the 1890s in Russia: a period of rapid industrialisation in which millions of young peasants were being uprooted from medieval conditions and transplanted into high-tech modern industrial factories. That economic boom in Russia ended in a general strike, the birth of Soviets and the 1905 revolution – events that transformed the international working class and ushered in an era of world revolution. The rate of recorded strikes and worker protests in China doubled in 2015, to a total of 2,774[114]. The impending entry of the Chinese working class as a political force could transform the face of the world labour movement as dramatically as did the German working class in building the Socialist International, or the Russian working class the Communist International – or indeed the British trade unions in creating the fundamental bedrock for the First International.

What is necessary today is to draw together the forces fighting capitalism the world over into a new broad anti-capitalist front, to build an international forum in which new programmes, strategies and tactics can be thrashed out democra-tically, in the traditions of Marx and Engels at the time of the

First International.

The actual course of revolution is always more flexible, imaginative, and daring than can be predicted by any dry theory. The forms of struggle that have erupted largely outside the traditional organisations – in the Occupy movement, the Arab Spring, the South African miners' strikes, the Spanish indignados demonstrations, etc. – confront socialists with new challenges.

What is needed is not preaching, though whatever theoretical lessons might be learned from history need to be absorbed and placed at the disposal of the new generation of fighters. But today, from Athens to Cairo to Santiago to Seoul to South Africa, millions have been marching, mobilising, striking... and talking. Their debates have at least as much to teach us as whatever abstract lessons we may have gleaned from the textbooks. We need to learn from their experience, and to find ways to engage in mutual discussion of the way forward.

Workers everywhere are beginning to rise to their feet again. But their struggles are diffuse and unco-ordinated. There is no international; no organised programme to change society. Now more than ever we need a single party of the working class. Civilised life, war and peace, and environmental survival all depend upon it. Dark forces stalk the world: nationalism, racism, bigotry, fascism, fundamentalism, nihilistic terror. Rosa Luxemburg's aphorism "socialism or barbarism" once seemed little more than a rhetorical flourish, but now it is literally the nightmare choice imminently facing humanity.

The creation of a worldwide party of the working class is not at all an abstract or unreal idea. Every day, in every continent, we see new evidence that such a party is straining at every nerve to materialise. Mass communications and the "information revolution" have made the present generation incomparably better informed than their grandparents. The world has drawn together and a new global consciousness has arisen. The size and specific weight of the proletariat have grown everywhere.

In 2003, 30-million people worldwide marched to protest at the impending war on Iraq. In 2011 the Occupy movement spread across the planet. On 14th November 2012, workers across Southern Europe held a one-day international general strike.

In his preface to the *Communist Manifesto*, written on the first May Day in 1890, as workers throughout the world rallied and struck for the eight-hour day, Engels wrote:

> True, the International itself lived only nine years. But that the eternal union of the proletarians of all countries created by it is still alive and lives stronger than ever, there is no better witness than this day. Because today, as I write these lines, the European and American proletariat is reviewing its fighting forces, mobilized for the first time, mobilized as *one* army, under *one* flag, for *one* immediate aim... And today's spectacle will open the eyes of the capitalists and landlords of all countries to the fact that today the proletarians of all countries are united indeed. If only Marx were still by my side to see this with his own eyes![115]

When tens of millions protest – on the same issues, with the same slogans, often on the same day in internationally synchronised action – that means that the world party of the future is almost a reality now. The international movement against capitalism needs to be embodied in a permanent thriving organised movement. It is the task of socialists to give conscious expression to this process.

Who is to say that the embryo of a revolutionary international is not already being created right now, in the debates that must be raging in workplaces, street corners and shanty towns across the world? A new, stronger, more cohesive international class is taking shape, bestriding every continent, and rapidly learning afresh the strategy and tactics of class struggle.

The people of Greece have rocked the continent and shaken

the complacency of the world's ruling kleptocracy. They may
have lost the latest engagement, but they will not lightly relinquish their cause. Let the troika remember the centuries of heroic
guerrilla struggle that brought modern Greece into existence; let
them remember the Greek people's rout of Mussolini's invading
army in 1940; the unparalleled mass resistance that single-
handedly overthrew the Nazi occupation; the years of civil war
against first the British and then the US military. Let them not
forget how one single uprising of the Greek youth in 1973 against
a brutal military dictatorship was enough to set in motion a
process that ended with the colonels literally packing their bags
and running away. The current era of resistance will not end any
time soon.

The last word has not yet been written. Events up to now in
Greece will come to be seen as a mere preliminary skirmish in the
struggles that lie ahead. What happens when the next debt crisis
comes, the next bailout and the next memorandum? Spain's debt
now amounts to more than a trillion euros (€1034 billion), and
Italy's more than two trillion (€2166 billion), compared to which
Greece's debt of €317 billion is pitiful. Spain's debt-to-GDP ratio
stands at 100%, Portugal's 130% and Italy's at 132%. Fifty percent
of Italy's debt matures in the next two years. These are all ticking
time bombs, all the more explosive on the eve of a likely new
financial crash, a crisis that could once again put in jeopardy the
very survival of the euro.

Greater catastrophes than that of Greece are looming ahead;
and they could have world-shaking consequences. The financial-
and-political-trends forecaster and publisher of the journal *Trends*
Gerald Celente wrote in 2011:

What's happening in Greece will spread worldwide as
economies decline... We will see social unrest growing in all
nations which are facing sovereign debt crisis, the most
obvious being Spain, Ireland, Portugal, Italy, Iceland, the

Ukraine, Hungary, followed by the United Kingdom and the United States.[116]

A real storm is coming.

APPENDIX

The Need for a Plan B in Europe

By Eric Toussaint

Eric Toussaint is a historian and political scientist, spokeperson of the Committee for the Abolition of Third World Debt, and coordinator of Greece's Truth Commission on Public Debt.

After the Greek government's capitulation to the creditors and the European institutions in July 2015, it is urgent for a Plan B to be developed. If we want to break away from the neoliberal orientations that have been applied for decades, a number of measures have to be taken simultaneously: implementing a different taxation system (both to take as much as possible away from the rich to put it in the coffers of the State, and to drastically reduce the unfair taxes that weigh on the majority of the population); developing measures regarding the debt and the banking sector; introducing complementary currency (especially, but not only, in the context of the euro); obviously doing away with a series of unjust austerity measures; and launching a democratic constituent process, based on active participation by all citizens. The purpose of our coming together in a European Citizens' Assembly on Debt is not to become some batch of experts that will discuss the issue of debt in all future debates, and repeat the same points over and over; our purpose is to discuss amongst ourselves, among all the organisations and movements that are participating in the debt movement and the general movement to resist neoliberalism, in order to bring our struggles closer together while seeing to it that demands and alternatives that include refusal of illegitimate debt are well represented.

In Europe the movement for a citizen audit of debt is still very young. It is a new movement that must be consolidated. I'll give just a few dates: the movement in Greece came into being in March-April 2011 – the Committee for a Citizens' Audit of Greece's Debt, known as ELE in Greece – and 3,000 of us participated in its launch in May 2011 at a university in Athens[117]. It then rebounded, or developed almost simultaneously, in Spain, as part of the Indignadxs movement in March-April-May 2011 when a series of economic committees in that movement, and in particular the economic committee of the Puerta del Sol in Madrid, began to raise the question of the debt, challenge its legitimacy, and use the tool of citizen audit. Out of the Indignadxs movement came the Citizens' Debt Audit Platform[118]. Then it arrived in Portugal, where a debate over challenging debt repayment arose, with an audit as a preliminary step. An initial conference took place in Lisbon in June 2011, which led to the creation of the Initiative for a Citizen Audit (IAC) of the Debt in December 2011[119]. The IAC produced an initial report in 2012[120]. In France the movement was born in September 2011 after ATTAC and the CADTM joined with a number of other movements in launching the Collectif pour un audit citoyen[121]). In Belgium it took some more time since the Citizen Debt Audit (ACiDE) came into being in February 2013[122].

At the level of Europe and the Mediterranean, the first initiative for coordinating citizen audit initiatives occurred in Brussels in April 2012 when the International Citizen Audit Network[123] was formed at the invitation of CADTM Europe. The first Euro-Mediterranean meeting of the ICAN was held on 7 April 2012 in Brussels. Twelve countries were represented – Greece, Ireland, Portugal, Spain, Italy, Poland, the UK, France, Germany, Belgium, Egypt, and Tunisia. In all these countries, citizen debt audit initiatives and/or campaigns against austerity that include the problem of debt had just come into being[124].

It is a new movement that has run into problems from the

start. A number of radical political groups say "Why audit the debt? Debt needs to be abolished, and to audit debt is a way of legitimising it," consequently the representatives of these groups leave the movement and refuse to support a citizen debt audit initiative. In Greece, the majority of the radical Left decided not to support the citizen debt audit (including the radical Left coalition Antarsya, a large part of SYRIZA, and the Communist Party, which even went so far as to treat us as enemies). Fortunately there were members of some organisations of the Left (part of SYRIZA, a few NAR members who were members of Antarsya, and union members) who joined us; but most members were individuals or else citizens' organisations mobilised around the issue of the debt, without the support of political organisations. Meanwhile we're still waiting for the political organisations who refused to support the debt audit in Greece to tell us, after having read the reports we issued in June[125]) and in September 2015[126], whether our work has indeed served to legitimise a portion of the debt or not. One thing that is certain is that if these organisations, instead of criticising us or remaining on the sidelines, had participated in the audit and presented arguments in favour of cancellation, it would have given more strength to those who wanted to mount a real alternative to the capitulation by Alexis Tsipras and his government.

Such problems have been faced by the debt-auditing movements in all countries. What is obvious is that we have not been at all well received by the governments. As Zoe Konstantopoulou, who was Speaker of the Greek Parliament from February to September 2015, said (see the video of her speech in English[127]), governments don't want to audit the debt because they don't want to radically challenge its legitimacy, its odious nature, or its sustainability from the point of view of respect for human rights. The height of irony is that there is a European Regulation, dated May 2013, which requires states receiving financial assistance to audit their debt. Until now, no government has initiated such an audit, let alone successfully completed one. Fortunately, in March 2015, the Speaker of the Greek Parliament decided to do so, as an extension of the citizen debt audit (ELE)[128]. At first, she succeeded in winning support from the government, but in the end they chose not to use the weapon of the audit or to rely on the findings of the preliminary report published in June 2015 in opposing their creditors.

One of the fundamental lessons to be learned from what happened in Greece is that the citizen audit movement, which had begun very well in 2011, did not gain sufficient strength, was not maintained, and did not create the pressure – in particular on the different political groups, and not just on SYRIZA – that needed to be brought to bear to get the assurance that if they came to power, conducting an audit of the debt with citizen participation would constitute an obligation and an indispensable priority. And yet that was a part of the platform SYRIZA had put forward in the elections of May-June 2012.

Whereas SYRIZA had obtained 4% of the vote in the 2009 elections, in May 2012 it succeeded in getting 16% of the vote, then 26.5% one month later in the elections held in June 2012 – just two points below New Democracy, the major party of the Right. SYRIZA had thus become the second-ranking party in Greece. Between the two rounds of the election, Tsipras put forward five concrete proposals for beginning negotiations with the parties opposed to the Troika (except Golden Dawn, which was excluded though also opposed to the Memorandum of Understanding):

- abolition of all anti-social measures (including the reductions of wages and retirement pensions);
- abolition of all measures that reduced workers' rights as regards protection and negotiation;
- immediate abolition of parliamentary immunity and reform of the election system;

- an audit of the Greek banks;
- the forming of an international debt audit committee combined with suspension of repayment of the debt until the end of the committee's work.

Citizens who had mobilised did not manage to put enough pressure on SYRIZA for these five tenets to be kept as priorities. The commitment to conduct an audit of the debt and in the meantime suspend repayment gradually disappeared from the discourse of Alexis Tsipras and the other SYRIZA leaders. This all happened unobtrusively and the fifth measure proposed by Tsipras in May 2012 (see above) was replaced by the proposal to hold a European conference to reduce Greece's debt. When SYRIZA formed a government after its victory in the 25 January 2015 elections, suspension of repayment and the audit had, wrongly, been taken off the table. This should reinforce the idea that energy needs to be devoted to strengthening citizen audit initiatives, so that political parties who seek to enter the government make strong commitments to adopting radical measures to face the challenge of paying illegitimate debt.

I participated in the audit committee formed by the government of Ecuador in July 2007. We worked from July 2007 through September 2008 and, based on our findings[129], the government suspended repayment of a portion of the debt, thus defeating its creditors. This enabled the State to save 7 billion dollars, which were reinvested in social expenditures. It was a total victory for Ecuador as regards a partial suspension. But that victory didn't just happen; we had been building a campaign since 2000. We had carried on a six-year battle to demonstrate to the population that the issue of the debt was central. We began with something very concrete: Norway was demanding that Ecuador repay a debt that had served to purchase five fishing boats. What became of these five fishing boats that Norway delivered to Ecuador? The activists in the debt movement showed that the vessels had in fact been converted for use in transporting bananas for a large private exporter in Ecuador. We had begun attacking that problem in 2000. Who took part in that movement? One person was Ricardo Patiño, who is now Minister of Foreign Affairs, after serving as Economy and Finance Minister while we were conducting the audit in 2007-2008. In other words, among the people who led the citizen audit initiative, some went on to hold positions in the government and honoured the commitment they had made to solve the problem of illegitimate debt. It has to be recognised that at least as regards that particular issue, they have been consistent and courageous. From within the government, they took initial unilateral action by launching an audit committee that neither the creditors nor the international community wanted. Then, they took a second unilateral action on the basis of the findings of the audit committee: suspending repayment of the debt, without asking anyone for permission to do it. And the situation in which they did it was rather remarkable: Ecuador actually had the money to repay the debt. Thus it was particularly scandalous, for the creditors, for Ecuador to say, "I'm ceasing repayment of a debt I have identified as being illegitimate, whereas I have the oil money with which I could pay it. As the State of Ecuador, I want the oil revenues to serve the people, and not illegitimate creditors." We succeeded in Ecuador because a balance of power had been built from the grass roots up on the foundation of the political forces that sought and won power and because the president of the Republic and several ministers in key positions supported the idea of forcing the creditors to make concessions. What I have just described applies to the first three years of the government – the period 2007-2009.

If this experience could be applied to other countries, starting with Spain, that would be a great step forward. Make sure that PODEMOS and other allied forces, should they come to power, cannot drop their commitments on the debt, in the name of pragmatism. Try to put PODEMOS and its allies under real pressure from the Spanish popular movements who will not reduce their pressure and activism on the question of the debt. If the Citizens' Debt Audit Platform does not apply the same pressure as it did in 2011-2012 PODEMOS could decide that "Finally, illegitimate debt is not a central question". The Spanish media's pressure on PODEMOS and its allies is very great; they say that "if PODEMOS gets into power Spain will suffer the same fate as Greece has". In reply several PODEMOS spokespersons try to get around the question by declaring that Spain has no debt repayment problems. They insist that Spain has no problems raising funds on the financial markets, as opposed to Greece that no longer has access to the financial markets. Thus they affirm that Spain has no serious debt repayment problems. They are wrong, even more so since several factors that are currently making debt repayments sustainable may very well change for the worse. One of these factors is the bad health of the banks. If the citizens' movements, the social movements, PODEMOS members and other progressive forces ease their pressure on Spain's debt question there will be another disillusionment like the Greek one. We must therefore keep in mind the importance of this struggle and not hesitate to put all possible effort and energy into it.

Another lesson to be learned from the Greek and Ecuadorian experiences, among others, is the need to take unilateral actions of self-defence. Unilateral action is not, at first sight, a pleasing idea; we have a tendency to seek multilateral actions. We denounce the unilateralism of the US that seeks to impose its will on the rest of the world. We refuse the unilateralism of the State of Israel that transgresses many resolutions of the United Nations and its Charter and oppresses the Palestinian people. Nevertheless, the unilateralism of the oppressed is a fundamental right. A government that comes to power through popular legitimacy has a duty to resist institutions that impose repayment of

illegal, illegitimate, odious and unsustainable debts. A
government brought to power through popular support should
have the courage to act unilaterally to suspend debt repayments.

In reply to affirmations that there will be dire consequences
for Greece if doesn't pay its debts it should be pointed out that
the country has transferred €7 billion to its creditors since
February 2015, whereas the plan to relieve the humanitarian
crisis only amounted to €200 million. €200 million against €7
billion! Between February and June 2015 Greece's accounts were
wiped out without the creditors having to make any concessions
whatsoever[130].

If you are repaying a creditor your debt is not his problem. As
the saying goes, if you owe your bank a hundred pounds, you
have a problem; but if you owe a million, the bank has a problem.

Remember, three weeks after SYRIZA's victory in the Greek
elections and the forming of the Tsipras government Greece had
to face a stark refusal by the creditors, represented by the Dutch
socialist Jeroen Dijsselbloem, to consider the popular will. The
Eurogroup, which would now represent the Troika in the negotiations with the Greek government, basically said that "the
January 2015 elections were of no importance and that 1) Thou
shalt continue to repay the debt, 2) Thou shalt continue the
austerity measures until the end of June 2015 and 3) Thou shalt
propose new measures to show your obedience to austerity and
neoliberal programmes. We shall see if we approve of your
proposals". What if, in the name of the Greek government, on 20
February, Tsipras or Varoufakis had inverted the situation by
saying "Over the last three weeks of negotiation we have been as
conciliatory as is possible but you offer nothing in return, you
have no respect for the mandate that the Greek people have
given us, we have no choice but to apply Article 7, Paragraph 9
of European Union regulation No. 472, dated 21 May 2013 that
requires a member State under financial assistance to conduct an
audit of its debt. During the period of audit we suspend all

repayments. We shall see 1) whether you respect the desires of the Greek people and 2) whether your intentions towards us are honourable [or] whether you are trustworthy and reliable." If Tsipras had done that there would have been an inversion in the balance of power.

That would have been a unilateral action of self-defence. In the situation that Greece was in, if there is no unilateral action by the debtors, nothing positive can be expected from the creditors.

Now that the Greek government has capitulated, what will happen to Greece's debt? It is not impossible that the ECB and the Eurogroup follow up their ukases with a small offering of appeasement to the second Tsipras government, but they will never give up on the greater part of the Greek debt because for them it is a means of pressure and blackmail. The most likely outcome is that the creditors, in the best of cases, restructure the repayment schedules over a longer period.

It is very important to read the report drawn up by the Greek Debt Truth Committee. It can be downloaded free[131]. In no more than 65 pages it presents many key arguments and definitions.

The Truth Committee on the Greek Debt was made up of thirty members from eleven different countries. Among them were eminent specialists on international law, economists, an ex-president of a central bank, highly experienced auditors and comptrollers, banking specialists, and representatives of social movements who have competence in many fields and a profound knowledge of the effects of the creditors' policies on the Greek people. One of the first tasks was to define the terms of reference[132] and the definitions: what does it mean to say that a debt is illegal, illegitimate, odious or unsustainable? These terms of reference and definitions, which may still be improved upon, may be useful for audits in other countries[133].

Resolving the problem of illegitimate debt is a primary condition of a necessary rupture with austerity policies, but it is not the only one. As suggested in the opening paragraph a coherent and fully comprehensive alternative policy should include auditing the debt and suspending repayments, but also solving the banking crisis, i.e. the socialisation of the banks (in Greece this would have meant winding up private banks and replacing them with a healthy public banking system that protected deposits); launching a complementary form of money; implementing tax measures aimed at increasing the tax participation of the rich and reducing the tax burden on the poor; repealing socially unjust measures; putting a stop to privatisations; deprivatising; developing public services; sharing available work time; introducing a programme towards an ecological transition. If leaving the Euro becomes necessary, it must be managed along with redistributive monetary reforms[134]. A constituent process must also be launched in order to democratically change the country's constitution. Not only must national constitutions be changed but Europe must also be refounded, starting with the abrogation of unacceptable treaties. A constituent process implies very broad public debate: European citizens must again become involved in political issues and choices, and achieving this empowerment of the many starts with drafting new constitutions. We can draw this important lesson from the South American experience, where successful constitutional processes occurred in Venezuela (1999), in Bolivia (2006-2008) and in Ecuador (2007-2008), where constitutional changes included elements as important as totally prohibiting the socialisation of private debt.

In Belgium or in France, private illegitimate debt has not yet become a central issue, but in Spain if you do not raise the matter of the hundreds of thousands of illegitimate mortgage repayments that are demanded from Spanish families you are not facing up to a fundamental injustice. Between 2008 and the second quarter of 2015, 416,332 homes were repossessed from families unable to repay their mortgages. The foreclosures are one of the consequences of the crisis but the "mortgage law" goes back to a much earlier date, in fact to a decree issued under the Franco regime in 1946 and still in force.

How do you expect overindebted and humiliated people, who have been abused by the banks, thrown out of their homes, and still have a part of the burden of debts to repay, to find the strength and hope to get together to cancel the State's public debts? If they have been defeated in their personal struggle because there was no sufficiently strong and organised resistance to prevent them from being evicted they cannot be expected to feel concerned by illegitimate public debt. Fortunately a big anti-foreclosure movement has developed in Spain since 2010. The mortgage victims platform (PAH) highlights the fact that "many abusive articles are tied to the loans and that the values of the properties, in their functions as guarantees, were very much overvalued and should be considered to be toxic financial products". Ada Colau, the new mayor of Barcelona since 2015, has made her name as one of the forces of the anti-foreclosure movement and has taken part in numerous bank occupations[135].

In the UK, where neoliberalism is even more entrenched than on the Continent, if you do not talk of the illegitimate student debt, you are ignoring an essential issue. In the US also, illegitimate student debt amounts to $1,000 billion and since the outbreak of the crisis over 14 million homes were foreclosed, at least 500,000 of these evictions being illegal. Many victims, assisted by social movements, in particular "Strike Debt," have been at the forefront to face off bailiffs and refuse foreclosures. Thousands of writs have been issued against banks. Between 2010 and 2015, US authorities came to out-of-court agreements with banks so as to avoid their being brought to justice for their scandalous activities in the mortgage sector. They all got away with fines.

In Belgium, although the overindebtedness of impoverished households has not reached the same alarming proportions as in the US, Greece or Spain, 352,270 people could not pay their debts (mortgage, electricity bill, etc.) in 2015 and the average rate of indebtedness has steadily increased since the beginning of the crisis. Austerity measures obviously increase the vulnerability of the most indebted households. Since over-indebtedness is not an issue that can be solved on an individual basis a new initiative is underway that raises the question of debt-auditing and of the cancellation of illegitimate private debts; it brings together the CADTM, the Walloon network against poverty, a service for the mediation of debts in Brussels, other associations and overindebted people.

Illegitimate private debt is also causing great problems and challenges for movements in struggle against the debt system outside of the most industrialised countries. In India more than 300,000 overindebted small farmers have committed suicide over the last fifteen years[136]. In Morocco the victims of shady micro-credit systems are getting organised, with the help of ATTAC/CADTM Morocco.

There is no longer any time for procrastination regarding the possibility of negotiating with the creditors of illegitimate debts. It has been clear for years now that they are not looking for compromise, nor for amicable arrangements, but that they are bent on putting all possible means in place for maximising their profits. And they will do it regardless of the human cost – which the people are already bearing, from Athens to Delhi, from the US university campuses to the streets of Bamako. Nor can we blindly count on the good intentions of political parties of the radical Left any longer, despite the increasingly rare hope they represent – SYRIZA is the sad proof of that. Only massive mobilisation around strong demands can bring about a real and lasting change towards a more just society, one that respects nature and the fundamental rights of all human beings.

References

1. *The Guardian*, 18/1/2016
2. http://archives.chicagotribune.com/1965/08/13/page/7/ article/athens-crowd-defies-police-melts-away
3. The royal houses of Jordan, Saudi Arabia and Iran respectively
4. http://dangerouscitizens.columbia.edu/1936-1944/epitaphios/1/
5. C. M. Woodhouse, *The Struggle for Greece*
6. For further details see https://www.marxists.org/history/etol /revhist/backiss/vol3/no3/acrocamp.html
7. Eudes, *The Kapetanios*
8. Ibid.
9. All these quotations are cited at http://www.oxidayfoundation.org/quotes-world-leaders
10. Sarafis and Eve, *Background to Contemporary Greece*
11. Eudes, *The Kapetanios*
12. Rees, *World War 2 Behind Closed Doors*
13. Iatrides, *Revolt in Athens*
14. http://www.theguardian.com/ world/2014/nov/30/athens-1944-britains-dirty-secret
15. *London Review of Books*, 4/12/14
16. Sarafis and Eve, *Background to Contemporary Greece*
17. Ibid.
18. https://www.youtube.com/watch?v=U3J4v4KNDQI
19. Ibid.
20. Eudes, *The Kapetanios*
21. Sarafis and Eve, *Background to Contemporary Greece*
22. Papandreou, *Democracy at Gunpoint*
23. http://www.arts.yorku.ca/hist/tgallant/documents/mcdonlad.pdf
24. Weiner, *Legacy of Ashes: the history of the CIA*

25. Contemporary press reports
26. Papandreou, *Democracy at Gunpoint*
27. Ibid.
28. http://www.helleniccomserve.com/thecoupat40part3.html
29. https://www.facebook.com/permalink.php?story_fbid=766552173394871&id=435723086477783
30. https://en.wikipedia.org/wiki/Talk%3ANikos_Sampson
31. https://news.google.com/newspapers?nid=950&dat=19721018&id=K1lQAAAAIBAJ&sjid=wFcDAAAAIBAJ&pg=4548,1082201&hl=en
32. http://www.24grammata.com/wp-content/uploads/2013/06/Kariotis-Papandreu-24grammata.com_.pdf
33. Contemporary press reports
34. Eudes, *The Kapetanios*
35. *Financial Times*, 21/6/2011
36. Colovas, *A Quick History of Modern Greece*
37. Pettifer, *The Greeks: A Land and People Since the War*
38. Manolopoulos, *Greece's 'Odious' Debt*
39. Ibid.
40. http://www.spiegel.de/international/europe/generations-of-pork-how-greece-s-political-elite-ruined-the-country-a-772176.html, 5/7/11
41. https://euobserver.com/political/32363
42. Manolopoulos, *Greece's 'Odious' Debt*
43. http://www.ekathimerini.com/140898/article/ekathimerini/news/pangalos-stands-by-we-all-ate-together-statement
44. http://cadtm.org/Preliminary-Report-of-the-Truth
45. *Financial Times*, 11/1/2010
46. *Financial Times*, 25/3/2010
47. *Financial Times*, 2/2/10
48. https://thenextrecession.wordpress.com/
49. Kalyvas, *Modern Greece: What Everyone Needs to Know*
50. http://tbinternet.ohchr.org/_layouts/treatybodyexterna

l/Download.aspx?symbolno=E/C.12/GRC/CO/2&Lang=En
51. Ovenden, *SYRIZA: Inside the Labyrinth*
52. https://xaameriki.wordpress.com/faq/
53. http://jailgoldendawn.com/2014/11/27/the-resistible-rise-of-golden-dawn/
54. http://www.bbc.co.uk/news/world-europe-24363776
55. https://www.marxists.org/history/etol/newspape/ni/vol01/no03/v.htm
56. http://www.internationalviewpoint.org/spip.php?article3858
57. http://www.bradford-delong.com/2015/07/highlighted-failing-to-manage-the-eurozone-economies-how-we-are-not-making-our-own-new-mistakes.html
58. Eichengreen, *Hall of Mirrors*
59. German Institute for Macroeconomic Research IMK, affiliated with the Hans Böckler Foundation
60. http://www.analyzegreece.gr/topics/left-goverment/item/314-nasos-iliopoulos-the-burdens-of-syriza
61. http://yanisvaroufakis.eu/2013/12/10/confessions-of-an-erratic-marxist-in-the-midst-of-a-repugnant-european-crisis
62. https://www.warhistoryonline.com/war-articles/germany-paying-pensions-for-wwii-spanish-volunteers.html/2
63. http://greekdebttruthcommission.org
64. http://www.independent.co.uk/news/world/europe/greece-crisis-alexis-tsipras-announces-referendum-on-creditors-unbearable-austerity-demands-10349543.html
65. http://www.theguardian.com/world/2015/jun/26/greece-calls-referendum-on-bailout-terms-offered-by-creditors
66. http://costaslapavitsas.blogspot.co.uk
67. https://www.jacobinmag.com/2015/07/tsipras-syriza-greece-euro-debt
68. http://www.theguardian.com/business/economics-blog/2015/feb/19/greece-runs-up-the-austerity-white-flag-in-brussels
69. http://www.ft.com/cms/s/f908e534-2942-11e5-8db8-

References

c033edba8a6e,Authorised=false.html?siteedition=uk&_i_loc
ation=http%3A%2F%2Fwww.ft.com%2Fcms%2Fs%2F0%2F
f908e534-2942-11e5-8db8-c033edba8a6e.html%3Fsiteed
ition%3Duk&_i_referer=https%3A%2F%2Fwww.google.co.
uk%2F6666cd76f96956469e7be39d750cc7d9&classifi-
cation=conditional_standard&iab=barrier-app#axzz3sJ
psui2k

70. http://krugman.blogs.nytimes.com/2015/07/12/killing-the-
european-project/?_r=0

71. http://www.independent.co.uk/news/world/europe/greek-
debt-crisis-alexis-tsipras-given-ultimatum-push-through-
cuts-this-week-or-quit-euro-10384084.html

72. http://yanisvaroufakis.eu/category/greek-crisis

73. *Financial Times,* 15/7/2105

74. Pentaraki, "The New European Economic Governance
(NEEG)"

75. http://blogs.ft.com/the-world/2015/07/tsipras-is-master-of-
all-he-surveys-in-greece

76. Pentaraki, "The New European Economic Governance
(NEEG)"

77. http://yanisvaroufakis.eu/2015/07/14/on-the-euro-summits-
statement-on-greece-first-thoughts

78. http://apokoronasnews.gr/wolfgang-munchau-i-am-
sceptical-about-another-round-of-extend-and-pretend-
dishonesty

79. http://www.ekathimerini.com/199552/article/ekathimer
ini/news/syriza-committee-members-slam-greece-
agreement

80. https://www.jacobinmag.com/2015/07/tsipras-syriza-
greece-euro-debt

81. http://analyzegreece.gr/topics/greece-europe/item/288-zoi-
konstantopoulou-n-to-ultimatums-n-to-the-memoranda-of-
servitude

82. http://cadtm.org/Black-days-4th-August-1914-Germany

83. http://www.counterpunch.org/2015/08/26/the-catastrophic-international-consequences-of-the-capitulation-of-syriza-and-the-criminal-responsibility-of-mr-tsipras/
84. https://www.jacobinmag.com/2015/08/greece-memorandum-austerity-coup-tsipras-syriza-interview
85. https://www.marxists.org/archive/lenin/works/1920/lwc
86. http://www.analyzegreece.gr/topics/left-goverment/item/314-nasos-iliopoulos-the-burdens-of-syriza
87. https://www.jacobinmag.com/2015/08/tsipras-debt-germany-greece-euro
88. http://www.theguardian.com/world/2015/apr/26/greek-finance-minister-hints-at-strained-eu-relations-i-welcome-their-hatred
89. http://www.bbc.co.uk/news/world-europe-33925781
90. http://www.reuters.com/article/2015/08/28/us-eurozone-greece-syriza-idUSKCN0QX1SF20150828
91. In personal correspondence
92. http://www.telegraph.co.uk/finance/economics/11694446/Another-bout-of-hyperinflation-may-be-whats-needed-to-bring-Greeks-to-their-senses.html
93. http://www.ekathimerini.com/201078/article/ekathimerini/news/kammenos-says-syriza-independent-greeks-coalition-explored-drachma-option
94. https://thenextrecession.wordpress.com/2015/03/14/greece-keynes-or-marx
95. In personal correspondence
96. http://indefenseofgreekworkers.blogspot.co.uk/2015/07/what-would-kke-do-if-it-were-in-syrizas.html
97. http://www.telesurtv.net/english/bloggers/This-is-a-Betrayal-Interview-with-Professor-Spyros-Marketos-20150715-0003.html
98. Pentaraki, "The New European Economic Governance (NEEG)"
99. http://www.marxist.com/the-lessons-of-greece-the-failure-

of-reformism.htm

100. http://www.socialismtoday.org/191/greece.html
101. *Financial Times*, 16/7/15
102. http://www.azquotes.com/quote/262398
103. The references are to mass occupations of public squares in Beijing, Bucharest, Prague, Cairo, Madrid, Barcelona, New York, Hong Kong, Cape Town, Mexico, Wisconsin and Athens respectively.
104. *Guardian*,2/2/16
105. https://www.marxists.org/archive/lenin/works/1920/lwc/
106. https://www.marxists.org/history/international/social-democracy/1912/basel-manifesto.htm
107. Reed, *Ten Days that Shook the World*
108. Silverman and Grant, *Bureaucratism or Workers'-Power*
109. https://www.marxists.org/archive/grant/1969/lat/5.htm
110. http://www.forgottenbooks.com/readbook_text/The_Coming_Revolution_in_Great_Britain_1000212138/131
111. In personal correspondence
112. http://www.counterpunch.org/2015/07/24/black-days-august-4th1914-germany-and-july-13th-2015-greece/
113. Silverman, *The Future International* and *Preparing for Revolution*
114. *The Guardian*, 22/1/2016
115. Marx and Engels, *The Communist Manifesto*, Preface to the 1890 German edition
116. http://trendsresearch.com/stories/Global-Anti-Govt-Protests-Whats-Next,1642?
117. http://elegr.gr/details.php?id=134
118. PACD, http://auditoriaciudadana.net/
119. http://auditoriacidada.info/
120. http://cadtm.org/Portugal-Connaitre-la-dette-pour
121. http://www.audit-citoyen.org/texte-reference/ and http://cadtm.org/France-The-citizens-debt-audit
122. http://www.auditcitoyen.be/lacide/

123. http://cadtm.org/ICAN

124. http://cadtm.org/Coordinated-efforts-in-Europe and http://www.citizen-audit.net/

125. http://cadtm.org/Preliminary-Report-of-the-Truth

126. http://cadtm.org/Greece-Assessment-of-the-debt-as

127. http://cadtm.org/Zoe-Konstantopoulou-at-the

128. http://cadtm.org/4-April-2015-a-landmark-in-the -

129. http://cadtm.org/Rafael-Correa-actively-supports

130. http://cadtm.org/What-if-the-Greek-government-had

131. http://cadtm.org/Preliminary-Report-of-the-Truth

132. http://cadtm.org/Terms-of-reference-for-the

133. http://cadtm.org/Definition-of-illegitimate-illegal

134. http://cadtm.org/Greece-an-alternative

135. See her biography: https://en.wikipedia.org/wiki/Ada _Colau)

136. http://cadtm.org/The-Debt-Relief-Package-of-Rupees

Map of Greece

Recent General Elections

	New Democracy	PASOK	SYRIZA	GOLDEN DAWN	KKE
Oct 2009	2,295,719	3,012,542	315,665	19,624	517,249
	33.47%	43.92%	4.6%	0.29%	7.54%
May 2012	1,192,103	833,452	1,061,928	440,966	536,105
	18.85%	13.18%	16.79%	6.97%	8.48%
June 2012	1,825,497	756,024	1,655,022	426,025	277,227
	29.66%	12.26%	26.89%	6.92%	4.5%
Jan 2015	1,718,694	289,469	2,245,978	388,387	338,188
	27.81%	4.68%	36.34%	6.28%	5.47%
Sept 2015	1,526,205	341,390	1,925,904	379,581	301,632
	28.1%	6.28%	35.46%	6.99%	5.55%

Glossary

Andartes: Wartime resistance guerrillas.

ANEL: Independent Greeks, a right-wing nationalist party founded in 2012 after a split in *Nea Demokratia.*

ANTARSYA: Front of the Greek Anticapitalist Left, a small coalition of left groups.

Armatoloi: Greek militia police originally deployed by the Ottomans against the *kleftes,* who switched allegiance and fought with them in the war of independence

Aspida: A secret grouping of junior army officers formed in the early 1960s to oppose IDEA and resist a military coup.

Chrysi Avgi: Golden Dawn, a fascist party owing allegiance to the traditions of the deposed military dictatorship and responsible for physical attacks on migrants and left activists.

DSE: Democratic Army of Greece, the army established by the KKE during the civil war.

EAM: National Liberation Front, the main Greek wartime resistance movement.

EDA: United Democratic Left, a political party in the 1950s–60s; originally a legal front for the banned KKE.

EDES: National Republican Greek League, a pro-British anti-communist resistance force during the occupation.

EENA: The colonels' secret conspiracy, linked to the Athens CIA station, which executed the 1967 military coup.

ELAS: People's Liberation Army, the armed wing of the EAM.

Enosis: union with Greece.

Enosis Kentrou: Centre Union, the liberal "Venizelist" party founded by George Papandreou in the 1960s.

EOKA-B: a Greek-Cypriot paramilitary organisation led by Colonel (later General) Grivas, which fought for *enosis.*

ERE: National Radical Union, a right-wing party founded by Konstantin Karamanlis in the 1950s.

ESA: Greek Military Police, an elite paramilitary force within the military dictatorship responsible for torture and death squads.

Filiki Etaireia: The Society of Friends, a secret society of Greeks dedicated to independence from Ottoman rule.

IDEA: a secret right-wing conspiracy of the generals and the palace in the 1960s.

Kapetanioi: guerrilla fighters.

KKE: Communist Party of Greece.

Kleftes: originally brigands who became insurgents against Ottoman rule.

Kremlin: the fortress in Moscow that is the seat of government in Russia, often used as a metaphor for the Soviet leadership.

Megali Idea: The Great Idea, the goal of establishing an independent state for all Greeks.

Nea Demokratia: the right-wing party founded by Konstantin Karamanlis on his return to Greece in 1974.

OPLA: Organisation for the Protection of the People's Struggle; the KKE's paramilitary security force during the occupation.

Organosis X: Organisation X, the fascist paramilitary militia established by Colonel Grivas during the Nazi occupation.

PASOK: Panhellenic Socialist Movement, the party founded by Andreas Papandreou in 1974.

PEEA: Political Committee of National Liberation; the KKE's "mountain government" established at the beginning of the civil war.

SYRIZA: Coalition of the Radical Left, a coalition of left parties founded in 2004, which became a unitary party in 2014.

Triple Entente: the alliance of Britain, France and Russia during the First World War.

Bibliography

Colovas, Anthone C., *A Quick History of Modern Greece*, PublishAmerica, 2007Eichengreen, Barry, *Hall of Mirrors: The Great Depression, the Great Recession, and the Uses and Misuses of History*, Oxford University Press, 2015

Eudes, Dominique, *The Kapetanios: Partisans and Civil War in Greece, 1943–1949*, NLB, 1972

Financial Times, *If Greece Goes…: The Impact of a Greek Default on Europe and the World Economy*, FT Publishing International, 2014

Gelis, V. N., *How the IMF Broke Greece: Role of the Fake Left*, CreateSpace, 2011

— (ed.), *The Greek Civil War*, CreateSpace, 2011

Hewitt, Gavin, *The Lost Continent*, Hodder and Stoughton, 2013

Iatrides, John O., *Revolt in Athens: The Greek Communist Second Round, 1944–1945*, Princeton University Press, 2015

Kalyvas, Stathis N., *Modern Greece: What Everyone Needs to Know*, Oxford University Press, 2015

Laskos, Christos and Euclid Tsakalatos, *Crucible of Resistance: Greece, the Eurozone and the World Economic Crisis*, Pluto Press, 2013

Manolopoulos, Jason, *Greece's 'Odious' Debt: The Looting of the Hellenic Republic by the Euro, the Political Elite and the Investment Community*, Anthem Press, 2011

Marx, Karl and Friedrich Engels, *The Communist Manifesto*, German edition, 1890

Ovenden, Kevin, *SYRIZA: Inside the Labyrinth*, Pluto Press, 2015

Palaiologos, Yannis, *The 13th Labour of Hercules: Inside the Greek Crisis*, Portobello Books, 2014

Papandreou, Andreas, *Democracy at Gunpoint: the Greek Front*, Penguin Books, 1971

Pentaraki, Maria "The New European Economic Governance

(NEEG): EU's austerity project, its effects on the welfare state and struggles of resistance", Alternatives Futures and Popular Protest Conference, 25–7 March 2013

Pettifer, James, *The Making of the Greek Crisis*, New Revised Edition, Penguin, 2015

— *The Greeks: A Land and People Since the War*, Penguin, 1993

Reed, John, *Ten Days that Shook the World* (1919), CreateSpace, 2011

Rees, Laurence, *World War Two: Behind Closed Doors: Stalin, the Nazis and the West*, Vintage, 2009

Sarafis, Marion and Martin Eve (eds.), *Background to Contemporary Greece*, Volumes 1 and 2, Merlin Press, 1991

Varoufakis, Yanis and Paul Mason, *The Global Minotaur: America, Europe and the Future of the Global Economy*, Zed Books, 2015

Weiner, Tim, *Legacy of Ashes: The History of the CIA*, Doubleday, 2007

Woodhouse, C. M., *The Struggle for Greece*, Hurst & Company, 1976

Contemporary culture has eliminated both the concept of the public and the figure of the intellectual. Former public spaces – both physical and cultural – are now either derelict or colonized by advertising. A cretinous anti-intellectualism presides, cheerled by expensively educated hacks in the pay of multinational corporations who reassure their bored readers that there is no need to rouse themselves from their interpassive stupor. The informal censorship internalized and propagated by the cultural workers of late capitalism generates a banal conformity that the propaganda chiefs of Stalinism could only ever have dreamt of imposing. Zer0 Books knows that another kind of discourse – intellectual without being academic, popular without being populist – is not only possible: it is already flourishing, in the regions beyond the striplit malls of so-called mass media and the neurotically bureaucratic halls of the academy. Zer0 is committed to the idea of publishing as a making public of the intellectual. It is convinced that in the unthinking, blandly consensual culture in which we live, critical and engaged theoretical reflection is more important than ever before.

ZERO BOOKS

If this book has helped you to clarify an idea, solve a problem or extend your knowledge, you may like to read more titles from Zero Books. Recent bestsellers are:

Capitalist Realism Is there no alternative?
Mark Fisher
An analysis of the ways in which capitalism has presented itself as the only realistic political-economic system.
Paperback: November 27, 2009 978-1-84694-317-1 $14.95 £7.99.
eBook: July 1, 2012 978-1-78099-734-6 $9.99 £6.99.

The Wandering Who? A study of Jewish identity politics
Gilad Atzmon
An explosive unique crucial book tackling the issues of Jewish Identity Politics and ideology and their global influence.
Paperback: September 30, 2011 978-1-84694-875-6 $14.95 £8.99.
eBook: September 30, 2011 978-1-84694-876-3 $9.99 £6.99.

Clampdown Pop-cultural wars on class and gender
Rhian E. Jones
Class and gender in Britpop and after, and why 'chav' is a feminist issue.
Paperback: March 29, 2013 978-1-78099-708-7 $14.95 £9.99.
eBook: March 29, 2013 978-1-78099-707-0 $7.99 £4.99.

The Quadruple Object
Graham Harman
Uses a pack of playing cards to present Harman's metaphysical system of fourfold objects, including human access, Heidegger's indirect causation, panpsychism and ontography.
Paperback: July 29, 2011 978-1-84694-700-1 $16.95 £9.99.

Weird Realism Lovecraft and Philosophy

Graham Harman

As Hölderlin was to Martin Heidegger and Mallarmé to Jacques
Derrida, so is H.P. Lovecraft to the Speculative Realist philoso-
phers.

Paperback: September 28, 2012 978-1-78099-252-5 $24.95 £14.99.

eBook: September 28, 2012 978-1-78099-907-4 $9.99 £6.99.

Sweetening the Pill or How We Got Hooked on Hormonal Birth
Control

Holly Grigg-Spall

Is it really true? Has contraception liberated or oppressed
women?

Paperback: September 27, 2013 978-1-78099-607-3 $22.95 £12.99.

eBook: September 27, 2013 978-1-78099-608-0 $9.99 £6.99.

Why Are We The Good Guys? Reclaiming Your Mind From The
Delusions Of Propaganda

David Cromwell

A provocative challenge to the standard ideology that Western
power is a benevolent force in the world.

Paperback: September 28, 2012 978-1-78099-365-2 $26.95 £15.99.

eBook: September 28, 2012 978-1-78099-366-9 $9.99 £6.99.

The Truth about Art Reclaiming quality

Patrick Doorly

The book traces the multiple meanings of art to their various
sources, and equips the reader to choose between them.

Paperback: August 30, 2013 978-1-78099-841-1 $32.95 £19.99.

Bells and Whistles More Speculative Realism

Graham Harman

In this diverse collection of sixteen essays, lectures, and inter-
views Graham Harman lucidly explains the principles of

Speculative Realism, including his own object-oriented philosophy.
Paperback: November 29, 2013 978-1-78279-038-9 $26.95 £15.99.
eBook: November 29, 2013 978-1-78279-037-2 $9.99 £6.99.

Towards Speculative Realism: Essays and Lectures Essays and Lectures
Graham Harman
These writings chart Harman's rise from Chicago sportswriter to co founder of one of Europe's most promising philosophical movements: Speculative Realism.
Paperback: November 26, 2010 978-1-84694-394-2 $16.95 £9.99.
eBook: January 1, 1970 978-1-84694-603-5 $9.99 £6.99.

Meat Market Female flesh under capitalism
Laurie Penny
A feminist dissection of women's bodies as the fleshy fulcrum of capitalist cannibalism, whereby women are both consumers and consumed.
Paperback: April 29, 2011 978-1-84694-521-2 $12.95 £6.99.
eBook: May 21, 2012 978-1-84694-782-7 $9.99 £6.99.

Translating Anarchy The Anarchism of Occupy Wall Street
Mark Bray
An insider's account of the anarchists who ignited Occupy Wall Street.
Paperback: September 27, 2013 978-1-78279-126-3 $26.95 £15.99.
eBook: September 27, 2013 978-1-78279-125-6 $6.99 £4.99.

Find more titles at www.zero-books.net